The Daddy Shift

How Stay-at-Home Dads,
Breadwinning Moms, and Shared Parenting
Are Transforming the American Family

Jeremy Adam Smith

Beacon Press
Boston

Beacon Press
25 Beacon Street
Boston, Massachusetts 02108-2892
www.beacon.org

Beacon Press books
are published under the auspices of
the Unitarian Universalist Association of Congregations.

16 15 14 13 12   8 7 6 5 4 3 2

This book is printed on acid-free paper that meets the uncoated paper
ANSI/NISO specifications for permanence as revised in 1992.

Text design and composition by Wilsted & Taylor Publishing Services

Library of Congress Cataloging-in-Publication Data

Smith, Jeremy Adam.
  The daddy shift : how stay-at-home dads, breadwinning moms, and shared
parenting are transforming the American family / Jeremy Adam Smith.
     p. cm.
  Includes bibliographical references.
  ISBN-13: 978-0-8070-2121-7 (paperback : alk. paper)
  1. Househusbands—United States. 2. Stay-at-home fathers—United States.
3. Working mothers—United States. 4. Work and family—United States. I. Title.

HQ756.6.S65 2009
306.3'6150973—dc22   2008047404

This book is dedicated to my father and to my son.

A Note about Names and People

Unless otherwise indicated in the endnotes, all quotations appearing in this book (of both parents and researchers) come from personal interviews. The couples I interviewed requested varying degrees of anonymity. Some agreed to let me use their full names; some asked me to drop or change their last names; others ("Mike Rothstein" and "Lisa Holt" in chapter 3 and the "Hoffman" family in chapter 8) requested that I change their entire name and alter certain personal details. In every case, I obeyed people's wishes, if they expressed any.

Some readers might notice that even though I write about my family life, my wife appears in these pages only in name, not as a full-blown character. This is simply because she is not a public person and she does not wish for her personal choices and feelings to be subjected to public scrutiny. I obeyed her wish as well, even if it gives the mistaken impression of her absence.

As a result the autobiographical passages primarily concern my own responses as a caregiver, which I felt needed to be there in order to complete this snapshot of male caregiving in the early twenty-first century. The reader should not construe this to mean my wife is unimportant to me. On the contrary, I love her and my son more than words can express.

Contents

Introduction

Twenty-first-century Dad

In 2004 my son Liko was born. Everything—the tree outside the window, the dreams I had at night—changed.

For the first year of his life, my wife Olli stayed home with Liko. Then she went back to work and I quit my job, joining the ranks of caregiving dads.

Now it was just the two of us boys, and it was scary. Liko, a confirmed breast addict, could not nap without his mother. When I would lay him down, he'd wail inconsolably, relentlessly, reaching out to me. But when I picked him up, he'd kick and arch his back, his little hands pushing against my chest. This would go on for hours.

I'd put him in the stroller and walk. He'd cry and fall asleep, but if I stopped—in a bookstore, a coffee shop—he'd wake and cry again, so I soon learned to keep moving through our San Francisco neighborhood, sticking to the side streets, going up the hills and down, up and down.

Time slowed, and with every minute I'd feel more and more isolated, more and more anxious. I wondered: "Is my life now no more than this?" I'd see people laughing in a picture window and want to be one of them.

In time, I learned to let that go, let myself get lost. On foggy days the hills of the city floated around us like deserted islands, the stroller a lonely raft. I'd study the cornices and gables on the Victorian facades, watch the tsunami of fog spill over Twin Peaks.

Later, Liko learned to fall asleep in my arms. I'd carry him through all the rooms in our apartment, stepping carefully around the bouncy seat, the swing, the baby gym, the high chair, the toy basket. I'd do this for hours.

Then one momentous day, I sat down in a rocking chair and he stayed asleep. I took a book down from the bookshelf. It was the best book I'd ever read; I don't remember its name. One afternoon as the room darkened, his eyes snapped open and they met mine. He smiled and said, "Dada," and his small fingers curled around my forefinger.

He was glad to see me there with him. And I was glad to be there.

New Model Family

It is strange to think that such an intensely private moment might be the product of a tectonic shift in society and the economy.

Although I felt acutely isolated when I was learning to take care of my son, in fact I was not alone. Since 1965 the number of hours that men spend on child care has tripled. Since 1995 it has nearly doubled.[1]

In 2007 the Census Bureau counted 159,000 stay-at-home dads in the United States, up from 64,000 in 1995.[2] But these numbers tell only part of the story of male caregiving, because they exclude stay-at-home fathers who also do paying work. When we add fathers who work part-time or from home, and who are primarily or equally responsible for taking care of kids, the number of male caregivers increases. According to a 2008 census report, for example, one in four preschool children spend more time in Dad's care than any other arrangement while the mother is working,[3] though most of the fathers work at least part-time and probably do not call themselves "stay-at-home dads."

Many studies find that twenty-first-century couples divide paid work, household labor, and child care far more equitably than couples in the past.[4] Some professional dual-income couples have even achieved rough equality in their domestic divisions of labor,[5] and one-third of working-class couples work different, complementary shifts and share care of young children.[6] A great deal of evidence also indicates that more fathers would adopt caregiving roles if they felt it was financially feasible to do so: For example, a 2007 survey by Monster.com found that 68 percent of American men would consider staying home full-time with their kids.

The bottom line is clear: during the past decade, the number of caregiving fathers has risen dramatically. Dads now spend more time with their children than at any time since researchers started collecting longitudinally comparable data.[7] This does not mean that Americans have achieved an egalitarian utopia. The census counts 5.6 million stay-at-home moms, compared to 159,000 dads.[8] The University of Wisconsin's National Survey of Families and Households says that the average mother is doing *five times* as much child care as the average father. When both parents work for pay, Mom still beats Dad by a four to one ratio.[9] If men as a group have indeed increased their contributions at home—and they have —they still don't come close to matching what mothers do.

However, averages can be deceptive. They reveal the big picture but, by doing so, obscure the many smaller pieces and countertrends that give it shape. In truth, we are in a period of transition when inequality coexists with progress. Some groups of men have adopted flexible gender roles and embraced cooking, cleaning, and taking care of kids, while other groups have not. The negative examples, often glorified, are everywhere, while the positive ones are often hidden and hard to find, especially for boys and young men.

It is time for twenty-first-century dads to go on the offensive. In this book I tell the stories of fathers who have embraced caregiving and egalitarian marriages, explore the hopes and ideals that inform their choices, and analyze economic and social developments that have made their choices possible.

As we will discover, stay-at-home dads represent a logical next step of fifty years of family change, from a time when the idea of men caring for children was inconceivable, to a new era when at-home dads are a small but growing part of the landscape. This is the "daddy shift" of the title: the gradual movement away from a definition of fatherhood as pure breadwinning to one that encompasses capacities for both breadwinning and caregiving.

Stay-at-home dads are the leading edge of the daddy shift, pioneers who are quietly mapping new territory for all fathers. I focus on stay-at-home dads for the same reason anthropologists study lost tribes and obscure subcultures: to reveal the variety and potential of human experience—and thus to suggest new possibilities for organizing our lives.

But in many ways, this book is really about male caregiving writ large. Stay-at-home dads represent one extreme of a continuum that includes the growing number of dads who split work and child care equally with their spouses, widowed or divorced custodial dads (a group that has quadrupled in size since 1970), two-dad families, and working fathers who have restructured their jobs in order to make more time for their children. Many of the facts, ideas, and trends I describe apply to all dads who have chosen to prioritize, for one reason or another, care over paid work.

This is also a book about female breadwinning, which is, of course, the main economic factor that makes stay-at-home fatherhood possible. Prior to the 1960s, as we will discuss in chapter 1, it was uncommon for mothers to work and nearly unheard of for them to make more money than their husbands. Today, 80 percent of mothers have jobs and one-third of wives make more money than their husbands[10]—and we have every reason to believe that these trends will intensify: today in America, for example, young women outnumber men on college campuses, and they outearn young men in many American cities.[11]

As women's incomes continue to rise—and they will—men will be called upon to do even more housework and child care. According to a growing number of studies, there is a direct relationship between the amount of money women earn and the amount of housework and child care men do. In 2006, for example, Pennsylvania State University sociologist Jennifer L. Hook analyzed forty-four time-use studies from twenty countries, and she discovered that men's housework and child care increases with national levels of women's employment, as well as the availability of paternity leave.[12]

Hook also found that widely available day care and preschool correlates with higher levels of father involvement.[13] At first glance there might seem to be a conflict here: Wouldn't more easily available child care *limit* men's participation in raising their kids? Wouldn't one trend counteract the other?

In point of fact, day care and father care are not antagonistic categories. Though the pie representing total time with children might shrink for dual-income couples using paid child care, moms and dads must still find a way to slice up the hours and responsibilities that remain. And, as we will explore in chapter 3, in relatively egalitarian countries with subsidized, widespread day care and early childhood education, the pressure is strong for fathers to match mothers' involvement. Most of the stay-at-home fathers I interviewed for this book—like many stay-at-home moms—pay for some amount of child care in order to do housework, work part-time for pay, search for jobs, take classes, or carve out time for themselves. Pitting paid care against stay-at-home parenthood sets up a false dichotomy. Child care isn't just for working mothers; it's for all parents.

In this regard American parents are disadvantaged when compared to their counterparts in Canada and Europe, as today's economic and social changes crash into the structures that govern parenting in America. For example, paternity leave remains a rare benefit, especially for working-class men, whose wages are stagnating. High-quality child care is expensive and sometimes hard to obtain. These are only two of the factors fueling a conflict between what women need and what men feel capable of delivering. Indeed, many forces in our society and economy limit male caregiving, as we will see in the pages to follow. Countering those forces will open new horizons for men, but it will also allow women to have more choices and more options—and, sometimes, more doubt and confusion.

For many people, male and female, the question of whether

men can effectively take care of children and homes remains open. But, after thirty years of research and growing male participation at home, we are now beginning to understand that the answer is yes, they can. The stay-at-home dad is important because he sweeps aside myths and stereotypes about what men can and can't do for their families, tears down the walls that divide men from their children, and fulfills the promise of feminism, which has always been as much about transforming gender roles as fighting inequity.

"Will women ever achieve real equality with men?" writes Rhona Mahony in her 1995 classic *Kidding Ourselves: Breadwinning, Babies, and Bargaining Power.* "I propose that the answer to that question is another question: Can a father raise babies and can a woman let him do it? That is the key question, because in order for women to achieve economic equality with men, *men will have to do half the work of raising children.*"[14]

Can we get to half? Mahony thought it was possible for men to do half the work—day care and preschool don't preclude the need for full participation—and I think it is too. Certainly men, women, and our entire society have a stake in the future of male caregiving.

Changing Attitudes, Changing Homes

This book is based on three years of research and hundreds of conversations with families all over the United States, including twelve in-depth interviews with dads who are the ones most responsible for children. I also interviewed the breadwinning partners of half of those men. These couples were drawn from every walk of life. Some are affluent; some are struggling. They are white, black, Asian, and Latino. They live in many places, from San Francisco to Chicago to Kansas City to New York.

Most of the couples are heterosexual, but some are gay. Though this book focuses primarily on what happens when biological fathers and mothers switch their traditional roles, gay men can be stay-at-home dads, too, and lesbian moms do, of course, serve as breadwinners. The issues facing gay couples with children are complicated and fascinating and, it almost goes without saying, different in many ways from straight couples.[15] Even so, as we will explore in chapters 7 and 9, the stories of gay and lesbian couples can yield new insights into why parents fall into breadwinning and caregiving roles—while also revealing possible new models of egalitarian co-parenting.

In trying to understand the origins and development of stay-at-home dads, I also delved into history, economics, sociology, demography, anthropology, psychology, biology, and neuroscience. I read every word I could find in peer-reviewed scholarly journals about caregiving fathers, breadwinning moms, and the science of sexual difference, and I interviewed dozens of researchers.

At root, however, this book represents a sustained effort to understand my own choices and feelings, which are very different from those of my father and grandfathers—and indeed there is an aching chasm between the dads of yesterday and today. *The Daddy Shift* is not primarily a memoir, but, like most books about parenthood written by a parent, it is a labor of the heart. I have tried to use my personal experiences to illustrate what it feels like for a man to take care of a child day after day—experiences that are seldom written about in our culture.

When I was born in 1970, men spent an average of three hours a week with kids, and my parents debated only whether my mom would work or stay home. They opted for her to stay home, and she didn't go back to work until my brother and I were teenagers.

In contrast, when I became a father, my wife and I saw our parenting roles as something to be negotiated. I started out as the breadwinner. As such, I did my best to be an involved father: I took on as much housework as possible, and I tried never to shirk changing diapers, getting up at night, or making doctor's appointments. This was also true of the other fathers I knew: we adhered unquestioningly to a set of unspoken expectations that seemed to arise spontaneously, though I know now that they were the product of at least a half century of historical change. I am not saying that our actions matched our ideals—that's for our wives and partners and for empirical studies to say. Rather, I intend only to describe the expectations that we strived to meet.

And yet home still felt to me like an alien, albeit happy, territory, teeming with unfamiliar emotions and strange possibilities. In truth, I understood little of what my wife was going through on a day-to-day basis, and I felt a gap growing between us. And so when my career reached a crossroads, it seemed desirable for me to take my turn as primary caregiver and for my wife to try going back to work.

We had little preparation to become parents, but we both quickly discovered that nothing at all had prepared us for our role reversal. My wife struggled with separation from her baby and was plagued by feelings of anxiety and depression. For my part, I felt overwhelmed by the daily minutiae as well as the emotional demands of taking care of an infant. Our old life had vanished; a new one was still in formation.

In my too-brief time taking care of Liko, I never replaced his mother. (Quite the opposite: to this day, she is still number one is his eyes.) For seven or so hours a day, I simply adopted a role that in my father's day was automatically assigned to the female. When my parents were children in the 1950s, only a tenth of mothers worked for pay, and women earned half as much as men. But from 1980 to 2007, their pay jumped from 60 to 77 percent of men's. Today, women are the majority owners of 7.7 million privately held companies, up 42.3 percent from 1996.[16] This is not equality, but it does represent a critical shift in economic power.

As a result, young twenty-first-century couples share a fundamentally different set of expectations about their roles and goals than our twentieth-century parents and grandparents did. Mine is the first generation of men to date a cohort of women who were born into feminist consciousness and who expect to have careers, financial self-sufficiency, reproductive freedom—and a man who is willing to share (not *help with*) domestic labor. Many of us, men and women, have seen our parents divorced, which has made marriage seem simultaneously more fragile and more precious, and has underscored the importance of cooperation and empathy.

This makes for a convoluted and confusing path to love, marriage, and children—not necessarily in that order. It also boosts pressures that were not as intense for previous generations. A study from the Families and Work Institute found that, while women of my generation experience about the same amount of conflict juggling work and family as their mothers did, men's sense of frustration has climbed precipitously: In 1977 one-third of men reported tension in balancing work and family. In 2002 more than half said they felt the squeeze.[17] These young men feel caught in a pincer movement: The economy (through factors like the rising cost of health care as well as weakening job protection) has intensified demands on their time, even as expectations of family involvement have increased. This is another dimension of the "shift" in the title of this book: As fatherhood is redefined to include both caregiving and breadwinning, men's hopes and anxieties are roughly converging with those traditionally felt by mothers.

In their twenty-year study of contemporary couples making the transition to parenthood, psychologists Philip A. Cowan and Carolyn Pape Cowan found that couples face less support and more isolation, new expectations and new emotional burdens, and more choice and more ambiguity than their parents did. The Cowans also found that, for today's parents, traditional and unequal family and work roles are actually associated with *more* stress for parents.[18] The problem, Carolyn Pape Cowan tells me, "is that in many ways the traditional family structure doesn't conform to the shape of contemporary life and couples' expectations. The new structures that are emerging are a response to a changing environment."

Jeff Cookston, a San Francisco State University psychologist who studies father involvement, put it to me this way: "We've had this remarkable shift in which we're all helping out more to bring in the resources, but we haven't quite reached a place culturally where we're able to balance that. Instead of saying, 'In a family of this type [egalitarian and gender-neutral], this is how we're going to define what everybody does,' instead everybody tries to do everything, and we're all burned to the limit. We don't have good models for this, especially fathers. We're a pilot generation, trying to find our identities within this transition time." Cookston, incidentally, is a thirty-eight-year-old dad who cut back on work two days a week so that he could equally share the care of his first child with his wife.

Families are evolving, but curiously both journalists and scholars have long focused on moms and kids when they study the impact of social change on families. Only recently has it been recognized that conceptions of fatherhood must likewise be changing, and so must the fathers themselves.

And yet at the beginning of the twenty-first century, after almost fifty years of radical upheaval in family life, the traditional ideal of father as breadwinner and head of the household persists as the baseline against which fatherhood is measured. Thus many people perceive evolution as a form of decline. A great deal of news reporting and activism around fatherhood—on both the left and the right—is crisis-oriented.

"The greatest social tragedy of the last thirty years has been the collapse of fatherhood," writes Wade Horn, former president of the National Fatherhood Initiative and assistant secretary for children and families in the George W. Bush administration. Noting the rising rates of fatherless children, Horn rejects the "new nurturing father ideal" as "an awfully uninspiring model for most men" and calls for men to reclaim their historical place as head of the household.[19]

In many respects, however, such attacks on caregiving, egalitarian dads are covers for the real target: working moms. In their 2007 book *The Natural Family: A Manifesto,* for example, veteran right-wing activists Allan C. Carlson and Paul T. Mero argue that working mothers undermine male confidence and earning power. "Government economic data indicates [*sic*] that once men take on the role of the breadwinner—a role traditionally defined as complementary to the wife's homemaker role—they become more productive," Carlson and Mero write.[20] "The goal of androgyny, the effort to eliminate real differences between women and men, does every bit as much violence to human nature and human rights as the old efforts by the communists to create 'Soviet Man' and by the Nazis to create 'Aryan Man.' "[21]

They might compare parents like my wife and me to Nazis, and confuse the goal of equality with androgyny, but even Horn, Carlson, and Mero call for dads to be "more involved" and "loving" with their families, deploying rhetoric about fathers that only rarely appeared prior to World War II. "There is now general agreement, even among men, that fathers should expect to become more nurturing than men have traditionally been in the past and plan to spend more time in domestic pursuits," writes conservative sociologist and activist David Popenoe in *Life without Father*. "Parenting should be a cooperative activity, a true partnership, between husband and wife." Even so, Popenoe stops short of endorsing stay-at-home fatherhood: "Unlike the workplace, family organization is necessarily based to some extent on the incontestable biological differences between the sexes."[22]

Can conservative activists have it both ways, endorsing parenting as a cooperative activity while still attacking what they call "androgynous parenting," in which partners have the capacity to switch roles? Will one position eventually be forced to give way to the other? Evangelical Christians, who form the social base of the contemporary conservative movement, do not have a well-defined position regarding stay-at-home fathers. My survey of articles in Christian evangelical publications about working women and stay-at-home dads reveals largely sympathetic coverage. My own evangelical cousins were supportive of my staying home to take care of Liko when I mentioned it; they thought it was best that one parent stayed home, regardless of gender, and they seemed to applaud a choice that put family first.

This raises a question: Are we seeing the emergence of a new, societywide (but still contested and unevenly adopted) consensus about what a good father does for his family?

The Daddy Dilemma: Who Are We?

In the middle of 2006, motivated by a need to overcome my personal and intellectual isolation, I launched the blog Daddy Dialectic (www.daddy-dialectic.blogspot.com) and began discussing the meaning of fatherhood with hundreds of dads I met, both online and in person. In those conversations I discovered that the traditional image of father as sole breadwinner and disciplinarian held little relevance or attraction, but none of us felt a sense of decline. Far from it, we in fact shared a positive image of father as nurturer, partner, and, in perhaps one point of continuity with the past, protector. Contrary to what Wade Horn asserts, we did find the "new nurturing father ideal" to be far more inspiring than the alternatives.

This applied across the cultural and political spectrum. On Daddy Dialectic, one evangelical Christian argued against stay-at-home fatherhood: "Men should be out there doing whatever it takes to insure that mom can spend as much time as possible with her family because she is uniquely equipped by God for the role of managing the household and the kids on a daily basis." But another evangelical responded: "Scripture commands [that men provide for their families] and leaves it at that. It doesn't specify a paycheck. If my family needs income, and my wife is better suited to earn it, why risk my family's stability by forcing my way into the workforce?"[23]

Guest blogger Chip, a former stay-at-home dad in upstate New York, rejected a masculinity that was defined solely by work: "As a guy I'll say very clearly, I would not trade my time with my kids for the best job with the highest pay in the world. Those hours were more fulfilling and enriching to me than the best novel I've read or the most lucrative account I've ever managed." Chip urged dads to spread the word and call more dads to caregiving roles. "What will change things?" he asked. "The kinds of discussions we are seeing among dads, especially stay-at-home dads, who have grappled with what Jeremy calls the dialectics of dad-hood. The kinds of shift in values that leads guys to actually want to stay at home with their kids, to downsize career and status expectations in order to have relationships with their children."[24]

This change in paternal attitudes is reflected in popular culture. Since the 1983 film *Mr. Mom,* stay-at-home dads have appeared more and more frequently in such movies as *Little Children* and *Trust the Man* (both of which came out in 2006), as well as recent TV series like *The Bernie Mac Show* and *Desperate Housewives.* Meanwhile, Hollywood stars Matthew McConaughey, Ben Affleck, the late Heath Ledger, Michael Douglas, Garth Brooks, and Rick Moranis (a widower) took on high-profile stints as stay-at-home dads—doubtless with teams of domestic servants and publicists to help them.

Perhaps as a result, news media coverage of stay-at-home dads proliferated. A Lexis-Nexus search reveals that newspapers published 458 articles about stay-at-home dads in 2000. That number had increased to 781 in 2006. That same year, *Time* columnist Nancy Gibbs claimed it was high time for the "daddy wars" to replace the "mommy wars," in which working moms and stay-at-home moms supposedly battled each other for moral supremacy.

"You can sense that the landscape is changing," she writes. "The Mommy Wars story has been around literally for decades; the Daddy Dilemma is only slowly catching up, partly because the economy has changed and pressures have grown, but also because attitudes evolve as well." She continues:

> All of which, I figure, is good news. It's no easier to generalize about the private choices of millions of men than it is about the choices of women. But nor is it any use for the public conversation to suggest that only women care about these choices in the first place. The social activists who have been working for decades to make parenting easier, make the workplace more friendly to families, make career paths more flexible, make it easier to be a "good parent"—however you define that goal—can only be helped when men care just as much about the goal as women do.[25]

New Frontiers in Fatherhood

Numerous books have told stories of paternal dysfunction and decline. This one tells the positive (but complex) stories of men and their partners who are building a new alternative on the ruins of the old. I write it in hopes of making the alternative visible, and viable, to more people. For dads, their partners, their extended families, and people who care about gender roles, this book tries to provide a companion and a road map into rough new terrain.

It is not my intention to somehow turn every family into a reverse-traditional family—as the years have gone on, my own family structure has been traditional or dual-income more often than it has been reverse-traditional. If this map has a destination, it is a world in which gender roles are more flexible and the division of family labor is negotiated, not imposed. It is also a world in which public policy supports the choices of twenty-first-century families by providing paid leave to both parents as well as high-quality day care, universal health care, and protection against discrimination, among other programs that have been shown to fuel father involvement and family health.

This is not, however, a work of propaganda. I am a journalist as well as an advocate, and I try to reveal the stresses and troubles of these families as well as their successes. The stories of the individual families are complicated and challenging, for none of these families, including my own, is a utopia. Both stay-at-home dads and their breadwinning partners struggle against feelings of social isolation, familial disapproval, role ambiguity, emotional failure, anxiety about the future, and the financial pressures and work/family conflicts many couples face.

And yet their stories suggest that people, far from being helpless victims of social change, are extraordinarily resilient and creative. Instead of wasting time lamenting the fall of the so-called traditional family, or confining themselves to rigidly ideological gender roles, they are pioneering new roles and relationships. Fathers are looking to mothers and wives for guidance, while mothers create new expectations and role models for themselves as breadwinners.

This is not a portrait of decline, but of cross-pollination, innovation, and adaptation.

The importance of reverse-traditional families goes well beyond their still relatively small numbers. stay-at-home dads and breadwinning moms reset expectations for all parents: stay-at-home dads increase the pressure for all fathers to participate in child care and housework—and create a constituency of men who might be concerned with so-called women's issues—while breadwinning moms are fashioning a new model of the working mother, one who is willing and able to accept full financial responsibility for her husband, as well as her children and herself. At the same time, fathers are helping forge a new kind of homemaking style, one in which the at-home parent unashamedly carves out time for himself and often tries to combine paid work with primary care. This transformative potential has negative as well as positive implications. For every couple that embraces new roles, at least one resists.

And yet in many ways traditional roles are no longer meeting the needs of our society, or individual mothers and fathers, or children. Something new must emerge, and it is emerging. In *The Daddy Shift,* I try to capture and describe a tricky, momentous change that is already happening on playgrounds and in living rooms, in countless casual exchanges and public debates, and in the most private moments between dads and their kids, when the child's eyes open and see Dad in a way that the sons and daughters of earlier generations never could.

Part I

The Fathers of Yesterday and Today

1

A Stay-at-home Dad's History of North America

My great-grandfather was born in rural Quebec. At the age of twelve he immigrated with his widowed mother and four sisters to Lowell, Massachusetts, and all of them started work in the city's textile mills. In Lowell my great-grandfather married and had thirteen children. My grandfather, Raymond Proulx, was born in 1923. Starting at the age of eight, my grandfather worked side by side with his father at home, tending the garden that helped feed them and taking care of the pigs, chickens, and cows they kept.

I asked my grandfather what lessons he learned from his father. He replied: "You do what you have to, and if you don't, you don't eat." Their relationship was not an intimate one. Discipline was strict and enforced with the back of a hand. The whole family worked together to maintain the household. They had meals together. Then the children would scatter outside and play with their friends. This was how families had lived for generations. For most of recent human history—that is to say, the past fifty thousand years—the vast majority of families worked together as a single economic unit, growing their own food or managing family businesses in small towns or villages where they were born, lived, and died.

"The organization of family life was not based upon people's desire for intimacy or love but on the fact that most production was organized and carried out through the family rather than through separate economic institutions," says historian Stephanie Coontz. For this reason a marriage was more often a business decision than a romantic one; the home was a center of production as well as a system of authority.[1]

Patriarchy—a system that requires men to lead families and women to serve them—was intrinsic to that system of authority. All over the world, in all social classes, for tens of thousands of years, fathers (or sometimes grandfathers) were the undisputed heads and masters of households, by both law and custom—and by extension, they ruled society and government.

"Models of idealized family structure lie metaphorically at the heart of our politics," writes linguist George Lakoff. "Our beliefs about the family exert a powerful influence over our beliefs about what kind of society we should build."[2] An authoritarian patriarchal family model shaped—or at least metaphorically defined—patriarchal social structures. Even in the most advanced democracies, women could not vote or stand for public office until the early twentieth century. Right up until the 1970s in the United States, husbands could get away with beating or raping their wives. The laws of many states tolerated abuse up to certain levels, and even at the worst extremes, men could and would receive the equivalent of a slap on the wrist.[3]

Thus the traditional image of the father is one of lawgiver, moral arbiter, disciplinarian, and CEO of the home economy—the opposite of the mother, who submissively cared for husband, children, and home. Mythologies from around the globe have enshrined and amplified the dyad of man and woman, sharply defining complimentary roles of punishment and reward, hunting and nurturing, death and life, sky and earth, sun and moon.

Yet, as the Jungian psychologists Arthur and Libby Colman point out, a countermythology has also persisted from ancient Egypt until the present day, in which mother and father switch places, so that, for example, the male becomes fertile earth and the female the all-encompassing sky.[4] These magical, ideological images flit in and out of history, merge, fly apart, and swap places, driven to and fro by social and economic forces that are anything but mystical.

Even in the practical realm of economics, the separation of feminine and masculine spheres has never been neat. Though many societies throughout history have formally barred women from paid work, owning property, and partaking in public debate, mothers have held much greater informal economic and political power than the writings and laws of a given time period suggest. They have shared in farmwork, brought goods to market, and performed essential productive tasks, such as food preservation and clothing making. In short, working mothers are not new. Women have always combined mothering and production, even if they did not control what they produced.

Likewise, the stern image of the family patriarch obscures the emotional and spiritual importance of fathers to their families. Until the Industrial Revolution, fathers and sons worked side by side on farms and in artisanal shops, while daughters might run the poultry business with their mothers and help serve breakfast, lunch, and dinner in the family kitchen—a way of life that immigrants carried to the New World.

"Contrary to what is often assumed," writes historian Ralph LaRossa, "colonial fathers played a very important role in the daily lives of their children. Although mothers may have been responsible for children under the age of three, fathers were the ones who were expected to guide older children and young adults."[5] It was fathers who made sure that the children learned to read and write; it was fathers who oversaw their religious instruction.

The term *stay-at-home dad* would have made scant sense to a colonial father—or, for that matter, to a Native American: before the Industrial Revolution, the vast majority of fathers and mothers were always stay-at-home. And Africans who were brought to America as slaves viewed children as a communal responsibility for men and women alike, drawing on their own traditions in order to cope with the breakup of families as members were sold off to various owners.[6]

Until late in the nineteenth century, all members of most families contributed to the home economy, though the father was deemed the natural leader and owner. The power resided with him, but most men were not heartless—in fact, letters and diaries reveal great tenderness between fathers, their wives, and their children, and a strong desire to be close to them. Reviewing hundreds of letters from Civil War soldiers to their families, Stephen M. Frank concludes:

> The evidence of these letters suggests that fathers expected to participate intimately in the rearing of young children, both sons and daughters. The separation from toddlers and infants was a source of distress and even guilt for some fathers, who believed that their presence was required at home for the proper socialization of young children and to serve as helpmeets to their wives.
>
> "The extra duty of caring for [our infant daughter] May will add much to your labors which cannot be shared by me so long as I am absent," wrote George Trowbridge, a surgeon, to his wife, Lebbie. "I have added to your cares without rendering aid and comfort."[7]

Cynical readers might say that Trowbridge is merely telling his wife what he thinks she wants to hear, but Frank quotes many letters in which fathers describe yearning to take care of their children or weep over separation from their wives. Can we reconcile the authoritarianism of this family system with the tenderness expressed by fathers like Trowbridge?

It might be most accurate to say that the severe patriarchal ideology of fatherhood was often at odds with the love and care that fatherhood engendered, in the minds of individual men as well as the culture at large. Trowbridge (an evangelical Christian) might not have seen his wife as an equal—and in the eyes of the law and economy, she was not—but when he longs to help care for his daughter, we catch a glimpse of the twenty-first-century dad who sees himself as co-parent, not patriarch.

The Civil War, with its submarines and submachine guns, is often called the first technological war, and it aptly symbolizes the sea change that came with the rise of steam-powered machines and mass production. Farm boys fought the Civil War, but many of their sons and daughters would quit the family farm and find work in urban factories and offices. The family as an economic unit declined.

The process was most intense for newly emancipated African American men, who fled the Jim Crow agricultural South for industrial jobs in big northern cities, often sending money back home to their extended families. "I want to be a free man, come when I please, and nobody say nothing to me, nor order me around," explained one African American migrant.[8]

But for blacks and whites alike, this process weakened the father's emotional and spiritual hold on his family, even as it gave him new importance as breadwinner. "He was a dutiful father," recalls one working-class son, "but he never kissed me, never talked to me and had conversations with me. He never hugged me—he never hugged anybody."[9]

At just the turn-of-the-century moment when industrial labor conditions were driving fathers from their families, however, middle-class reformers started urging them to spend more time with wives and children and help with housework—a tug-of-war pattern that would recur throughout the next hundred years and that continues today.

"It is far more needful for children that a father should attend to the formation of their character and habits, and end in developing their social, intellectual, and moral nature, than it is that he should earn money to furnish them with handsome clothes," wrote Catherine Beecher and Harriet Beecher Stowe in 1869. Later reformers would take this sentiment a step further. "The home is a man's affair as much as woman's," wrote the economists Martha and Robert Brueres in 1912. "When God made homemakers, male and female created He them!"[10]

Some men and women might have taken their ideas to heart. In the culture at large, however, too lively an interest in child rearing was viewed suspiciously. Nineteenth- and early twentieth-century literature and popular culture offer numerous examples of middle- and upper-class fathers raising children, but the literary critic David Leverenz found that, "typically, fathers who try to raise their children by themselves, either by patriarchal discipline or more nurturing attentiveness, become dangerous or degenerate"—as they do in Nathaniel Hawthorne's "Rappaccini's Daughter" (1844) and Henry James's *Watch and Ward* (1878).[11]

In this way, a gendered division of labor was increasingly encoded in American culture. Despite the efforts of advocates like Martha and Robert Brueres, history was driving typical fathers and mothers into separate economic and domestic spheres. Most men and women of the period would likely have agreed with this sentiment, expressed by an unemployed father during the Depression: "When a man is at home all day he cannot possibly command as much respect as when he returns to the family for a few hours of concentrated conversation."[12]

The trend did not affect blacks and whites equally: large numbers of black mothers began working for pay as soon as they were emancipated from slavery. In 1870, 40 percent of black married women reported working outside the home; in contrast, 98 percent of white married women identified themselves as housewives.[13] In 1911, 51 percent of black wives in New York City were employed, compared to 30 percent of German and 5 percent of Irish wives—numbers that held in many northeastern cities.[14]

Sociologist Bart Landry reports that ever since emancipation, black mothers have been much more likely to work than white women of the same income level. Thanks to this heritage, Landry argues that "black middle-class wives pioneered an egalitarian ideology of the family that contrasted sharply with the cult of domesticity so prominent among whites"[15]—and, as we will see later in this chapter, they provided role models that would influence the course of the civil rights and feminist movements in the 1960s.

Regardless, most white and black men embraced the breadwinning role, even if they could not always fulfill it. By the beginning of the twentieth century, the transformation of agricultural patriarch into industrial breadwinner was complete, though the patriarch still loomed in the background as a lost ideal. The obligations of breadwinning bound "men across the boundaries of color and class, and shaped their sense of self, manhood, and gender," writes Robert L. Griswold in *Fatherhood in America: A History*. "Supported by law, affirmed by history, sanctioned by every element of society, male breadwinning has been synonymous with maturity, respectability, and masculinity."[16]

A man who didn't make money was not a man at all. Men of all races and social classes did not, or were not supposed to, care for children.

The Modernization of Fatherhood

It is tempting, from our more comfortable, therapeutic twenty-first-century perspective, to accuse our great-grandfathers of being remote, uninvolved parents, but in fact fatherhood of this time, especially for poor and working-class fathers, entailed tremendous sacrifice.

"None of us had ever taken thought that Father wanted anything in this life, except the privilege of working twelve to sixteen hours a day to keep a roof over the heads of the rest of us," wrote W. O. Saunders in 1923. "It is an inconspicuous part that fathers seem to play in life. Yet how unselfishly, how resolutely they set their faces to the task of building and maintaining homes that families may be raised."[17] The ideology of breadwinning gave disenfranchised and alienated men a sense of duty and dignity; it gave their wives some measure of psychological security, by assuring them of support as homemakers.

But when men were robbed of the ability to support their families, the results could be brutal. Men who were put out of work

9

would not merely lose a job; they would lose their very identity. Chronically un- or underemployed men did not turn their energies to the care and rearing of children and the maintenance of a home, even as their wives took jobs; instead, they built walls around themselves. "He loves kids and plays with them all the time, except when he's out of work," testified one mother in the 1920s. "Then he won't play with them, but just says all the time, 'Don't bother me, don't bother me.' And of course the kids don't understand why he's different."[18] In *Fatherhood in America*, Griswold provides example after example of early twentieth-century fathers who were destroyed by unemployment. African American men were particularly hard hit, coping with institutional barriers to education and employment as well as the vagaries of economic boom-and-bust cycles. These fathers may as well have died or abandoned their families, as many did.

And yet, the widespread unemployment of the Great Depression had the ironic effect of allowing more caring and cooperative conceptions of fatherhood to gain a hearing. To be sure, all the evidence indicates that men became less involved with children during the Depression.[19] At the same time, however, more and more books and magazines promoted the idea of a "new father," who would be caregiver and role model to his children as well as breadwinner. One empirical study shows that debate and interest in fatherhood, as measured by articles in popular magazines, peaked in the 1930s, higher than any time since.[20] "A poor economy can make new ideas more attractive," writes Ralph LaRossa in *The Modernization of Fatherhood*:

> This would seem to be especially true if the ideas being circulated provide a respite from financial woes—perhaps because they valorize identities that give less weight to financial responsibility. Measuring virility and manliness in ways that were *independent* of whether one had a job [served] to counterbalance the emasculating effects of the Depression.[21]

Another, related factor that LaRossa does not note may have helped to uncouple masculinity from paid work: As men were tossed out of work, more and more women found jobs. "In 1900 less than 6 percent of married women in the United States worked outside the home," reports Stephanie Coontz. "By the mid-1930s more than 15 percent of wives were recorded as employed, and many households held jobs off the books."[22]

Even in the Depression, the growth of urban white-collar jobs offered women previously unknown opportunities. Women made up only 2.5 percent of the clerical workforce in 1870. But by 1930, women were 52.5 percent of all clerical workers.[23]

"You Work for Me"

At fifteen, my grandfather found a job in a slaughterhouse butchering cows. He quit school and never went back. The year was 1938, and the country was in the throes of the Great Depression. My grandfather stayed put in Lowell, but all over the world, people were on the move. Indeed, throughout the first half of the twentieth century, masses of people quit farms and small towns for cities—and, often, poor countries for rich ones—looking for work. Extended families fragmented, the nuclear family emerged as the dominant family form, and individuals became increasingly independent.

With each decade of the twentieth century, more women went to work, but the biggest jump occurred during World War II, when women were hired to replace men who went to fight. "I think it changed the dynamic—and gave women confidence," says one Chinese American woman of her experience during the war years. "You didn't have to be dependent on the male. Being a housewife is an honorable job. But with women who were out in the world, they didn't feel subservient to the man anymore."[24]

In 1945, my grandfather was drafted and served in World War II. In 1946, he married my grandmother and started work at a quarry—a job he would do for the next forty years. "My wife was so poor," he said. "They didn't have nothing. I took her out of poverty when I married her. At the quarry, I got fifty cents an hour, working like a horse. There wasn't a union, we just worked. If you asked for a raise, you'd get four cents," he said.

A year later my mother was born; my two uncles both came within the following decade. "It was my wife's responsibility to take care of the kids, and I used to go to work," said my grandfather. He told me that he wanted to play a role in the development of his children—which he defined as making "sure they do what they're supposed to do"—but the main measure of his success consisted of going to the quarry every day and putting a roof over their heads. "I used to go to work, come home. I didn't drink at all. I didn't spend my money foolishly. Everything went to feed the kids and buy their clothes."

I've never heard any of his children say otherwise; my mother says that she often saw my grandfather work seven days a week, for up to twelve hours a day. By the standards of his time and social class, my grandfather was an excellent father. His sacrifices were enormous, but my grandmother, Cecile Proulx, seemed almost crushed by the burdens of her life. I can't include her voice here—she died years before I conceived this book—but I have pictures and memories of a woman who seemed to be always battling against herself and the world, her lips set, her eyes fearful.

"She worked for me," said my grandfather of his wife. "I always said, 'You work for me.' She took care of the kids, and I took care of the money; I brought it home, so she would have enough." When I asked him if he faced any challenges in raising the kids, he replied: "I never did. My wife took care of all that. She brought the kids up."

Morlocks and Eloi

We think of the 1950s—when my parents were children—as the apotheosis of the father-knows-best family, consisting of a wise and strong breadwinning father, a submissive and happy homemaker mom, one towheaded little boy, and one homemaker-in-training little girl. In the 1950s, approximately 80 percent of children were raised in two-parent homes,[25] but, perhaps ironically, their parents were being driven even further apart. Postwar prosperity made it possible for the first time for middle-class families to live comfortably on the earnings of one male breadwinner, and the brand-new suburbs built a Great Wall of highway between the places where a man worked and where his family lived—reifying a divide that was a century in the making.

Men and women came to live in worlds as different from each other as the worlds of the Morlocks and the Eloi in H. G. Wells's novel *The Time Machine,* with mothers becoming almost wholly dependent on the labor of men for food and shelter. At the beginning of the decade, only 12 percent of married mothers worked—down from the Great Depression and World War II but still higher than earlier decades (and it would rise again as the 1950s ended). Crucially, many women resented losing their jobs after the soldiers came home. The layoff of those women lit a fuse that would burn straight through the Eisenhower years and set off a bomb when their daughters launched the second wave of the feminist movement.

This subterranean crisis wasn't just about jobs; it was also about community and values. The flight from farms to cities that started in the nineteenth century quickened after World War II. Following jobs, young couples moved away from the small towns and neighborhoods where they had grown up—which had the effect of even further isolating women from such support structures as extended family, whose female members might help with child care or provide a shoulder to cry on.

"The call for young couples to break from their parents and youthful friends was a consistent theme in 1950s popular culture," writes Stephanie Coontz. "In *Marty,* one of the most highly praised TV plays and movies of the 1950s, the hero . . . turns his back on mother, aunt, and friends to get his new marriage and a little business of his own off to a good start. Other movies, novels, and popular psychology tracts portrayed the dreadful things that happened when women became more interested in careers than marriage or men resisted domestic conformity."[28]

In 1955 the sociologist Talcott Parsons could write that "the

American family has, in the past generation or more, been undergoing a profound process of change."[27] The changes were economic and cultural, but they were also emotional. And many of the changes were contradictory. For though we might see the 1950s as the golden age of the breadwinning father who cultivated a behind-the-newspaper authority at the breakfast table—an image with some basis in fact—at this time many men were simultaneously embracing, or trying to create, a deeper, more cooperative relationship with their wives and children.

Their halting and awkward efforts were the fruit of the "new fatherhood," whose seed was planted in the dirt of the Great Depression. This is the 1950s version of today's Daddy Dilemma: As economic forces were pushing them away from their families, cultural and emotional forces were pulling them back in. It's a cruel and familiar dynamic. Though we might see a vast gulf between the stay-at-home fathers of today and our allegedly stern and distant grandfathers, from a longer historical perspective the two generations are more alike than different.

"The traditional conception of the family holds that the father is head of the house," wrote the sociologist Rachel Ann Elder in 1949. "Today, these values are being discarded by those who are creating developmental families, based on inter-personal relations of mutual affection, companionship, and understanding, with a recognition of individual capabilities, desires and needs for the development of each member of the family, be he father, mother or child."

Mark the date in which Elder's paper was published: 1949. In a qualitative study that was nearly unique for its time, Elder interviewed thirty-two fathers in Des Moines, Iowa, all of them veterans of World War II, about their conception of their roles within the family, including the nature and variety of what they did with their kids. While the sample size was small, I doubt Elder could have found a more typical slice of postwar American manhood. She defined "traditional parenthood" as emphasizing discipline, obedience, and a strict division of labor between man and woman; by contrast, developmental conceptions of parenthood emphasized emotional well-being and being the kind of person the parent wishes the child to be, among other qualities.

"Nearly three-fourths of the fathers interviewed gave primarily developmental conceptions of a good father,"[28] writes Elder, though a majority of the men had much more traditional ideas about motherhood and children's behavior. Seventy percent of the developmental fathers whom Elder interviewed said that husbands should help regularly with housework, while nearly half of the traditional fathers defined housework as "women's work" and only 20 percent indicated that they might help on a regular basis. "Helping with housework helps us to be together instead of me in here reading and her out in the kitchen working," said one developmental father. But not everyone agreed: "Helping with housework is out," said a traditional father, echoing my own grandfather. "She can do it." [29]

Thus at precisely the moment when we now think the family was supposedly at its most "traditional," new conceptions of fatherhood were spreading to compete with more traditional notions—not in ultramodern New York or bohemian San Francisco, but in the Iowa homes of the men who fought in World War II. Likewise, the basis of marriage was becoming increasingly fragile and voluntary. As the 1950s sped along, the postwar economic boom called more and more moms into the workforce. Prosperity turned Americans' attention from survival to fulfillment.

By the end of the decade, people were restlessly searching for alternatives. In 1957 divorce rates started once again to rise, after a thirty-year decline. That same year J. M. Mogey of Oxford University, in a paper entitled "A Century of Declining Paternal Authority," confidently predicted that, thanks to increasing fatherly participation in child rearing and family activities, "the divorce rate should continue to decline for some years to come." The stability of the nuclear family, he argued, "rests upon a new base, the redefinition of the father role."[30]

Mogey was not the only one who could not hear the earthquake starting to rumble underneath placid suburban sidewalks. "As late as 1963 nothing seemed more obvious to most family experts and to the general public than the preeminence of marriage in people's lives and the permanence of the male-breadwinner family," writes Stephanie Coontz.[31] But countertrends were brewing, often under the social-scientific radar.

In 1963 Betty Friedan published *The Feminine Mystique,* which denounced the full-time homemaker role for women and provided a crucial intellectual impetus for the modern feminist movement. The following year the Civil Rights Act formally abolished workplace discrimination against women.

The Second Shift

My parents met in Dracut High School in 1963 as well. I was born in 1970. "I wanted to be closer to you than my father was to me," said my dad, Dan. "I wanted to participate more in my kids' lives. I didn't want to just come home at five and leave everything up to your mother."

My parents were not part of the counterculture or New Left of the 1960s. My mother was not a militant feminist; my father was not a hippie or a sensitive New Ager. They were children of the white working class, and they followed their parents' expectations and trod the path to a materially better life: youthful marriage, college and career for him, stay-at-home motherhood for her, houses in a series of suburbs.

As we have seen, fatherhood—and motherhood and family life in general—had been changing for decades. New ideals spread from avant-garde social reformers in the nineteenth century to an urban, magazine-reading, middle-class group in the 1930s to many dads in America's postwar heartland to a truly huge number of baby boomers.

But as the 1970s and 1980s went by, my dad's hopes for himself as a father clashed with reality—a pattern that practically defines his generation of fathers, caught as they were between two evolutionary stages. He helped with housework more than his father ever did (a fact my mother confirms), and certainly I would not describe him as absent or remote, the way he describes his own father. Nonetheless, my dad's daily practice fell considerably short of his ideals and my mother's hopes, especially as his career in health and rehabilitative services advanced and he became the executive director of a facility. My mother, Louise Proulx, reports that the new responsibilities, on the job and at home, weighed heavily on my dad. "He was always worrying about work," she said. "It consumed his life."

Outside of the office, he pursued career-related volunteer activities, serving in professional associations and on review boards, sometimes as president or director. "It was always challenging to handle that and still be around to participate," my dad said. "I think I managed to make most of your Little League stuff, soccer stuff, and recitals, and races, those kinds of things. I felt like I was there and involved, much more than my father was."

There were also limits to what gender roles my parents were willing to consider: They debated whether my mother would work at all, not who would take primary responsibility for child care, which was her domain from the outset. "We opted for her to stay home," said Dad. "That was the question of the day. The idea that a mother could have a career and be a mom was the radical thought of the time. The thought that Dad would stay home was not considered. If it was, nobody told me, and the thought never entered my head."

Or anyone else's head, apparently. Almost certainly men were sometimes taking care of children in 1960s and '70s America, but I have never found a contemporary study that attempts to measure their numbers or gauge their behavior as caregivers. I have never read a novel or short story of the period that portrays fathers as anything other than bystanders to rearing young children. Such 1950s TV shows as *My Three Sons* and *Bachelor Father* portrayed men raising older kids, usually for laughs, but by the 1960s, caregiving dads had been replaced by fathers like Mike Brady of *The Brady Bunch,* a widower whose new wife Carol ran the household. "I used to be a pretty good cook in my day," says Mike in one episode. "Then your can opener broke and you had to get married," quips Carol. The laugh track roars.[32] Caregiving dads did exist in the 1960s and '70s—the father of Ta-Nehisi Coates, whom we will meet in chapter 6, was one of them—but their stories were not told.

On the other hand, plenty of anecdotal and empirical evidence indicates that men of this time—including the most politically and culturally radical guys—hardly provided even minimal help to their partners with child care or housework. For many of them, the resurgence of feminism (which had previous peaks in the middle of the nineteenth and beginning of the twentieth centuries) came as an ugly shock. When white women traveled south to join the civil rights movement, they found new role models in local black women activists. "For the first time," said one white woman, "I had role models I could really respect."[33]

When these activists went back to their college campuses, they launched a revolutionary new challenge to traditional gender roles. By all accounts it was a heady time for women and a confusing one for some men. But only for a minority. "By the end of the 1960s most women still did not support even the more moderate ideas of women's liberation," writes Coontz. She continues:

> As late as 1968 two-thirds of women aged fifteen to nineteen, and almost as many aged twenty to twenty-four, still expected to become full-time homemakers. A 1970 Gallup poll reported that more than three-quarters of married women under age forty-five said the best marriage was one in which the wife stayed home and only the husband was employed.[34]

Based on data like these, it is tempting to dismiss the feminist movement as a minority movement, not representative of working-class white women like my mother. But the 1970s saw social and economic changes that supported key tenets of the feminist movement, crystallizing trends that in retrospect seem to have been unstoppable.

In the 1970s the period of postwar prosperity ended. Prices went up; wages went down. Manufacturing jobs—which traditionally employed breadwinning men—started to go overseas, even as service and health-care jobs—by and large staffed by women—expanded. At the same time, high-technology and knowledge-based jobs multiplied, and educated women started to reach the higher rungs of the corporate, nonprofit, and government worlds. Men as a group saw their economic prospects dim; women as a group saw their real wages rise and opportunities brighten.

In many respects the genders traveled through the twentieth century on separate tracks—but by the end of the century women were catching up, economically, socially, and politically, and the trains were on the verge of collision. "It was inevitable that women would rise out of property status," writes the novelist and social critic Jane Smiley. "Capitalism wants every consumer, and ultimately distinctions among consumers according to gender, age, geographical location or ethnic background must break down as the market extends itself."[35]

Women responded more quickly and nimbly to social and economic change, and so they benefited in the evolution of capitalism from industrialism to postindustrialism. Meanwhile, men who were overly invested in the status quo fell behind. Feminism did not cause these social and economic changes, but by preaching equality between genders, it tried to teach women and men how to live with them.

"We reject the current assumptions that a man must carry the sole burden of supporting himself, his wife, and family, and that a woman is automatically entitled to lifelong support by a man upon her marriage," says the 1966 statement of purpose for the National Organization for Women, written by Betty Friedan. "We believe that a true partnership between the sexes demands a different concept of marriage, an equitable sharing of the responsibilities of home and children and of the economic burdens of their support."[36]

The implications of this statement were revolutionary, but in general, post-1966 feminism did not ask fathers to give up their jobs and become stay-at-home dads. Its dominant demands were to end discrimination at work and to split housework and child care fifty-fifty between spouses.

Fathers had been pioneering more equitable and caring roles for decades prior to 1966, but when push came to shove in the decades that followed, the average dad was apparently unwilling or unable to give up the power and comfort that came with being "lord and master" of his household. In fact, men's behavior at home changed only slightly during the 1970s and '80s, even when their wives worked just as many hours as they did. When sociologist Arlie Hochschild studied the work and domestic habits of fifty dual-income California couples in the late 1980s, she found overwhelming evidence that working mothers were still primarily responsible for child care and housecleaning. Hochschild famously described this after-work domestic burden as "the second shift."[37]

Enter Mr. Mom

In 1985 my mother got the first full-time job she'd had since my father graduated from college. Working as a secretary in a real estate office, she remained largely responsible for household and kid-related tasks. While this was an individual decision driven by her particular circumstances, millions of women were making the same decision. By 1988—the year I graduated from high school—only 29 percent of children lived in two-parent families with a full-time homemaking mother.[38] Meanwhile, new kinds of families proliferated: single parents, stepfamilies, multiracial families, and so on. The first openly gay and lesbian families started to appear.

As family types diversified, ideals of fatherhood fragmented, with each piece rooted in a different historical period and marked with a high level of cognitive dissonance. In the 1990s evangelical Christians still promoted the ideal of biblical patriarchy that predominated through the middle of the nineteenth century, though heavily modified by contemporary circumstances: they reframed leadership as a form of service, allowed for the possibility of female employment, and pressured men to be more committed and responsive to their wives and children.[39] Meanwhile, large numbers of men clung to self-images as authoritarian breadwinners, refusing to help with dishes or vacuuming, even as their wives went to work. Tens of thousands of divorced or never-married fathers, freed from community pressure to "do the right thing," abandoned their families or failed to keep up with child-support payments.

Others tried to forge more positive roles for themselves, an effort reflected in popular culture. The 1979 film *Kramer vs. Kramer,* starring Dustin Hoffman and Meryl Streep, depicted one divorced dad's transformation from emotionally neglectful, self-absorbed breadwinner to sensitive caregiver. The film, which won that year's Academy Award for best picture, struck a cultural nerve: Ted Kramer's journey reflected (in a hazy, idealized way) that of a minority group of mostly educated middle-class men who were struggling to share housework, rear children, make a living, provide emotional support to working wives, and cooperate with ex-wives.

In the early 1980s signs appeared that younger men and women were open to the possibility of a reverse-traditional arrangement, with female breadwinners and male caregivers. This momentous cultural change did not, of course, happen all at once. There was no epochal thunderclap and no storming of the Bastille—just an accumulation of decisions made by ordinary fathers and mothers who only wanted what was best for their kids and themselves.

In 1983 the film *Mr. Mom* marked the screen debut of the stay-at-home dad. Jack Butler, played by Michael Keaton, is a Detroit assembly-line engineer who loses his job in a wave of corporate downsizing. His wife, after eight years of taking care of their three children, returns to work in the advertising industry. This premise mirrors real life: the Michigan-based auto industry had entered a terminal decline as Asian companies took their market share and manufacturing became globalized. Tens of thousands of workers were laid off, creating a situation regionally more akin to the Great Depression than a recession, as economists and politicians of the time called it. Had this film been made in the 1930s, *Mr. Mom* would have been a tear-jerking melodrama: Jack would have sunk into alcoholism and domestic violence while his wife endured the humiliation of employment. In *Mr. Mom,* Jack certainly does struggle with the tasks of being a househusband, and his clumsy efforts to cook, clean, and change diapers are milked for slapstick comedy.

The stay-at-home dads of today often resent the *Mr. Mom* caricature of a bumbling at-home dad, but I found the film to be more complex than this stereotype suggests. Jack and his wife both grow into their new roles—they even help each other along, trading advice and support in crucial moments, drawing on their respective experiences—and by the end, Jack is a competent and confident homemaker, and his wife is a successful advertising executive. As during the Great Depression, a lousy economy uncoupled fatherhood and breadwinning, but the growing social and economic power of women allowed both women and men to pioneer new kinds of roles.

The real significance of *Mr. Mom* lies in the fact that it tries to teach guys how to behave when they are faced with domestic responsibilities: The film preaches that family men must embrace, not flee housework and child care when those tasks fall to them. When their identities as breadwinners are destroyed by economic change, argues *Mr. Mom,* family men must build new identities as homemakers. Moreover, it argues that men ought to support their wives' economic power and career aspirations—especially since lifelong male employment was no longer guaranteed and a middle-class lifestyle was no longer affordable on one income. In this way necessities are turned into virtues, as often happens.

Mr. Mom was marketed as a light comedy, but in retrospect, it marks a cultural watershed: the stay-at-home dad was now a part of the landscape—as a real option, not just as the butt of a joke. In a 1990 *Time* magazine poll, 48 percent of men between the ages of eighteen and twenty-four claimed that they would consider staying at home with their children.[40] When my mother and father were born, such a question could not even have been asked. When I was born, it could be raised only in jest. By the 1990s, however, the definition of fatherhood as breadwinning, secure for a century, was suddenly on the ropes.

Imagining Fatherhood

In 1990, I was a sophomore at the University of Florida. I could not have imagined myself one day becoming a father. If asked what a father ought to do—and I never was, not by family, teachers, peers, or, for that matter, *Time* magazine—I would have said, liberal, right-thinking gentleman that I was, that a father and mother ought to share in everything equally.

At the time, four visible ideological currents on campus aspired to influence male behavior. One came from campus conservatives, who argued for an old-fashioned brand of sexism and masculine supremacy. That held little appeal for me. A second came from campus feminists, who fought against the most negative forms of male behavior, especially such aggressive acts as rape and sexual harassment. This I supported, and I was an active member of the campus chapter of the National Organization for Women. I wasn't alone at our meetings and demonstrations; many guys participated, and none of us felt like a traitor to our gender. We were just seeking a way to address the worst forms of male stupidity—and since no leadership on these issues was coming from other campus organizations, NOW seemed like the best way to do it.

A third force tried to redefine manhood and provide a positive vision for guys to live up to: the so-called "mythopoetic men's movement," launched by the poet Robert Bly. This movement was easy to parody and mock, and it still is: leaders organized gatherings of men in the woods, asking them to get back in touch with their rough and wild masculine essence through activities like howling at the moon and running through the trees dressed only in a loincloth.

I read Robert Bly's 1990 manifesto *Iron John,* and I attended a local "men's movement" meeting, prodded by a friend. I was surprised to see several professors. They seemed to cringe as I said hello, perhaps concerned that the student-professor barrier was being breached. They needn't have worried: I didn't make it to a second meeting. Frankly, the "men's movement" (I can't bring myself to remove the quotes from around the term) seemed vapid, reactionary, and neurotic to me: vapid, because it failed to account for differences in social power between men and women; reactionary, because it looked back into premodern fables and rituals instead of forward in search of masculine meaning and standards of behavior; and neurotic, because it preached a brand of masculine primitivism that seemed fundamentally at odds with the technological real world in which we lived.

A dark, frenzied, subterranean current was sweeping through the minds of men in those years, one that was more visible, but less coherent, than the upright, marriage-minded conservative or the mythopoetic wild man. I saw warnings of this fourth force in bars near campus, as when a wasted frat brother stalked through the tables shouting, "Bitch!" in the faces of random women. I saw it in politics, when George Bush Senior bragged that he had "kicked a little ass" after his vice-presidential debate with Geraldine Ferraro and called himself a "macho man" for invading Panama. But the purest distillation of this current ran through suburban multiplex theaters in the form of action films. Coifed gym rats like Sylvester Stallone, Bruce Willis, Steven Seagal, and Arnold Schwarzenegger punched and shot their way through every constituency of Jesse Jackson's Rainbow Coalition and refought every battle America ever lost. And for good measure, they smacked around some journalists[41] and blew the brains out of their evil ex-wives.[42] These were the not-so-secret heroes of the Reagan/Bush years: violent, nihilistic conservatives who had lost hope for the future and renounced the responsibilities of caring for new life.

My grandfather mocked these guys. I seem to remember once watching TV with him and seeing a commercial for a Stallone movie. "That guy wouldn't have lasted two minutes in the quarry," I remember my grandfather muttering. To him, it seems Stallone was not a real man at all; instead, Stallone was a hideous parody of manhood. My grandfather had been a soldier and a breadwinner, and those were the two things he was proudest of. I have always had the impression that he defined those two roles by duty, modesty, and steadfastness—not qualities we saw in the action heroes of the 1980s and '90s.

In reading through my journals of those years, I am surprised to see many small reminiscences about my grandfather. Though I didn't see him more than twice during my undergraduate years, his appearances in my journals outnumber those of both my parents. In one entry I recall an incident when he had accidentally killed a man at the quarry and we found him at the kitchen table, head in his hands; on another page, I describe a bicycle he built for me, "the best bike I ever had, the fastest in the neighborhood."

We were never close. Why did I write about him so often? I think in many ways I was haunted by how different he seemed to be from me; I was quite simply incredulous that we were related. He apparently represented some rough masculine quality that I never had and didn't want, but which still held the same attraction that the image of Havana seemed to have for the second-generation Cuban-Americans whom I knew in my Miami high school. My friends had no desire to go back to Cuba—they felt their families led freer, richer lives in Miami—but they still romanticized Havana's shark-finned cars and crumbling buildings, which cast a long shadow over their lives. My family had not crossed an ocean strait, but in many ways I was just as far away from my grandparents.

Looking back, it is remarkable to me how little preparation I received for one day becoming a father, which is easily the single biggest event in my (and many another guy's) life. My culture defined manhood as Rambo with his machine gun or my art history professor in the woods, dressed in a loincloth and howling at the moon—and both definitions were fundamentally escapist. I had gotten sex education in high school, but no education in fatherhood. My grandfather and my father did not discuss with me what it might mean to take responsibility for a family, though of course they provided many lessons through examples. For previous generations, this might have been enough. But when I was young, a single definition of the "good father" as provider and protector was coming apart at the seams.

Unsurprisingly, images of fatherhood on TV sent mixed messages. Fathers like Homer Simpson of *The Simpsons* or ladies' shoe salesman Al Bundy on *Married . . . with Children* got a paycheck but provided little else to their families. Al's nemesis in *Married . . . with Children* is his neighbor Marcy D'Arcy, a female breadwinner and high-ranking bank officer whose very existence seems to taunt Al and remind him of his failures. Homer Simpson's nemesis is neighbor Ned Flanders, an evangelical Christian whose fatherly competence and concern serve only to highlight Homer's shortcomings. To me, Al and Homer both represent the eviscerated ruins of the breadwinning father, clinging to the vestiges of privilege and unwilling to embrace something new, feeling attacked by feminism on the left side and Christian "new dads" on the right.

Positive images of fatherhood also appeared in popular culture, often in unexpected places like science-fiction television programs or comic books.[43] In one story line on *Star Trek: The Next Generation,* which first aired in 1987, the gruff, hypermasculine ship's security officer, Lieutenant Worf, is stuck with raising his son after the mother is killed. Initially Worf resists the emotional dimensions of his responsibility, retreating to a Klingon traditionalism that sounds an awful lot like Christian Right ideals of the patriarchal father. But as the series proceeds, Worf gradually learns to genuinely care for his son as a single father.

In another corner of popular culture, James Robinson's *Starman* comic book series, which started in 1994, portrays a father-and-son superhero team who are locked in generational conflict. Jack Knight, a tattooed twentysomething slacker, inherits his father's mantle as the superhero Starman, but refuses to embrace his father's black-and-white worldview or wear superhero tights, preferring instead to fight crime in a T-shirt and leather jacket.

In the last five issues of the eighty-issue series, Jack becomes a father. Jack's dad, the original Starman, dies, and so does the baby's mother. Instead of retreating into superhero fantasy, Jack becomes a stay-at-home dad. "My son is more my life than . . . crimefighting," says Jack. In the panels of the comic book, we see an exhausted Jack, changing, feeding, and burping the baby, often in the dead of night, surrounded by laundry and dirty dishes. "My boy needs feeding. He needs changing. My boy needs love so he can begin to understand I'm his dad and not just some weird guy he got stuck with. He cries for his mom. He misses her. I cry too sometimes for my losses."

Later Jack seeks the counsel of Superman. "I have a son," he tells the Man of Steel. "He needs me now. I don't want him to become an orphan. And . . . I don't know . . . something's gone. Some part of me. I'm not motivated like I was. Suddenly there's an unknown vista ahead and none of them involve crime fighting. Is that wrong?" He asks Superman's permission to quit. "You met evil with valor," Superman replies. "Now let others."[44]

In the end Jack does quit and passes the "cosmic rod" that gives him his power to a female superhero. (The phallic symbolism here is too obvious to dwell upon, but the reader has my permission to giggle.) Back in the golden age of comic books, Superman or the original Starman never would have given their power over to a woman so that they could step into a woman's role. The superheroes of their time—archetypical masculine images—were muscle-bound warriors, not stay-at-home caregivers. But in the end, Jack Knight doesn't reject his fathers, both biological and metaphorical —instead, he integrates their images into a new context of gender equality and embarks upon his new role with their blessings.

There are limits to this brand of superheroic fatherhood: the wealthy Jack is not dependent on a woman for food and shelter, and he has no need to confront the trade-offs that a normal modern couple faces when a baby is born.[45] But in the end—and this is the important thing—giving it all up for his child is the most heroic thing Jack can do.

Though *Starman* might not have had the audience and influence of a show like *The Simpsons*, it embodies a radical new vision of fatherhood that valorizes caregiving as well as self-sacrifice. *Starman* is too culturally marginal for anyone to claim that it spoke for a new generation of fathers, but Jack Knight might be the closest image of fatherhood I can locate in the 1990s that makes any sense to me. That we find it on the vibrant margins, instead of the vacuous center, of our culture says a great deal of how fragmented and disorganized fatherhood had become.

Living on the Bridge

In 1991, while I was home from school, my parents separated. That day my mother drove my brother and me to the dentist. As we got our teeth cleaned, she cleaned her clothes and personal possessions out of our house and moved them to an apartment that she'd secretly rented.

There was nothing extraordinary about this divorce. My father was not abusive; my mother was not crazy. They were good parents, but their dissatisfactions with each other had been building for years. My mother's employment gave her the financial basis she needed to escape her frustration and move on to the next stage of her life. That night my father sat on the couch, sipping a beer. I sat down next to him and told him that I thought he had been a good father—it was the only thing I could think of to say. Indeed, as his son it was the only thing I had to offer. He looked down and didn't say anything.

Today I see my dad as caught between two images of fatherhood, living on a bridge he could never cross. On one side stands the remote breadwinner; on the other, the caring co-parent. He had both qualities; he could not fully embody either one. This might be why baby boomers are the most scorned generation of fathers in recent history—an empirical study of newspaper comic strips by Ralph LaRossa and colleagues found that mockery of dads peaked in the 1960s and surged again in the 1980s, as the last boomers started families. At the same time, portrayals of fathers as nurturing and competent climbed steadily through the second half of the twentieth century, peaking in 1995–1999[46]—and roughly paralleling women's rising economic power.

History—that is, the past that shapes our present, a conveniently amorphous and abstract force—would not allow my father to be one thing and not the other. If this chapter has one message, it is that we must make our individual choices within the limits that history creates. In turn, however, our choices shape history. History required our grandfathers to work long hours and put their emotions aside, which left their families emotionally stranded and economically dependent. It required our fathers to find those emotions again and shoulder the burdens of social change, though too often this quest led them to flee from their responsibilities.

And what about my generation of guys, the ones born after 1968? As we became fathers, we would indeed take on more housework and child care than our dads—Generation X dads do significantly more child care than baby boomer men, continuing a trend that we did not start and will not finish. It is laughable to believe, however, that we are a superior sort of man; our female partners still do twice as much child care and housework as we do.[47] We stand on the shoulders of the generations before us—and our children will stand on ours.

The same year as the divorce, I met the woman who would one day become the mother of my son. For over a decade, we lived together as partners and equals, sharing the housework, splitting the rent. When parenthood loomed in 2004, I anticipated that the structure of our relationship would remain fundamentally unchanged. I imagined our life as it had been, but with a baby added on. I occasionally discussed it with other dads-to-be: We all took it for granted that our wives would work and we would share housework and child care. We agreed that it would be better if one parent stayed home for at least the first year. We all thought it would be *nice*—in the abstract, in principle—to serve as the primary caregivers of our children.

We had no idea how enormously difficult this would prove to be.

2

Searching for Role Models
Ed and Rachelle's Story

Juno lifts rock after rock, his round two-year-old face focused, searching. "Bug!" he cries triumphantly, pointing to a salamander. "Bug!"

His dad, Ed Moon, squats down. "It's a salamander. That's a kind of amphibian, Juno."

Ed plucks the pinky-length salamander off the ground and slides him into Juno's hand.

"Gentle," he says to his son. "Be very gentle."

It's a warm, sunny day in February. We're standing outside their rented two-story home in Oakland, California, tramping around in a thin spit of yard, our shoes crusted in mud made by the morning rain.

"Tell me about your dad," I say.

Ed laughs sarcastically and doesn't say anything. In another person, this would seem self-dramatizing. I sense, however, that Ed is only thinking. Ed is forty-three years old, but he's boyish and stocky, and he has a scholar's face, quiet and a little sad. Words come slowly to him.

I prompt him: "What kind of role model is he for you, as a father?"

"He saw himself as a breadwinner and not much else. His attitude was, 'I'm your father and you will respect me, because of all the things I've done for you.' He didn't see our relationship as going two ways. It was more of a one-way thing, from him to me."

Ed's parents divorced when he was eleven. At first he and his sister lived with his mom, then one day when he was fourteen, Ed was caught smoking marijuana. It was decided that he would go live with his father in suburban Atlanta.

"I have a lot of fond memories from before, but after I went to live with my dad, I don't know. It was a closed atmosphere. I didn't have a lot of friends. The attitude about me was, 'He's done drugs before, so let's keep him in a cage so that he'll never have a chance to do drugs again.'"

Later I ask Ed to describe his teenage bedroom to me: long and dark with brick walls, no windows, mirrored ceiling, and a deep red shag carpet. Against one wall stood a homemade bar with leather-backed barstools, installed by the previous owner. "The whole room came complete with disco ball," Ed tells me. "The owner of the house must have been a midlife divorcé whose marriage had spoiled his chance to be a swinger in the 1970s."

I imagine a fifteen-year-old Ed lying in bed, staring at his own reflection on the ceiling, enveloped by silence. What's he thinking about? I'm guessing someplace else, perhaps a city far from his family, where he's free to be another person. Or maybe it's the opposite: he daydreams of sitting down to dinner with his dad, mom, and sister, all of them together.

"What was your father like during this period?" I ask.

"My dad was an alcoholic . . ."

"Look at me, Daddy!" cries Juno.

We look. He is standing on a pile of wood chips, legs spread, with one foot propped on a nearby fence, smiling as though he just completed a triple somersault.

"Way to go, Juno, good job!"

"About your father," I prompt again.

"He was a mean drunk. He picked on the family . . ." Ed stops talking.

31

"What do you think he did well?" I ask.

Ed is quiet for a time. "I can't think of anything," he finally says. "I don't have a good relationship with my dad."

When Ed went to college, he became a serious bicycle racer. He'd take classes for a semester, then race for a year. This went on for twelve years, until he got his undergraduate degree.

"I wasn't getting rich, but I'd make a couple hundred dollars a week, enough to get by with some other work, and I raced with professionals, some pretty famous guys. My dad wasn't supportive, except when I won a race. I won about fifty races. I think winning was the only thing that made it worthwhile to him."

On the walls of their house I see photos of Ed racing. In them he looks like a different person, decked out in mud-splattered blue and red spandex, the top of his face shielded by wraparound sunglasses and the shadow of his bike helmet. And yet you can see in the hard set of his mouth how angrily and competitively he raced. These are photos of a man who thinks only of reaching the finish line.

As Ed talks I imagine an invisible and distant figure on the other side of that line: Ed's father. How many times did Ed cross the finish line in second or third place and feel the absence of his father's approval? *Look at me, Daddy!* We all want to hear the same answer: *Way to go! Good job!* When we don't, the silence cuts deep.

Alone Together

Ed is more than an interview subject; he is a friend. Ed and his wife Rachelle went through child-care classes with me and my wife. Together we hired a professional midwife to come into our home and teach us how to perform such basic tasks as changing diapers and bathing a baby—jobs which previous generations of women learned from their mothers and grandmothers. We didn't know how to do these things. No one, male or female, had taught us how to take care of babies.

At this point in my life I lived in San Francisco. My father lived in Massachusetts, and my mother lived in Florida. My wife's father lived in Hawaii, and her mother lived in Nevada. As my wife and

I prepared to become parents, we knew only one other couple in our circle of Bay Area friends who had a child—and they divorced shortly after Liko was born.

Research shows that many, perhaps most, parents face the same challenges that we did. When the Stanford University sociologist Michael J. Rosenfeld analyzed 150 years of census microdata, he discovered a strong link between growing geographic mobility, rising independence for both men and women, and the emergence of new family types such as interracial, gay and lesbian, and reverse-traditional. "In the past, the surveillance of parents and neighbors prevented nontraditional unions," Rosenfeld says. "Today, however, young adults are more independent than they've ever been, and much more mobile—and that helps explain why we have so much more diversity in family types now than we had in the past."[1]

But that independence can turn into loneliness once a baby comes and childfree friends run for the hills. "Increasingly, new families are created far from grandparents, kin, and friends with babies the same age, leaving parents without the support of those who could share their experiences of the ups and downs of parenthood," write University of California at Berkeley psychologists Philip A. Cowan and Carolyn Pape Cowan. "Most modern parents bring babies home to isolated dwellings where their neighbors are strangers."[2]

The Cowans studied two hundred nuclear families over two decades and found that today's parents face a range of challenges that earlier generations did not. In addition to the timeless problems of sleep deprivation, putting food on the table, and learning to take care of a baby—stressful all by themselves—the Cowans found that *most* husbands and wives with new babies come to feel isolated from each other, as well as from their friends, families, and communities.

What's more, the Cowans found that "strained economic conditions and the shifting ideology about appropriate roles for mothers and fathers pose new challenges for these new pioneers, whose journey will lead them through unfamiliar terrain."

In other words, not only are we geographically isolated from family and friends, but we're cut off from tradition as well. Modern conditions make it difficult—if not impossible—to emulate older family models, leaving us with few clear templates for what our families should look like. My grandfather, for instance, told me that he always expected to be the same kind of parent his father was, and he deliberately married a woman cast in his mother's mold. "Your grandmother was just as strict as my mother," he said proudly. In contrast, I have never felt obligated to base my parenting on the examples I saw in my own family; quite the opposite.

As we will discuss later in this chapter, that is typical of the children of baby boomers. And certainly Ed and Rachelle did not feel they could look to their own parents as role models. As I discovered, they see their parents as figures to rebel against, not to emulate.

The Same Wavelength

Ed went to college and lived in Atlanta for twelve years, racing bikes and sporadically attending classes. One day he met Rachelle, the roommate of the girlfriend of another bike racer.

Rachelle and I meet in her fourteenth-floor office at an international development agency, where she works as communications director. Her desk is tidy and surrounded by the brochures and magazines she designs for the agency, set near a picture window overlooking the streets and high-rises of downtown Oakland.

She leads me into a conference room and shuts the door. There is none of the childish chaos Ed and I experienced, no bugs or salamanders or muddy shoes. We hear only the hum of the air conditioner, the murmuring of coworkers outside the door. And unlike her reticent husband, Rachelle has an open face, and she laughs and talks easily.

"Tell me about the first time you met Ed," I ask.

"We met at a party. He was supposed to date my other roommate, but he and I just totally clicked," says Rachelle.

"What attracted you to him?"

"I was attracted to his sense of humor. There were a lot of things

34

about Ed that I admired. He was really active in the cycling community, and he was getting his PhD. In a lot of ways he's like my father, which freaks me out when I actually say it. But my dad is very reserved; he's a scientist, like Ed. There was something deep in Ed that resonated with me."

Rachelle's biological parents divorced when she was two years old, and her biological father was gone from her life by the time she was six. "I do remember some things about him, and everything I remember is scary," she says. "Like, I do remember him as a cruel person, mean and abusive."

Her mom remarried when she was six, and today she calls her stepfather *Dad*. Rachelle grew up in a trailer outside Birmingham, Alabama, and her voice contains the hint of a Southern accent. Her upbringing was traditional and religious.

"I'm close to my dad, and I love him dearly, but he was too strict," says Rachelle. "He has a militaristic point of view about parenting that I totally despise, and he knows it. I didn't want to emulate the model my parents set as a couple. My mom really believes that the dad is the head of the household, and she's submissive—she believes this for religious reasons. After my little sister was born, she stopped working, and she never went back."

When Rachelle's little sister died of cancer, her parents' faith deepened while her own waned. It's an event that pulled the family together in grief, while at the same time it drove them further apart in belief.

"Why didn't you end up like your mom?" I ask.

"We just had different opportunities. My mom didn't think about being a parent. My mom was so naïve. . . . She didn't know about sex or anything. She just got pregnant [when she was twenty years old], and she didn't have time to get used to being a mom or think about being a mom. For me, college was very formative. The second I stepped onto a college campus I never again set foot in a church. My mom never went to college. She went straight from high school to parenthood. I made all my best friends in college, and that's also where I formed my political beliefs. I didn't have any before, and my mom didn't have any either."

In college Rachelle took women's studies courses and became enamored with Simone de Beauvoir. "I admired the freedom that the existentialists had: the intellectual pursuit, the sexual freedom, and that was important to me when I was becoming an adult," Rachelle recalls. "I knew that who my partner was in life was going to have to have that same kind of philosophy. Even though Ed would never put it that way, we're very compatible that way. He's nonjudgmental, open to whatever you want to be."

Ed and Rachelle married. Three years before our interview, Rachelle became pregnant—an event that triggered a three-way confrontation between her ideals, her maternal desires, and her worldly ambitions. "When I was pregnant, I had a huge struggle about whether to work or stay at home," she says. "It was a political statement for me as an individual.

"My best friend was a stay-at-home mom," Rachelle goes on. "She embraced the label, and she was always careful to mention it when other women were stay-at-home moms, and I don't know why, but at the time that really bothered me. I was like, they're not just stay-at-home moms; they're people. When I was pregnant, I wanted to work as a statement. . . .

"But after he was born, it was a nonissue. I just wanted to be with Juno. It became much more clear. I felt sorry for anyone of any gender who doesn't have that choice. Not everyone can afford to stay at home. In some ways it's a privileged debate that some people don't even get to have, because they have no choice but to work."

For the first year of Juno's life, Rachelle worked as a freelance designer but spent most of her time caring for the baby. Ed worked as a research scientist for the U.S. Geological Survey, but he found himself increasingly dissatisfied with his job. He started restlessly sending out résumés and searching for new opportunities. Then one of his efforts hit pay dirt: Ed was offered an opportunity to work for the United Nations on a conservation project in China, "counting critters in a lake," as Rachelle describes it.

Looking for adventure, the family jumped at the chance.

In China they found themselves isolated from neighbors and

coworkers by language and culture, but Ed's schedule was flexible, and for the first time, he was able to spend more time with Juno. Their family bonds tightened, and Ed and Rachelle hatched plans to leave China and move back to Atlanta, to be near friends and family. But after almost a year in China, out of the blue Rachelle was offered the job she now holds. She took Juno, then almost two years old, with her to Oakland, where he went to day care while she was at work. Meanwhile, Ed completed his contract with the United Nations. When Ed joined his wife and son three months later, jobless and at a crossroads in his career, the couple talked over their options.

"I hated having Juno in day care," says Rachelle. "And when Ed came home, he said, 'Why do we have Juno in day care all the time? I should just take care of him.'" Rachelle and Ed weren't rejecting day care in principle or in practice (Juno later went to preschool two days a week so that Ed could do housework and freelance as a Web designer), but they both wanted the chance to take care of him.

And so Ed made the leap into stay-at-home fatherhood, while Rachelle entered the brave new world of breadwinning. At first Rachelle worried: Would Ed remember that after a certain time Juno got hungry? Would he remember about packing snacks and taking naps?

"I think Ed had to learn how all-consuming it is and how important it is to get Juno out and have the day planned," says Rachelle. "But Ed has completely moved into that place. Now when I come home, Ed and Juno are on the same wavelength. They're both relaxed, and Ed isn't stressed out at all. He never asks for relief—to the point where I'm like, Don't you want to go for a bike ride or something?—but he doesn't want that."

As she speaks these words, Rachelle beams. "I've seen Ed become more planned and organized than he probably was before," she says. "And he seems incredibly happy doing that."

"Do you ever feel jealous of Ed?" I ask.

The smile melts away. "Um, yeah. I totally miss it. I mean, I feel happy that Ed and Juno are having this experience, and I feel happy here at my job. I like my job. But yeah, sometimes, all things considered, I'd give it up and stay home with Juno. And that's strange. I didn't realize that I'd feel that way."

She adds, "I was talking to my friend who has a six-month-old, and she asked me about this. And I said, nope, I'd rather be home. I was happier. I was more sure and relaxed. At work I'm more fragmented and stressed out. I like the things I'm pursuing at work, and I believe in the organization, but it can't match watching my kid grow."

Cognitive Dissonance

Ideology can lag behind (or sometimes jump ahead of) behavior, creating a rift that breeds unhappiness in family life. Though most partnered women today work and most are committed to ideals of equity and advancement, when children come, many of them still feel, often unconsciously, that their rightful place is in the home. Of course, they might deny that and insist on their feminist modernity, yet I have spoken with many moms who share Rachelle's ambivalence.

In the first decade of the twenty-first century, women are serving as the sole breadwinners in roughly 7 percent of American homes—and, as stated in the introduction, a third of wives earn more than their husbands.[3] Women's average weekly pay has jumped 26 percent since 1980; during the same period, men's pay has increased just 1 percent.[4] Today women in their twenties earn more than men the same age in many American cities, including New York, Chicago, Boston, and Minneapolis. All this evidence suggests that the number of women breadwinners will continue to rise.

This circumstance can create a high level of cognitive dissonance, as traditional expectations clash with the new reality. Many women "are of two minds," says the historian Stephanie Coontz.

On one hand, they're proud of their achievements, and they think they want a man who shares house chores and child care. But on the other hand they're scared by their own achievement, and they're a little nervous having a man who won't be the main breadwinner. These are old tapes running in their head: "This is how you get a man."[5]

As in the case of stay-at-home dads, the small numbers of breadwinning moms belie their cultural importance. They are a carefully watched test case and an example that others may, or may not, follow. To date, the results have been mixed. In a 2007 essay for the *New York Times,* M. P. Dunleavey writes that breadwinning moms "are seething—with uncertainty, resentment, anxiety and frustration." While her own husband "cooks, cleans, shops and takes care of our son," Dunleavey is filled with "terror that I'll be the breadwinner forever."

She goes on, "Does the fact that he's doing so-called women's work have so little value in my eyes—or am I afraid of how others might view a man whose contributions can't be measured in dollars? Am I a Susie homemaker wannabe because I sometimes pray my husband will decide to go to law school and earn a good living?"[6]

Dunleavey's piece was part of a wave of first-person accounts by mothers fulfilling the father's traditional role that appeared in the mainstream media in 2007. Many of those pieces echoed the sentiments expressed by both Rachelle and Dunleavey. In an essay for the women's magazine *Marie Claire,* "Why I Left My Beta Husband," author Amy Brayfield writes that she initially loved it when her first husband Mark stayed at home with their daughter, which allowed her to focus on her career. But Brayfield found herself "mortified" when coworkers discovered that her husband was a stay-at-home dad.

"I had it all back then," she writes, "including a gorgeous toddler and a cool job. What I didn't have was a husband I felt proud of." She continues,

> I felt guilty about being glad to go back to work, and in my head, I made it Mark's fault. Because he couldn't find a job, I blamed him when I was working late and had to miss the

baby's bedtime; it was his fault I had to go in early every day, since the fact that he couldn't find a job meant that I couldn't afford to lose mine.

Brayfield divorced Mark, and got custody of their daughter. But the ending had a twist: "Nobody was more surprised than I was when I went ahead and fell for another stay-at-home dad." This, of course, allows Brayfield to continue to pursue her high-powered career—and gives us yet another example of a woman caught between her ambitions, her emotions, and her ideology.[7]

These two essays, and dozens of others like them, provoked a firestorm of criticism and debate in the blogosphere. Many breadwinning-mommy bloggers disowned the image of the "seething" working mom who doesn't respect her "subservient" stay-at-home husband. In her blog Half-Changed World, breadwinner (and public policy analyst) Elizabeth Lower-Basch asked if women like Dunleavey aren't measuring themselves by the wrong standard. One of the strains on mothers who support their families, she writes in another entry, "is that we rarely give ourselves mothering credit for being breadwinners. We often beat ourselves up for the things that we don't do, without giving ourselves corresponding brownie points for the things we do. Maybe we should stop worrying about whether we're good enough mothers, and decide that we're damned good fathers."[8]

The Good Father

Ed and I are sipping apple juice on the front porch, watching Juno continue his never-ending quest for bugs.

"What's most stressful about taking care of Juno?" I ask.

"Finding things to do, when we're alone. But I feel most stressed when Rachelle is around. She's a really good mom and she always catches things, but I don't worry about some things. She'll catch things, and I'll get defensive and think that I'm not a good dad. She's much more protective, I think, and I'm more laid back.

"I also worry that I'm not talking enough. That goes back to high school, when my dad and I didn't talk much and I didn't have a lot of friends. It's stuck with me. I think it's pretty typical, when you're part of an abusive, alcoholic family, to retreat."

"What does your dad think of you staying at home with Juno?" I ask.

"He's insulting about it. Not so much about me taking care of Juno. More about the fact that I don't have a job right now. He's in his sixties; his health is deteriorating, so he lashes out at anything." (During our interview Ed was learning Web design and taking on projects as a volunteer. Within a year after our interview, he had started getting paid for designing Web sites on a freelance basis.)

Juno wanders over to the concrete steps that lead down the hill from their street to the neighborhood below. Ed lets him stand at a railing, looking down at a ten-foot drop.

I say, "My wife would never let our son stand there."

"Rachelle's terrified of the stairs. She won't let him go near stairs like that."

"Are you more careless than Rachelle?" I ask.

"I wouldn't say careless. . . ."

We both laugh.

"He is more likely to get hurt with me . . . well, not, like, hurt. I'm careful with him, but I like to give him more room to, you know, experiment, see what he can do. He'd never learn to walk down the stairs otherwise."

"What are some things a good father does?" I ask.

For once, Ed doesn't hesitate. "A good dad is close to his kids. He's there emotionally. He's supportive and encouraging, whatever the kids want to do, within reason."

He pauses.

"But I think the most important thing is for a dad to set a good example. You have to be the kind of man you want your son to grow up to be. You can't impose your ideas on him. You have to *be* the idea and just hope he gets it. If they see you being kind to other people, they're more likely to be kind to other people."

We stop talking, both of us pondering his words, and we stand up and walk over to the yard where Juno now squats, intently watching another salamander traverse the landscape of his tiny hand. Juno starts to poke and prod at the salamander.

"OK, Juno," says Ed. "Let the salamander free."

He squats down next to his son and helps the salamander back into its home under the rock.

"You don't want to hurt him," says Ed, taking his son's hand.

No Role Models

"Fathers tend to parent more like their fathers than their mothers," writes a team of researchers, "but few fathers—ironically, even those who tend to take less responsibility for their children—say they learned to parent from their own fathers."[9] In 1993, Kerry Daly of the University of Guelph, in Ontario, interviewed thirty-two fathers about their style of fathering and their role models, asking many of the same questions that sociologist Rachel Ann Elder posed to Iowa veterans forty-four years earlier.

"One of the most striking findings was that these fathers perceived that they had no specific role models," Daly writes. "Although respondents frequently talked about their own fathers in response to the question about models, their fathers served only as a negative role model or a reference point for what respondents wanted to change in their own lives."[10]

Ironically, it was the baby boomers who had pioneered more caring, participatory ways of fathering, and they were not even the first. As we have seen from Elder's research, credit for that actually goes to *their* fathers, the so-called "Greatest Generation," who straggled and marched through the Depression and World War II.[11] Theirs was the first generation whose wives were called in large numbers to the workforce. And many of them mustered out of the army with a deep appreciation for the frailty and coziness of family life.

"I used to think I didn't want the responsibility of my family any more," said one of the vets, "but after seeing German kids wanting to eat scraps from my mess kit, I decided that I should accept the responsibility for my own family."[12] Other factors conspired to increase their emotional investment in family: as some of these men moved away from the places where they grew up, they formed nuclear families whose bonds were less economic, more cooperative, and less tangled with other families—which created intense emotional burdens.

Elder also reports, "About a third tried to be like their fathers, another third tried to be better than their fathers, and a third tried to be different." Here we see the beginning of a process that would accelerate as the century wore on: fathers rejecting their fathers as role models and seeking to succeed where a previous generation is judged to have failed.

By the time Kerry Daly interviewed his thirty-two Canadian fathers in the early 1990s, the hairline crack between generations had widened to a chasm—and dads were compensating by looking to their wives, mothers, and each other for guidance.

"In light of the perception that parenthood had changed so dramatically from the previous generation," Daly finds "a tendency to search for specific instances of good fathering behavior among one's peers." At the same time, however, "the men in this study viewed their mothers and wives as providing some of the more practical and tangible guidance for how to provide care for children." One father tells Daly: "I think my mom for the most part did a better job of getting me ready to be a father. When the child came home, there was more input from my mother in helping me out on how to handle things; where my father was pleased for me, you know, 'it's your child,' and that's what I got from my dad." [13]

These men did not look only to wives, mothers, and each other for role models. Just as Ed spoke to me of being "the kind of man you want your son to grow up to be," many of the men Daly interviewed spoke explicitly about trying to reshape themselves as *new* role models. "For most, the intergenerational continuity of fathering ideals and practices was being consciously severed," he writes and then goes on,

In light of this, they spoke of being role models to their children in a way that represented a departure from previous generations of fathers. Instead of presenting an inherited model of fatherhood to their children that is rooted in the past, these fathers appeared to be focused on the construction of a fatherhood model from the values of the present.

One dad explicitly rejected the patriarchal prerogatives of the past: "The idea of the father having license to do whatever he wants because he is the father, I think is wrong, and I think the father must be what he wants his children to grow up to be." [14]

Daly's findings are not isolated. In 2006, Trent W. Maurer and Joseph H. Pleck interviewed over a hundred parents in order to understand how feedback from others shapes parenting behavior and parenting identity. They also found that new fathers did not look to their own fathers for guidance. Instead they looked to mothers and also to fathers their own age.

"The more involved fathers perceive other fathers to be," they conclude, "the more they attempt to model the level of that involvement (and the more models they have)." Maurer and Pleck suggest that such peer influence is one of the most decisive influences on fathers' caregiving behavior—perhaps just as important as their wives' expectations. During a time when new families are isolated and separated from tradition, it makes sense that new parents would look to one another for guidance.

Maurer and Pleck's study produced one other interesting result. They note an earlier study by Pleck that found that the more a mother is involved with the *worker* role, the less time she *feels* she has to enact the *mother* role. In the new study, however, they found that this result did not apply to fathers, despite the fact that fathers reported working twice as many hours on average as mothers did. "These findings suggest that although caregiving and breadwinning behaviors may be competitively organized [internally] for mothers, they are not for fathers." [15]

This does not imply that mothers are somehow worse at organizing their time than fathers. As I understand their results, it means that fathers tend to see breadwinning as part of parenting—even though the two usually happen in different places—while many mothers see working as a separate activity that takes time away from their children. This explains why both stay-at-home dads and their breadwinning wives struggle with feelings of inadequacy, even as they continue to grow into new roles.

Blossoming

"I like working," Rachelle says. "I'm good at working. But I want to have another kid. So for me, our child-care situation is raising a lot more questions than it's answering. At work I do forget about Juno and Ed, because I'm so happy with Ed being home with Juno, and so secure with what Juno is doing with his day—where I wasn't before, when Juno was in day care. I was split, because I was worried about Juno all the time. But Ed being home has freed me up to push through this job, but at the same time, the job has taken me away from being the mother that I want to be."

However, Rachelle has few regrets.

"We're gaining so much," she says. "Juno is gaining a strong bond with Ed. We both feel like these are incredibly important years in Juno's life, and he's going to get to spend lots of time with both of his parents. I feel like most kids don't get that opportunity, especially with their dad. The way that Ed is a parent is so different from the way I'm a parent, and Juno gets to see both sides. I love the stuff they do together, and I love Ed's attitude. He never seems frazzled."

Rachelle has seen her husband change and grow as a stay-at-home dad, from a man who kept to himself and repressed a great deal of pain—the racer I saw in the photos, hell-bent on winning —to someone who is opening up to the world and discovering a capacity for love and caring that appears to surprise both him and his wife.

"He seems to have blossomed as a person, being a stay-at-home dad," says Rachelle. "And I try to tell him that lots of times so that he doesn't get discouraged about not having a job. Because at first, he didn't want to say he was a stay-at-home dad. He seemed a little bit ashamed. Now I hear him saying that to people—and they always say, 'That's so great.' He's really blossoming in his role."

Why Do We Love These People?

From one point of view—perhaps the dominant one in our culture —Ed and Rachelle's stories contain all the elements of the apocalyptic decline-of-the-family narrative: divorce, (mild) drug use, absent or abusive fathers, rejection of religion, and role reversals that call into question what it means to be a man or a woman. There is no question that Ed and Rachelle might have benefited from (and preferred) more stable and loving family situations, when they were growing up. Their individual stories are microcosmic distillations of fifty years of disruptive family change.

But decline is not the whole, or most important, story, for there is a positive side as well, chiefly the educational advancement and economic empowerment of women and their growing ability to bolt from dangerous marriages, such as the one Rachelle's mother appears to have had with her biological father. The economists Betsey Stevenson and Justin Wolfers found that in states that adopted unilateral divorce, suicide of married women fell 20 percent and domestic violence dropped significantly.[16] Higher rates of divorce also appear to lead to lower rates of homicide among wives and husbands.[17]

In Ed and Rachelle's stories we also see how men's range of emotional expression and experience has grown to encompass empathy, gentleness, and caregiving, even as men like Ed still fight to find the words that can describe their emotions and experiences. And instead of rejecting the new images of mother and father that have grown from these changes, Ed and Rachelle have embraced them and developed a profoundly cooperative relationship, one that depends not on the submissiveness and dominance that defined their parents' marriages, but instead on communication and mutual well-being. To be sure, they have their occasional arguments, and both speak of unresolved tensions, but neither feels trapped. Both feel like they have been able to live full lives in the context of their marriage, taking turns at work and care.

Is it possible that the decline of one type of family is giving rise to new types that might actually be better at cultivating the health and happiness of their members? Of course, divorce did not create stay-at-home dads. Women going to work did that. But as we have seen, divorce was an important part of a multidimensional package of changes that created the economic and emotional basis for the stay-at-home dad.

Po Bronson, author of the 2005 book *Why Do I Love These People?*, writes on his blog:

> Before my parents divorced, my father worked and my mother was a homemaker. . . . After the divorce, I watched my Dad constantly doing what had once been called 'woman's work.' He did the laundry every night, he cooked dinner. . . . I rarely got to see my Dad work at his job, but I constantly got to see him cook and clean.

Echoing the themes of *Kramer vs. Kramer,* Bronson continues:

> What if, in breaking homes into two, [divorce] actually helped give rise to a new type of father two decades later? All gender roles were blurred. We watched our moms work, and today we're comfortable with having working wives. We watched our dads clean and cook, and so we do more around the house as adults. . . . I think back to my guy friends from high school. Those of us today who are most "New Dad"—(including that we married women with careers) —all came from divorced homes.[18]

I had read Bronson's blog entry the week before I interviewed Ed, and I knew that Ed's parents were divorced, so when I asked Ed about his dad, I think I was hoping to hear another heartwarming story about how he saw his old man become a more caring, domesticated person as a result of the divorce—but that turned out not to be the case.

Ed, I discovered, is carrying around tremendous pain, but he deals with it, and one of the ways he does that is by trying to be the best, most caring dad he can be—that's how he is healing himself of the wounds that were inflicted on him in adolescence. In many respects, both Ed and Rachelle had the worst of both worlds: their parents divorced and yet their fathers remained cold and distant.

Several studies of stay-at-home dads have discovered that many of the men became more involved with their children because their own fathers were not involved in their upbringing. In other words, dads are more likely to get up in the middle of the night and change diapers if their own fathers rolled over and went back to sleep.

This insight might help explain Ed's evolution, but it is only one variable among many. Why will one guy repeat every unkind remark his father ever made to his own children, while another vows to be a different man? Why will one succeed at that task while another fails? We might never know for sure, but evidence we have seen in the studies by Pleck, Maurer, and Daly strongly suggests that providing positive role models and social support for caregiving is key to a father's—and a family's—success in navigating uncharted waters.

Postscript:
Legacies of Divorce

Ed and Rachelle's experiences are representative, but not universal. Many families manage to maintain a caring, connected environment in the wake of divorce. Many fathers step into new roles as a result of divorce and provide an image for sons to emulate. In her essay "Binuclear Man," the psychotherapist Ruth Bettelheim shares an experience that echoes Bronson's. Her divorce forced her ex-husband to take responsibility for all aspects of the children's lives.

"At first the task was overwhelming, but gradually he found a way to be a different kind of father than he had been," she writes. "Although certain kinds of empathy and nurturing behavior are still difficult for him, he learned to meet many of the children's needs that had been previously out of his sphere."

Bettelheim continues, "Study after study have found that adult children of divorce are more empathetic and have a greater devotion to honesty, kindness, and integrity in relationships than their peers." From her ex-husband's example, Bettelheim claims, her son "learned how to be a parent in ways that his own father was never taught as a child. Unlike his father and both of his grandfathers he has had a role model of a father who is hands-on and a primary caregiver."[19]

Bettelheim's conclusion is counterintuitive. Studies by Judith Wallerstein and others have found that divorce can have a profoundly negative impact on both children and families, and many of us know this to be true from firsthand experience. Bettelheim doesn't dispute the damage and pain that divorce causes, but her more subtle point is that families can, and do, make the best of bad situations. Both she and Bronson argue that children, especially boys, can gain emotional and domestic skills, such as empathy and caregiving, which will serve them well in a world where women are supposed to be equals.

Constance Ahrons, a psychologist who studied 173 children of divorced families over a twenty-year period, argues that it is the quality of family life after divorce—not the mere fact of divorce itself—that shapes outcomes, both positive and negative. "A good divorce doesn't destroy children's family bonds and relationships," says Ahrons. Her study found that most of the grown children "emerged stronger and wiser in spite of—or perhaps because of—their parents' divorces and remarriages."[20] Almost 80 percent, she reports in her 2004 book *We're Still Family,* said that their parents' divorce had positive outcomes. More than half felt that their relationships with their fathers actually improved after the divorce.[21]

No one knows what effects male caregiving will have on the divorce rate or the emotional quality of postdivorce families—the phenomenon is too new. Rhona Mahony, the author of *Kidding Ourselves,* argues that stay-at-home dads will probably not have any impact on the rate of divorce, but divorce will become "less harmful to children than it is today." Fathers who share the care for children will feel a stronger attachment to their children and will be less likely to stop visiting or helping, she argues, perhaps idealistically. More of them will have primary custody. And because breadwinning mothers start from a higher base of biological attachment than the average father today, they will also be less likely to abandon their children emotionally or financially. More of them will be paying alimony and child support.[22]

Already the terms of divorce are shifting: the percentage of men receiving alimony rose from zero in the past to 2 percent in 2001 to almost 4 percent in 2006, according to the U.S. Census Bureau. "The idea that men can receive spousal support from their wives may feel like a freakish concept, but as women have become higher earners, it's increasingly common," reported *Forbes* magazine in 2007. "'A lot of women are indignant now that the shoe is increasingly on the other foot,' says Carol Ann Wilson, a certified financial divorce practitioner in Boulder, Colo. . . . 'I've seen thousands of clients,' she says, 'and almost every time I've seen a stay-at-home dad seek alimony, the wife—she's usually a software executive—goes ballistic.'"[23]

It appears that equality, when it finally comes, will not be utopia. The best we can say is that it will be better than what came before.

3

Stay-at-home Economics, or Five Myths of Caregiving Fatherhood

Vince Janowski never wanted to be a stay-at-home dad. He got a good education and went to work in book publishing in New York City. He supported his wife when she went to law school. They envisioned a future as a professional, dual-income couple and bought a house in the affluent suburb of Hopewell, New Jersey, which in 2007 had a median household income of $77,270—almost $30,000 more than the national average.

In 1998, their daughter was born. That same year Vince was laid off in a wave of industry downsizing, but his wife had started work as a lawyer. So instead of seeking a full-time job, Vince freelanced two days a week and took care of his baby daughter the rest of the time. When his daughter turned four, Vince went back to work full-time in New York, and when their son was born in 2003, his wife went down to part-time and he supported the family. This arrangement lasted for two years, until Vince was laid off once again. His wife started again full-time as a lawyer, and he took on care of both kids.

If you find this narrative confusing, so does Vince. Indeed, their economic roller-coaster ride caused a great deal of stress for the family. "If things had been different, I'd still be working, and my wife would be doing the part-time thing," says Vince. "There's a certain amount of reluctance to accept the situation. You just don't want to admit that you have to settle for something that's different from what you wanted."

But a funny thing happened over the next two years. As he took care of the kids and the house, and his wife advanced in her career, they grew into their respective roles and came to accept them. "I like it," he now says. "It's not strange to me anymore. It seems like a natural thing." Today Vince calls himself a stay-at-home dad—and, his wife says, he "seems more like himself."

In Vince's story we see how one family has been shaped by the economic forces that have altered the family landscape during the past five decades: as men like Vince have faced increasing economic insecurity, women like his wife have gone to school and advanced in careers and earned more money. By doing so, mothers have gained the ability to support families.

This dynamic has changed the way some families make decisions about how to care for children. Once, as we saw in the first chapter of this book, a dad at home was beyond the pale. Today, for many families, it is an acceptable option—and an evolutionary adaptation to a new economy that is global, hypercompetitive, and unstable. If a father gets the sharp end of the stick of globalization, today's diversified families are not necessarily condemned to poverty, as were those of the past with a sole male breadwinner. Instead, moms can go to work and dads can stay at home—roles that can flip again as time goes on.[1]

Vince's story reveals that even relatively privileged people are not immune from economic disruption. It also seems to confirm one stereotype of at-home dads as a luxury of the educated and affluent. But what about a couple like Joey and Angela Dorantes?

Joey, who was raised in San Francisco's Mission district by Mexican-born parents, tends a bar part-time while his wife Angela works as a waitress and dance teacher. There's little in his upbringing—which sounds tough, at least to my ears—that would have suggested Joey might one day share child care with his wife. He was beaten, sometimes with belts, for disobedience, and his father was the undisputed head of the house. But most of his friends did not have fathers at all—they were dead, deported, jailed, or just out of the picture—and Joey loved, idolized, and feared his dad, feelings that are intertwined and inseparable in his mind. "I had somebody there," he says, "who was going to be there for me, that we could look up to, where the buck stopped."

But when Joey was sixteen, his father was killed in a car crash. Today Joey remembers him as "a great father."

Joey—who was once my neighbor in the Mission and is still my friend—grew up to be a sturdy, handsome, and good-hearted man. After his first child, Julius, was born, Joey wanted more than anything to be a part of his son's life—and he recognized that working was important to his wife. And so instead of seeking to ramp up his paid work, as most fathers do, Joey cut back on his hours so that Angela could keep her two jobs and they could share child care. This arrangement persisted after their second child was born (though when I interviewed them shortly after the birth, Angela had temporarily quit waiting tables), with each continuing to work complementary shifts.

When I ask why they crafted a child-care arrangement so different from their parents' generation, Angela replies, "We're a modern couple." As she says this, her eyebrows arch and her chin tilts up, almost as if she is challenging me to contradict her.

For Joey, fatherhood is not a vehicle for emotional growth. "We gain something, but parenting's not really for our personal gain. It's for the kids."

And yet Angela notes that since he started caring for his children, Joey has become more patient and thoughtful. "Now that he has to think about what children need, he's much better about time management and being prepared," she says. "He thinks about other people."

Five Myths of Caregiving Fatherhood

In both these examples we can see how the structure of the fathers' work lives altered the emotional landscapes of their families. Economics and emotion are not separate spheres; changes in one influence the other. This chapter explores how economic instability and employment conditions mold men's caregiving behavior—and how men's caregiving is in turn reshaping the economy. It also looks at how the persistence of sexism affects the economics of reverse-traditional families, even as they appear to transcend it.

This is a topic permeated by myths, half-truths, and lies, five of which I discuss below. But the big myth that encompasses all the others is that caregiving fathers each fit the same social and economic mold. What that mold is, exactly, depends on the prejudices of the person propagating the myth. To some, stay-at-home dads are all white, ponytailed, espresso-sipping liberals who quit creative-economy careers so that their Hillary Clinton–like wives could pursue theirs. To others, stay-at-home dads are moochers who can't hold down a job.

But taken together with the other profiles in this book, these two stories—one of a suburban, professional, Anglo-American couple and the other of an urban, working-class, Latino American couple—point to a fundamental empirical truth: Caregiving dads are ordinary guys of many cultures and educational levels who have a range of motivations for taking care of kids. They don't necessarily call themselves "stay-at-home dads"—and many of them work at least part-time, as Vince and Joey do—but they nonetheless take on many of the child-care tasks that once fell primarily to mothers.

As is often the case with new or minority social practices, a great deal of what people seem to believe about reverse-traditional families is actually the opposite of the truth. Their popular image has been shaped by rampant bias in the slice of families portrayed in the media. My survey of two years of newspaper and magazine articles about stay-at-home dads shows that most of the dads profiled are comfortably middle class, which means their particular circumstances set the terms of the debate the articles were often claiming to cover. Low-income and working-class fathers do not appear in most of these stories.[2]

Empirical facts underlie each of the myths we will explore, but the facts are more complicated than the myths would have us believe. Reverse-traditional and egalitarian families are affluent *and* they are poor—and everything in between. They can be found in every ethnic group. Sometimes couples choose their roles, and sometimes economic forces don't give them any choice at all. Sometimes they learn to be happy in their roles, and sometimes the stress of change drives them apart. If there is one truth behind all the following myths, it is that reverse-traditional families are diverse. Each family has strengths to draw on; each also has weaknesses to minimize.

Myth No. 1:
Stay-at-home fatherhood (and motherhood) is the luxury of educated elites.

As an example of this myth, I submit the very first post to my blog Daddy Dialectic: "Dads-at-home will be a tiny minority for as long as parents have to scramble to keep their heads above water, trying to make enough money to survive and give their kids the best life possible, under the circumstances."

At the time I wrote that, I had thought about the issue for all of two seconds. Like many other people who should know better, I reflexively assumed that stay-at-home parenthood is a luxury of the affluent. I was wrong. And if I had used my own experience as a guide instead of simply adopting a widespread assumption, I might have written something different. At the time, my own family was struggling to get by, and so were all the other families I knew with a stay-at-home parent.

When public policy analyst Elizabeth Lower-Basch (herself a breadwinning mom married to a stay-at-home dad, whom we encountered in chapter 2) looked at census data for couples with children under fifteen years of age, she discovered that families with stay-at-home parents, both male and female, actually had lower than average incomes. In part this is because families with a stay-at-home parent have lower incomes, period—there's one adult earning money instead of two. But being lower on the economic ladder also makes it more likely that one parent will stay home or that parents will split work shifts and share care as much as possible.

According to Lower-Basch's analysis, the families *most* likely to have a stay-at-home mother were those with annual incomes between ten thousand and twenty-five thousand dollars, and mothers were more likely to be employed as they went up the economic ladder. This result is roughly corroborated by many other studies, which show that the more educated and affluent a woman is, the more likely she is to be working.[3]

Then Lower-Basch dug deeper and found a fact that will surprise many people: families with a stay-at-home dad *had lower cash incomes* than families with a stay-at-home mom. Over 15 percent were poor—compared to 12 percent of families with stay-at-home moms—and fewer than 22 percent had family incomes above seventy-five thousand dollars—compared to the 31 percent of families with stay-at-home moms.[4]

Lower-Basch argues that this is in part a legacy of sexism. "On average, there's still an overall gender gap in earnings," she says, meaning that, in general, breadwinning moms have less earning power than male counterparts. But, she says, it's also "because reverse-traditional families specialize less than traditional families." In other words, women are less likely than men in traditional families to become "purely" breadwinners. Moms, with their tight biological bond with children and more culturally developed sense of family responsibility, will tend to keep their hours at work under control and stay as involved as possible at home, which potentially undermines their earning power over the long run. Meanwhile, stay-at-home dads are more likely to earn some money, even if the amount is small.

To many people, these facts are counterintuitive. Why should poor, working, and lower-middle-class parents be more likely to stay home with children (or split the care) if they are less able to afford it? Part of the answer lies in the cost of child care, which varies a great deal, depending on where you live, the age of the child, the type of care, and the number of hours the child spends in care. But it's not hard to figure out the bottom line: you are employing other people to take care of your children so that you can go to work. If your income is significantly higher than what a nanny or preschool teacher makes—and in our society, they don't earn nearly as much as they should[5]—it makes economic (if not emotional) sense to hire that person to take care of your child. However, if your income is lower, it doesn't.

Furthermore, a 2008 census report reveals that as your income shrinks, the percent of your income that you spend on child care increases: poor families who paid for care (as opposed to those who receive free or subsidized care) spent an average of 29 percent of their income on child care, while working- and middle-class families spent only 6 percent.[6] In other words, a family of four earning $21,000, considered poverty level by the federal government, might pay $5,000 a year for the two youngest kids to go to an off-the-books, in-home provider of questionable quality—and that will still have a bigger impact on their standard of living than a family earning $160,000 and paying $25,000 a year for two kids to attend the most expensive Reggio Emilia preschool in the city.[7]

And competition for child care is fierce, especially in major cities. According to the National Association of Child Care Resource and Referral Agencies, in 2007 the number of preschoolers with working parents exceeded the number of child-care slots by 25 to 75 percent in half the states, including California (where Joey and Angela live) and New Jersey (where Vince and his family live). In urban areas, the rising cost of child care has outpaced the national average by 17 percent.[8]

In short, poor, working-class, and even many middle-class parents can't afford for one parent *not* to stay home or for both of them *not* to split shifts and share care. Here issues of equity come to the fore: which parent will cut back on work and take on care? While breastfeeding mothers might seem like the obvious and traditional choice, what happens when Mom makes more money than Dad, or Dad loses his job? Suddenly, tradition doesn't seem to amount to much, and neither does biology.

Myth No. 2:
Stay-at-home dads are lazy men
and inattentive fathers.

This leads us to the second myth about stay-at-home dads: that a man who takes care of children cannot hold down a "real job" and usually avoids doing housework and child care. In this way of thinking, fathering is synonymous with breadwinning: the lack of a job equals a failure in fathering.

This came up when I was interviewing a thoughtful and committed doctor serving a low-income African American community in San Francisco. (Incidentally, half of all new doctors in the twenty-first century are women.) She told me that she never saw stay-at-home dads in her office—"just good-old-fashioned unemployed dads." But, I responded, the very fact that those dads were taking their kids to the doctor indicated some level of care and involvement. Might they be replacing one essential child rearing task with another?

The doctor paused. "I guess I never thought of it that way," she said.

She could see their presence in her office only as a sign of their failure as providers, instead of evidence of caring, involved fatherhood. I saw another, affluent application of this myth in the 2006 film *Trust the Man,* in which an unemployed father, played by David Duchovny, spends all day watching porn and neglecting his family.

According to this myth, stay-at-home dads are dysfunctional parents who are so demoralized by unemployment that they are incapable of pulling their weight around the house—and, as we saw in chapter 1, this did indeed happen during earlier periods of history, before women started going to paying jobs in large numbers.

When I started searching for stay-at-home dads to interview, I actually found chronically unemployed dads to be the most difficult group to pin down. In conversation I discovered that this is in part because such men are often not proud of their caregiving role and some are doing everything they can to escape it. When the doctor I interviewed tried to send fathers my way, none in the end would agree to a deeper conversation after the initial contact. "I'm not a stay-at-home dad," said one man, who refused to be interviewed for this book. "If I said that, it would be like giving up. I'm looking for a job." I'm sure other writers have had similar experiences; thus the bias I found so pervasive in the media is partially reflected in this book. Materially and emotionally secure fathers are apparently more willing to discuss their feelings and experiences, and to call themselves "stay-at-home dads."

To be sure, there's no shortage of guys who fit the negative image. When some dads are involuntarily out of work, they feel themselves to be "stuck" with child care. Society views them as failures, and it is inevitable that they might come to see themselves in the same dim light—as in the case of Vince Janowski, who had to struggle to build a new self-image.

But when a mother is out of work and taking care of her kids, we seldom call her "unemployed" and certainly not "a failure." It is generally assumed that she has just stepped into a different and necessary role, one that, according to the traditional view, comes more naturally to a woman. In fact, I suspect many people see a mother's being forced back into the home as having a certain "rightness" to it: she didn't choose to become a homemaker, but it's better for everyone if she is. It feels equally "wrong" when a man is in the same position. These attitudes are deeply encoded in the collective unconscious of our culture.

However, when sociologists like Paula England and Kathryn D. Linnenberg have studied the caregiving behavior of low-income unemployed dads, they've discovered that these dads did indeed take on more caregiving tasks—"because, duh, they're home," says England, who teaches at Stanford University. This starkly contrasts with previous generations of fathers, who plunged into drink and depression when they lost the ability to support families. New research also finds, not surprisingly, that their reversed roles are shot through with ambiguous feelings and conflict with their wives.

"Being unemployed tends to correlate with a lot of other things, like having been involved in drugs and crime and stuff like that," says England, referring to chronically unemployed low-income fathers. "So these weren't the best relationships." Instead of choosing to be stay-at-home dads, "they happen to be in this situation where he didn't have a job and she did. He was doing a lot of care and the women appreciated it, but it wasn't actually seen as the ideal situation for either of them."

England, who studies the sociology of gender, says that poor and working-class men often resist adopting a caregiving role. "It's a lot easier to get women's roles to change in a nontraditional way than men's roles," she says. "So more women get jobs, more women have careers. People have some resistance to that, but mostly they think that makes sense."

The problem is that women's traditional work has been denigrated for centuries. "We value the male stuff more than the female stuff, so when women had to step out of traditional gender roles to do the male stuff, everybody respected [their paid work] more," says England. The opposite is true of men doing women's work: their unpaid work is respected less. And England argues that, in the past, many men who were socially disadvantaged by their race or social class used "the trump card of gender" as much as they could in order to feel more powerful. "So you get this situation where the college-educated guy with a good job can afford to be more feminist," says England. This is an advantage Vince Janowski brought to unemployment: he'd been to college and had had a good job, and his liberal values allowed for the possibility of a role reversal.

But in spite of this, data show that even low-income and unemployed men today are for the most part doing more and more housework and child care. Economic distress is always bad for father involvement (and it's not so good for moms either). When parents are focused on survival, stress and despair can drive them away from their children. But when the Beloit College sociologist Kathryn Linnenberg studied fifty-seven low-income couples, she discovered unemployment could, under the right conditions, drive men into a positive role with their families.

"Men are often pushed into family-first fathering because they are not currently working for pay," she writes. But if the relationship with the mother is loving, and the couple has values that prize children and family-life, the reverse-traditional arrangement can work out. The men "wind up enjoying how the care work is distributed, [even if] it did not originate out of a desire for family time. The bond with the family is an unintended consequence, in part generated by the guilt such men feel for not fulfilling their role as breadwinners."

Linnenberg finds a pattern different from the one uncovered by earlier research into the caregiving behavior of low-income males—as well as a great deal of historical information—which showed that they did *less* work around the house. "Could it be," she asks, "that at the bottom of income distribution . . . men are now defining fathering as a worthy masculine endeavor?"[9]

And so it is true that economic dislocation—and inflexible workplaces—can push parents of both genders out of work and into the home, which causes stress and conflict. But when the right values and the right conditions are in place, it is also true that many families adapt to their new circumstances, and even thrive.

Myth No. 3:
The decision for a father to stay home
is always an economic one.

That said, for many families, low- and high-income alike, staying home is often a positive and noneconomic decision.

Parents of modest means intuitively distrust the quality of the child care they can afford and instinctively feel that they will do a better job of raising their kids—and their intuition is backed up by research. Numerous studies, writes Jane Waldfogel in *What Children Need* (2006), indicate that "children whose mothers work long hours in the first year of life or children who spend long hours in child care in the first several years of life have more behavioral problems. . . . Children do tend to do worse [in health, cognitive development, and emotional well-being] if their mothers work full-time."

Does this mean that working mothers are responsible for damaging their children?

Emphatically *no*.

First of all, the quality of paid care matters a great deal; parents who can afford it, or who get lucky or have help from relatives, can put their kids in good hands, and the kids will thrive. Indeed, decades of research show that a sensitive and responsive day-care worker can do a better job than an indifferent or depressed mother. But secondly, and more importantly for the purposes of this discussion, research shows that fathers can be the ones to take care of children. Waldfogel writes:

> We need to be careful in interpreting these results, given that in nearly all cases studied the fathers were either working full-time themselves or were not in the household at all. These results tell us the effect of having two parents working full-time or a lone mother working full-time. And so their clearest message is that children would tend to do better if they had a parent home at least part-time in the first year of life. They do not tell us that the parent has to be the mother.[10]

Whatever the research finds—and the controversies over the impact of day care on children are far from settled—families will choose a lower standard of living over questionable day care, and the economics of the situation will compel more paternal involvement even in the context of more traditional cultures. When the sociologists Ross Parke and Scott Coltrane, of the University of California at Riverside, conducted a five-year longitudinal study of how Latino and Anglo families in Riverside cope with economic stress, for example, they found that Latino families are often willing to accept much higher levels of material deprivation in exchange for time with children—and that this could contribute to greater paternal involvement.

"The middle-class profile of the Latino families would make them poverty level among the Anglo families," Coltrane told me in an interview, meaning that Latinos as a group have a lower economic floor and ceiling than Anglo-Americans as a group. "A lot of the mothers are not employed. In one sample, only a third of the mothers, in another, only 40 percent of the mothers, are employed, and that's very different from the Anglo families where [in our study] 80 percent of the women are employed."

Many other families, like Joey and Angela Dorantes, will split work and care equally—a situation that pertains in one-third of working-class families with young children.[11] Parke, Coltrane, and their colleague Thomas Schofield discovered that the decision of how to structure work is based more on an antimaterialistic ideology of family togetherness (which academics call *familialism*) than on an ideology of male supremacy, though obviously traditional notions of gender influence the division of labor. However, contrary to stereotype, their study found that Mexican American fathers tend to be significantly more involved with children (though not necessarily housework) than their Anglo American counterparts[12]—a result echoed in many other studies.[13]

"I do the housework but he also helps," one Mexican American mother told Texas Tech University researcher Yvonne Caldera. "I go to work at six in the evening and from there on he's in charge of the house. He feeds the children dinner and he leaves the kitchen clean for me."[14] This is echoed by Linnenberg's study of low-income couples. She found that, while couples sharing care and splitting shifts at work might save on day care, "economics do not seem to be the primary motivation, at least by the parents' accounts."[15] Instead, they were driven by a desire to share the care of their children.

We see this illustrated by the story of the Dorantes family. Joey does leave a disproportionate share of the housework to his wife, but he is a highly involved, caregiving father. "Before [Julius] was born, the plan was that we would do as much of the parenting ourselves," says Angela (who is primarily of Anglo descent). "We didn't even look into child care. Unless you're making tons of money at work, it's not worth it." But they both make it clear that staying home with their kids was ultimately *not* an economic decision. "The most important thing was that we wanted to be the ones to raise our kids," says Joey.

But what about families with more education and income? Even families that can afford high-quality child care will make sacrifices in order to care for their own children. The *Wall Street Journal* reports (based on data from the Bureau of Labor Statistics) that once the decision is made for one parent to stay home with the kids, many affluent families take a serious financial hit. Many of them lose the ability (at least temporarily) to save, invest, buy homes, or make discretionary purchases. In short, they are no longer affluent. They are simply getting by[16]—and generally speaking, they entered this arrangement fully aware of the consequences.

This has certainly been the case with my wife and me: as a teacher and a nonprofit manager, respectively, living in one of America's most expensive cities, we were never "affluent" in the conventional American sense. But in our child-free state we had money for things like travel, nice furniture, CDs and books, entertainment, and restaurants—and we had substantial savings to boot. After Liko was born and we voluntarily took turns staying home with him, our savings dried up, discretionary income vanished, and our debt rose.

And so staying home with Liko might be viewed in one light as a bad financial decision and therefore "irrational"—that is to say, from an economic perspective, insufficiently selfish—but I can't say we have any regrets. In fact, in retrospect it's clear that we had little choice. Liko wanted us to take care of him, and we wanted to take care of him. We simply did what we had to do—a statement I've heard echoed in almost all my interviews with parents.

This should not be read as a passive-aggressive criticism of dual-income parents with young kids: Children are different, and so are families. Many parents need to work, for financial and/or psychological reasons; some kids go to day care and seem to like it. That was not the case with my son when he was an infant and toddler. We sent him to preschool only when we thought he was ready and we were ready, starting at two half-days a week after he turned two and moving to five half-days when he was three years old.

At this writing, we both work and he attends preschool for much of the day. My point is not that one kind of family is good and another is bad; indeed, my own has gone through several stages. Instead, my point is that families are different and diverse and that today that diversity should be respected and supported.

This is why absolutist economic arguments against stay-at-home parenthood will mostly be ineffective. In her 2007 book *The Feminine Mistake,* journalist Leslie Bennetts provides a grim litany of financial warnings to women who stay at home with children, in an effort to scare them to go back to paid work. "So many women are unaware of practical realities that range from crucial changes in the divorce laws to the difficulties of reentering the work force and the penalties they pay for taking a time-out," writes Bennetts about the contents of her book. "I devoted two chapters to financial information alone."[17]

I agree with Bennetts that stay-at-home parenthood comes with substantial risks, and it is true, of course, that women are still the ones who disproportionately bear those risks. Much of her advice to mothers is sound—protect yourself, keep a hand in the job market, think about the future—and applies equally well to stay-at-home fathers. Families are intrinsically cooperative enterprises whose members are highly interdependent. Specialization is efficient, but it also makes each member more vulnerable to the negative effects of change. If the breadwinning spouse dies or leaves or loses his or her job, the whole family, especially children and the stay-at-home spouse, is at risk.

But Bennetts frames the problem as the fault of women (witness the title of her book: *The Feminine Mistake*), and her solution is to call for all women to work for pay and for families to hire babysitters. That's obviously fine for many families, especially affluent ones, but she glosses over the fact that the quality of day care is a function of income. She gives scant attention to other cultural and governmental solutions that might be better for children and contribute to greater social equality, such as more male caregiving (which she seems to dismiss as a chimera), flexible workplace policies, legal protections for caregivers, and a sensibly constructed social safety net. We will be looking more closely at many of these solutions later in the book.

In the end, the altruistic nature of family life makes it impervious to Bennetts's dollars-and-sense argument, which is mostly directed to middle- and upper-class women. Her recommendations are more likely to make individual women feel anxious and guilty than empowered and purposeful, because they might conflict with the commonplace desire of mothers to take care of their own children. And yet today women are not the only ones who feel guilty about not spending enough time with kids. Many men have evolved to a point where they, too, are intimately involved in care—and some struggle to contribute at least as much as moms.

Myth No. 4:
Men are marginal to networks of care.

In her 2001 book *The Invisible Heart,* the economist Nancy Folbre argues that two economies allocate the resources we need to survive—one governed by the "invisible hand" of the market, where everything is for sale, and the other animated by the "invisible heart," where relationships are based on empathy, altruism, and care. The two economies are divided by gender: traditionally, the invisible hand belongs to men, the invisible heart to women.

As women have gone to work, however, the caregiving sector has grown and come to be governed more and more by the invisible hand, which in recent decades has driven up the cost of care and made high-quality care inaccessible to those who cannot afford it. Unlike Bennetts, Folbre does not dismiss the value of the invisible heart. Instead, she argues that society must become more altruistic—and so must men. "There is nothing natural or inevitable about the way we associate femininity with altruism," she writes. "If we can reinforce caring behavior in women, we can also reinforce it in men." She points out that over the past century, we have seen some men play more caring roles in their families. "Most fathers also care for their children," she writes of today's dads. "They change diapers, get up in the night to warm their babies' bottles, and go to work to earn the money to buy the milk and bicycles and computers their children need."[18]

This leads to our next myth: that men are marginal to the economics of caring for children. When the sociologist Karen V. Hansen studied four "networks of care"—that is to say, the elaborate and delicate web of spouses, relatives, friends, and paid caregivers who take care of children while parents work—in 1990s California, she reported that she initially expected to interview only women. To her surprise, however, she found "four fathers, four uncles, a grandfather, and a male friend involved in the daily tasks of caring for and caring about children." When Hansen found so many men in the first network she studied, she dismissed it as an aberration. "However, by my third network, after repeatedly encountering men as essential cogs in the caregiving systems, I began to realize that perhaps my assumptions entering the field were ill informed."[19] (Note that Hansen conducted her fieldwork in the 1990s, when male caregiving was less common than it is now.)

Hansen isn't alone; many people, including many feminists, make the same mistake. Like many beliefs about caregiving dads, this piece of conventional wisdom falls apart when we bother to look at the numbers: census reports since the mid-1990s have consistently shown that one in four fathers takes care of the kids while the mother is working. In 2008, the U.S. Census Bureau reported that fathers cared for 30 percent of the preschool children of white mothers while they were at work. Fathers weren't as prominent with most other ethnic groups, but they still played a strong role in all of them. (Incidentally, grandparents provided roughly the same amount of care as white fathers, and more for other ethnic groups.)[20]

Hansen writes, "Swept up by my critique of the inequality of the big picture—where women do most of the work and take major responsibility for raising children, running kin systems, and caring for the elderly—I made light of the supplementary contributions of men." The people who participated in her study set her straight, "emphasizing the significant contribution of men to the networks and to the children."[21]

Folbre argues that unpaid care work is largely invisible to the marketplace, though it's essential for the economy to function and society to reproduce itself—but as Hansen's study shows, caregiving men are often a hidden force within that invisible economy. Their participation is usually concealed for ideological reasons: conservatives do not want to admit that men are capable of caring for children, I would argue, because they fear doing so will undermine male power; meanwhile, some feminists (such as journalist Leslie Bennetts, philosopher Linda Hirshman, and scholar Pamela Smock[22]) cannot seem to accept that men are participating more in child care, perhaps because they fear that admitting progress will diminish the urgency of appeals for change.

Note that no one is saying that deadbeat dads don't exist or that the gendered division of family labor has vanished. I am certainly not saying that men contribute equally to child care—it is still the case that men control the invisible hand and women by and large form the invisible heart. Instead, I am arguing that men *do take care of children* and that *their contributions matter a great deal*—to the mothers, the children, and society at large—and if we recognize and exalt their contributions, instead of denigrating them as "women's work" or as token efforts, more men will see them as expectations to meet and examples to follow. In an era of economic instability and rising maternal employment, this is not a luxury. It's a necessary adaptation that families must make in order to survive.

Myth No. 5:
Men would not take advantage of parental leave or flexible hours even if those benefits were more widely offered.

I hear it all the time: "I wonder how many fathers would take advantage of their year away from paid work to care for their child?" writes one commentator on my blog. "I notice now that while some larger companies offer paid paternity leave, it is rarely taken."[23]

If you look at the plain statistics today, this myth seems plausible. The federal government does not require that employers offer paid paternity leave, and only 13 percent of American companies do, but it is true that American men often do not take the full leave available. [24] For example, one Michigan-based company that offers six weeks of paid leave reports that only 10 men a year, out of 2,000 total employees, take advantage of the policy. A bank in North Carolina found that in 2001 only 12 new fathers took leave, out of 70,000 employees. That same year, 520 mothers took parental leave.[25]

The question is why. Is it because of an innate aversion to child care? An unwillingness to make sacrifices for their families? Or is there another reason?

Despite its obvious importance, there is little empirical data about this question—few researchers have gone out and actually asked fathers why they don't take advantage of paternity leave, on the rare occasions when it is offered. One 2000 survey of mothers and fathers found that 78 percent of new parents did not take leave because they didn't feel able to afford the pay cut that usually comes with it. Forty-three percent said leave would hurt their prospects for promotion; 32 percent claimed they'd lose their job if they took leave; 21 percent said their employer denied their request.[26] A 2008 Monster.com survey found that roughly half of fathers did not take paternity leave when offered. The reason? They couldn't afford it, because the leaves entailed either a pay cut or no pay at all.[27]

These stark numbers are underlined by plenty of anecdotes and speculation by human resources directors and corporate spokespeople. "One reason for not taking advantage of it is because they may perceive that it might hinder their climb up the corporate ladder," a spokesman for AT&T told *HR Magazine*. "The best way for companies to promote usage of the leave is for senior management to use it. My impression is that parental leave will take off with fathers after some high-profile CEO stays home for a few days to take care of his children."

His impression is supported by several surveys in the 1990s that showed a majority of managers believed that new fathers should *not* take advantage of flextime and parental leave policies.[28] And it is safe to assume that men's anxieties are fueled by watching what happens to women who take advantage of maternity leave or flextime: many studies have documented the harsh discrimination and penalties mothers can face at work. For example, when the sociologist Arlie Russell Hochschild studied one supposedly "family-friendly" company for her 1997 book *The Time Bind,* she found pervasive discrimination and sanctions against mothers who took time off for their children. When one manager explained to Hochschild why he refused to let an employee named Connie take the afternoon off to bring her son to the doctor, he made it clear that money was not the issue. Instead, the issue was power. "If I let Connie take Wednesday afternoons, I'll have Laura asking me for time off next," he said. "She's got three-year-old twins. Rena has the desk on the other side of Connie, and her dad just had a stroke. We have a *business* to run."[29]

The discrimination is real, and so is the intense pressure that men feel to make money after they become fathers. It's a role that many men have been prepared to take on. They understand it; they know what is expected of them; and they know the consequences when they don't meet expectations: criticism from partners and relatives, a stalled or deteriorating standard of living, and a catastrophically deflated ego.

Mike Rothstein of San Francisco, a chemical engineer and father of two, was threatened with a layoff when his start-up was swallowed by a big pharmaceutical company. After a tense month of restructuring, he found himself promoted instead of fired—but his new bosses made it clear that he had to prove himself. Today he leaves for his job as a chemical engineer before the sun rises and comes home late at night.

"For the position that I have, that's what's required," he says. "I have a big job title, eight people reporting to me. I make a lot of money and have a lot of responsibility. I can't just walk in the door at ten and stroll out at four." Why doesn't he get a new job with less responsibility and less money, in order to spend more time with his kids? "My wife doesn't want to work, but she wants a nanny two days a week and she wants to be able to buy clothes. She's depending on me to be the provider, and so are the kids." Not surprisingly, spending two hours alone with his children leaves him feeling "flattened"—just as I had been before my stint as Liko's primary caregiver. Mike is not accustomed to caring for his children. It's not his job.

To better understand the pressures that dads like Mike face, consider the feelings of many of the breadwinning moms interviewed in this book. Most—not all, but most—of these moms are uncomfortable with the burdens of breadwinning, and they live in fear that something will go wrong at work. Rather than wishing they had their partners' presence and help at home—the standard complaint of many a stay-at-home mom—they wish they had more help making money.

"I would have been more comfortable being one engine on a twin-engine plane," says breadwinning Chicago mom Debbie Wang. "Instead, I'm the single engine on a single-engine plane. This means I worry to no end about my employment situation. It's not even so much the income, but it's the health insurance, college savings, and retirement accounts. It's difficult to fly without a safety net, especially when others in the household are relying on you."

The main advantage dads have in this regard is that most of them have been raised to accept this responsibility—and, perhaps, they feel a weaker visceral tie to offspring than do women. But in interviews, I have found that breadwinning dads, breadwinning moms, and breadwinning gay and lesbian parents all sound similar when they describe what keeps them up at night. "I stress about work all the time," says Lisa Holt, a lesbian mom. "I feel like I have to work nonstop, because my family is so close to the financial edge." It is anxiety about supporting their families, not an aversion to spending time with kids, that drives many of them to work longer hours. For the most part, they are all too aware that they are missing time with their families, but they feel like they have little choice. For male and female breadwinners alike, this is often the great disappointment of their lives.

This casts the dilemma of the working dad in a different light: the strongest factors are situational and economic, not biological or inevitable. As the situation changes—as it has, throughout history—family relationships evolve. Indeed, many recent studies show that, as wives earn more money, men feel less pressure to bring home the bacon, and thus do more housework and child care. For example, one 2007 analysis of data spanning thirty-one years found that the more hours a woman works for pay, and the more experience she has as a worker, the more housework her husband does[30]—a result echoed in numerous studies.[31] The maid is not picking up the slack in most of these studies—the contributions of husbands and wives are being measured relative to each other. This, notes sociologist Sanjiv Gupta, represents a significant change from the past, when men who earned less than their wives were reported to do even *less* housework in order to salvage their manly pride.[32]

This pattern holds around the globe. When Jennifer L. Hook, a sociologist specializing in family demographics, analyzed forty-four time-use studies from twenty countries, she discovered that men's unpaid work (primarily housework and child care) rises with national levels of women's employment.[33] Swedish women, for example, have some of the highest average female incomes in the world, and the men they live with do the most housework and child care.[34] The United States, meanwhile, is plagued by a huge, uneven distribution of domestic labor and earning power, which leads to persistent poverty among mothers and children.

The differences between the United States and Sweden did not happen overnight, and they are hardly accidental. Instead, they are the deliberate products of decades of diverging social policy. Sweden didn't start out supporting father involvement. For most of the twentieth century, the social democracies of northern Europe extended support only for mothers to stay home with children. As a result, Scandinavian women have historically had jobs but not careers: one report by the International Labor Organization found that women held fewer leadership positions in Sweden than they did in the United States.[35]

But in Sweden, policy has evolved as Social Democratic leaders applied their ideas to every sphere of life. "Equality is an enduring goal for policy," proclaimed the 1969 national congress of the Social Democratic Party. "Equality cannot be 'achieved' at a certain point in time. Rather, it must be a permanent ambition permeating all political activities."[36]

This proclamation unleashed decades of reform whose goal was to increase the independence and equality of women. In 1974, Sweden invented paternity leave, which catalyzed long-term changes in patterns of work and care. "By 1986, more women were combining paid work and motherhood in Sweden than anywhere else in the world," reports journalist Ann Crittenden. "Some 90 percent of mothers of children under age sixteen were working outside the home. The proportion of women quitting their jobs after childbirth fell to less than 10 percent. Among university-educated Swedish men and women, the rates of participation in the labor force are now virtually the same."[37]

In Sweden today, fathers are entitled to 10 days of paid leave after a child is born, and 80 percent of them take it, often combining it with vacation time. Parents get a total of 480 days off after they have a child, with 60 days reserved for mothers and 60 for fathers. The rest can be divided according to the wishes of the parents. Of those days, 390 are paid at 80 percent of the parents' incomes, with the remaining 90 days paid at a set rate. In 2006, 20 percent of fathers took their share of extended leave.[38] That might not seem like a lot, but it compares very favorably to the minuscule number of American fathers who take advantage of the paltry amount of leave available to them. And after Swedish parents go back to work, high-quality day care is available to all parents, regardless of ability to pay.

The reforms had a sweeping impact on the culture of fatherhood in Sweden. When the Swedish researcher Anna-Lena Almqvist interviewed twenty French and thirty-five Swedish couples in an effort to understand why fathers did or did not take advantage of parental leave and how that related to their self-images as men, she found that Swedish fathers expressed a more "child-oriented masculinity" and actively negotiated for more time with children.[39] "By international standards, Swedish fathers take on a good deal of the day-to-day care of their children," writes the Swedish feminist Karin Alfredsson. "Mothers still stay home longer with newborn children, but the responsibility for caring for sick children—while receiving benefits from the state—is more evenly divided between mothers and fathers. It is almost as common for fathers as it is for mothers to pick up and leave the children at pre-school and school."[40]

Ann Crittenden has found the presence of men with children to be a striking feature of Swedish life, and so have other foreigners. "In my home country of England," writes former journalist Rob Hincks, "stay-at-home dads are something of a rarity." ("Rare" is relative: the number of stay-at-home dads in the United Kingdom is dramatically higher than it is in the United States.[41]) But when he moved to Stockholm with his Swedish wife, he found that culture and public policy allowed and even encouraged him to become the primary caregiver for their children. He continues:

> There isn't a father I know in Sweden (and I know many) who hasn't taken at least two months off in the first two years of their child's life. That's two months more than any fathers I have known outside Sweden. . . . More importantly, outside of the easily defined paid leave period, Swedish fathers contribute much more to the family unit than their international counterparts. The fact that during the writing of this article I have washed my daughters' clothes . . . picked [the children] up from day nursery and made an autumnal vegetable soup for their dinner is nothing that I can boast to my Swedish male friends about.[42]

Because of the sheer amount of paid leave available to parents in Sweden, it is virtually impossible to compare stay-at-home parenthood in Sweden directly to the United States. The context is too different—very few parents in America take care of their kids at even a fraction of their old pay—and that says a lot. The bottom line: Swedish citizens, male and female, are both more likely to stay home with young children *and* more likely to go back to work. They are not trapped into one role.

This pattern of female breadwinning and male caregiving is echoed in countries that have adopted similar policies. When Germany—which once had one of the most gendered divisions of labor in northern Europe—started offering a gender-neutral subsidy in 2007 for a parent to stay home with a child during the first year of life, fathers took advantage of the policy in unexpectedly large numbers. Twenty percent of the fathers who signed up planned to take a full year off; 21 percent planned 3 to 11 months at home; and 58 percent planned 2 months.

"I think many more men would stay at home if they had the opportunity," says a Berlin father who stayed home for two months with his infant son. "The politicians act as if it's a huge gift, but actually it's not—it's an improvement, but I think even more would stay at home if they could afford it."[43] This father's assertion is supported by Jennifer Hook's study of twenty countries: aside from high levels of maternal employment, the availability of paid paternity leave is the single most important factor driving men's level of housework and caregiving.[44] When the province of Quebec in Canada (where my great-grandfather was born) introduced a five-week paid leave solely for fathers, the number of Quebec men claiming parental benefits jumped from 32 percent in 2005 to 56 percent in 2006. "Fathers were two-and-a-half times more likely to dip into government-paid leave benefits if they had a spouse who earned the same or more than they did," says one Canadian report.[45]

The upshot: We know from the northern European and Canadian experience that men will take more advantage of parental leave if policy, workplaces, and culture support them. In America the culture is changing in advance of workplaces and public policy, and a new generation of fathers is more willing to take advantage of leave and rebel against workplace cultures, even at the expense of careers. When the American University Program on WorkLife Law studied sixty-seven trade union arbitrations in which workers claimed to have been punished for meeting family responsibilities, they discovered that two-thirds of the cases involved men taking care of children, elders, or sick spouses.[46]

In the meantime, more and more fathers are filing complaints with the federal Equal Employment Opportunity Commission (EEOC), claiming that their employers have discriminated against them because of their caregiving roles. In some cases, says the EEOC, "employers have wrongly denied male employees' requests for leave for child care purposes while granting similar requests to female employees."[47] "I expect that the number of men coming forward to claim caregiver discrimination will increase," says EEOC attorney Elizabeth Grossman. "Men are deciding to fight the stereotypes. Men are deciding they want to have a work/family balance." And a warning to their employers: Jury verdicts in their favor have reached as high as $11.65 million.[48]

As a result, more and more companies, large and small, are offering family leave benefits to men. "A few years ago, I would have told you that paternity leave wasn't that beneficial in terms of recruiting and retaining," Burke Stinson, a spokesperson for AT&T, tells *HR Magazine*. "But today, I would say these 20-something men are far less burdened by the macho stereotypes and the stereotypes about the incompetent dad than their predecessors. They are more plugged in to the enrichment of their children and more comfortable taking time off to be fathers."[49] It's an observation echoed by Howard Schultz, chair of the Starbucks corporation, in 2007: "Men are willing to talk about these things in ways that were inconceivable less than ten years ago."[50]

Men are evolving, but society, business, and government still drag their collective feet. The gap breeds unhappiness—not to mention lawsuits—but it also creates opportunities. Through all the twists and turns of their lives, guys like Vince Janowski, Joey Dorantes, and the other fathers interviewed in this book aren't waiting for a new world to be born. Together with their wives and partners, they are making it themselves.

Now we can ask: what does this new world look like?

4

Searching for Community
Chien's Story

"I'm really boring," Chien Nguyen tells me in e-mail. "There are no guarantees that I have stories to tell. In fact, I really don't know if I'm the type of 'stay-at-home dad' you would like to meet with."

Chien didn't seek me out—his friend and fellow stay-at-home dad Alan Wang put us in touch—and he seems reluctant to agree to an interview. But I'm always intrigued by people who describe themselves as "boring," and I figure it won't hurt to fit Chien into my Kansas City, Missouri, itinerary. We set our meeting at a Barnes and Noble bookstore near my hotel. He ends up being the first interview of the trip.

I spend that morning exploring the Westport neighborhood, which, one local warns me, is "funky and tough." But when I get there, I find the streets feel safer than those of most San Francisco neighborhoods, and a lot less funky. It's a gray, blustery Saturday. The only families I see on the sidewalks are African American, and I stop to chat with a gaggle of moms on their way to a church event, small children swarming around us.

"I love KC!" says one. "But I wish there were more jobs." She works as a hospital administrator, but her live-in boyfriend, who has been out of work for a year, serves as a part-time caregiver to her two school-age kids (sired by another man shortly after she graduated from high school). As we part, she invites me to come with them to a church barbeque; I regretfully decline. "OK then," she says. "Good luck with that book!"

Kansas City is a metropolis with a population three times the size of San Francisco's, and yet it feels smaller, or perhaps just more fragmentary. Sitting at the center of the continental United States, Missouri is one of the whitest (86.5 percent, according to the 2005 census) and most politically conservative states in America: George W. Bush won Missouri twice by double digits, and in 2004, 71 percent of voters passed an antigay amendment to the constitution of Missouri defining marriage as the union of one man and one woman.

Religious belief is widespread, and most religious people are either Roman Catholic or Baptist.[1] In the Barnes and Noble of an upscale pedestrian mall called Country Club Plaza, where I wait for Chien to arrive, I find five rows of books—more than a quarter of the vast floor—dedicated to facets of Christianity as lifestyle: Christian Inspiration, Christian Fiction, Christian Sports, and so on. Later on in Berkeley, California, I check the Barnes and Noble near my office, and I discover that it has only one shelf devoted to Christian life. In truth, I spend the first part of my week in Missouri feeling as though I am lost in a foreign country, separated from the natives by history, culture, and politics. I'm not proud of this, but it's a fact. And I find myself wondering how at home stay-at-home dads can feel in a place like Kansas City.

When we finally meet in the store café, Chien turns out to be a boyishly good-looking, well-built man of medium height, with a polite smile and somewhat reserved eyes. As I take out my recorder and notebook, he self-effacingly reminds me that he sees himself as a "really boring guy." I assure him—somewhat smugly, in retrospect—that it's my job as a writer to make his life interesting and that he should just tell me his story. I press the record button.

"Let's start at the beginning," I say. "Where you were born?"

Chien speaks, and his story unfolds. It's not the tale I expect.

His story humbles me, and it reveals a multifaceted Kansas City that I could never see on my short walk through its streets. In the days to come, I discover the stay-at-home dads and breadwinning moms of Kansas City are knitting together something uniquely American and thoroughly modern. Their lives contain lessons for parents everywhere who want to form new kinds of community and thrive in the twenty-first century.

Chien's Choice

In 1975—the year Chien was born—Vietnam had been embroiled for nearly thirty years in a succession of revolutions, occupations, and civil wars. The first American soldiers arrived in 1961 to support the anti-Communist dictatorship in South Vietnam, inaugurating a phase of conflict that the Vietnamese today call the "American War." By 1975, 1.5 million soldiers had been killed in the civil war, 58,000 of them Americans. Estimates for the number of dead Vietnamese civilians run as high as 2 million, many of them children, though no one will ever know for sure.

Chien was born two months prematurely in a small town outside Saigon, about a month before Saigon was overrun by North Vietnamese troops. Unfortunately, Chien's father was not an ordinary citizen. He was a South Vietnamese policeman, and as the last Americans fought for places aboard the last helicopters leaving Vietnam, he faced imprisonment and even death. And so he took his family, including his month-old, prematurely born son, and ran for his life. Chien should have been receiving special care, but instead he rode out of Vietnam with the rest of his malnourished and demoralized family on a cargo ship. "I shouldn't be living," says Chien with a smile. "I hear a lot of people say 'Oh, you're heaven-sent,' because they didn't think I was going to make it."

The ardently Roman Catholic family stayed in a series of refugee camps, waiting for some group of Americans to sponsor them. Help came from a Catholic community center in Kansas City, and so that's the city in which the family—including a clutch of Chien's relatives—ended up.

"Trust me," says Chien, "I still wonder why I'm in Kansas City, of all places."

Chien grew up with seven brothers and two sisters in a public housing project on the Kansas side of Kansas City, which is separated from its Missouri sister by the junction of the Missouri and Kansas rivers. "It was definitely a culture shock for the Afro-American people, and for us, and for the white people," says Chien. "Because they heard about the war far away, and then all of a sudden we were there in Kansas. They weren't very welcoming." (As of the 2000 census, less than 2 percent of the population of Kansas City, Kansas, is of Asian descent.)

But once they arrived, Chien's mother and father did not look back, at least not according to their son. As he grew up, Chien heard one message from his parents: "You lived. Now you're here. Now do something about it. Make something of yourself."

His parents were highly traditional and spoke Vietnamese at home, but they still embraced their new situation and pushed Chien and his siblings to study hard and to be assimilated into American society. "They didn't understand the American culture," says Chien. "But they did appreciate how everything came so freely here as far as food, clothing. Anything that you can afford you can get here."

There was a small community of Vietnamese refugees in Kansas City, but it was Catholicism that tied his family to mainstream American society as well as to Vietnamese families throughout the Midwest. In 1991, two years before graduating from high school, Chien met his wife, Ashley, at a religious retreat in Carthage, Missouri—she lived in Lincoln, Nebraska, but she was also raised in a family of Catholic Vietnamese refugees.

"It was funny because our tents were actually right next to each other," says Chien. "I'm pretty sure there was some kind of attraction there. She thought I was cute and I thought she was cute."

The two struck up a friendship, and yet many years passed before they started seriously dating. I can easily imagine Chien as a teenager: a good boy, polite, earnest, decent, and perhaps a bit awkward, especially when it came to the opposite sex. His good looks would not have gone to his head, and it's not hard to believe that it might have taken him years to work his way up the ladder of courtship, from first date to first kiss to marriage proposal.

Chien graduated from high school in 1993, went to the University of Kansas in Lawrence, and finished three years later with a degree in cellular biology. "I had one thing in my mind, which was to get out and work and earn as much as I could," he says. He interned as a chemist at a series of pharmaceutical companies and got a job as a scientist in pharmaceutical product development. His father had died shortly before he graduated from high school, and so after college Chien moved in with his mother. He saved as much money as he could.

"I didn't know why I was saving money," he says. "I just knew I was going to need it sometime later. I had that feeling and I did it."

He stayed in contact with Ashley, but the couple didn't get serious until she graduated premed from the University of Nebraska in Lincoln in 1997. She went to medical school while he continued to work as a scientist. They married in 2002. Shortly after, Chien used his savings to buy a home for his mother.

"Without a doubt we wanted to have children," says Chien. "We wanted to have lots of children." Their first daughter was born in 2004 and the second in 2006—and when I interview Chien, who remains a practicing Catholic, he says they plan to have more.

Both had been raised in close families with a traditional division of labor between mother and father, but after they became parents, the couple faced a new kind of problem, one we have already encountered many times in this book. Chien had a good career, but he couldn't advance much further without going to graduate school—not an easy thing to do after one becomes a father.

Meanwhile, Ashley already made more money than he did and had better prospects in her career as a doctor. When they became parents, she was in the third year of a pediatrics residency. The couple did not want other people to raise their children, but at that moment in her career she couldn't stop. Not without stopping altogether.

"I definitely loved my job as a formulation scientist," Chien says ruefully, yet after his first daughter was born, it was he, not Ashley, who cut back on hours at work. His mother took care of the baby while he worked in the morning, but in the afternoon, the baby was all his. Chien's co-workers gave him a hard time—"Some of the people I worked with said, 'Dang, Chien, you're working banker hours'"—but after his second daughter was born, he felt that even part-time was too much.

And so he quit, taking a path usually walked by mothers. "The most difficult thing to do was to let go of the job," he says. Nevertheless he became a stay-at-home dad. For the most part, his family didn't understand. His mother, in particular, at first accused him of throwing his life away.

The Outsider

Chien might laugh to hear it, but he is much more of a rebel against tradition than many of the other dads profiled in this book—and yet he also enjoys traditional familial connections that are a source of strength. Indeed, Chien appears to live in the difficult center of a Venn diagram in which multiple circles overlap: Vietnam and America, tradition and modernity, family and isolation, economics and emotion. It seems that one can't understand him (or anybody else, in my view) unless one is willing to embrace paradox and multiple identities.

As discussed in previous chapters, research has shown that modern mobility reduces pressure on young couples to adopt traditional family forms. But despite being immigrants and living far from the country where they were born, the bonds among Chien's family are actually much tighter than those of many native-born American families. Pressure to make money—for the extended family, not just for himself—was intense. His parents came from a hardscrabble, war-torn country and struggled all their lives for necessities, and they instilled an unyielding work ethic and sense of familialism in all their children. Chien used his savings to buy his mother a house when he got married, but his brother had to take over the mortgage a year after Chien started taking care of his daughters, a step that Chien describes as painful. He did it anyway.

Moreover, there was absolutely no precedent in his family for caregiving fatherhood and no readily available model they could use to understand his choice. No other dad I interviewed has faced such pressure, and yet only a few of them have embraced their roles as wholeheartedly as Chien. He portrays the decision as a practical matter—his wife had better career prospects than he—and yet there is nothing obviously practical about it. Both made professional salaries. They could have gone the dual-income route and placed their daughters in day care. Theirs was clearly an emotional, sacrificial, noneconomic decision, and in some ways a deeply traditional one.

Except that the couple made their decision in twenty-first-century America, and so the tradition reversed itself: he stayed home, she pursued her career. Where there once wasn't a model for their families, they created a new one. It's an arrangement that both extended families have come grudgingly to accept, says Chien, and they remain a fiercely cooperative and interdependent clan.

Ashley and Chien are not the first immigrant parents to translate the values of the Old World into the context of the New World, keeping what works and discarding what doesn't—and by doing so, helping to alter the American cultural landscape. "We often assume that immigration is a one-way process," write researchers Ross Parke, Scott Coltrane, and Thomas Schofield. "People from other countries come to the United States to settle and work, and they routinely adopt the values, customs, and practices of the host country. This is an oversimplified view that ignores the mutual influences between cultural groups." Their five-year study of Mexican American immigrant families reveals that many of the families pick and choose the aspects of American culture that seem to help them survive, while rejecting traditional ways that might hold them back.

Parke and his colleagues cite research into multiple immigrant groups by Raymond Buriel, Jeannie Gutierrez, and Arnold Sameroff, which, taken together, shows that bicultural orientation can come with clear benefits. "Both children and adults who straddle the cultural fence, in fact, have better physical and psychological health, including higher expectations and feelings of positive self-worth," they report. This bicultural orientation opens the door to a fusion of old and new. The authors argue that grafting egalitarian gender values onto traditional familialism can create a twenty-first-century family form "that is better anchored by extended kin, neighbors, and communities committed to the common good of our children."[2]

Their vision is not a fantasy: it is a living reality embodied by couples like Ashley and Chien.

The Secret Weapon

Chien draws upon his heritage and kin network as a source of power, but many stay-at-home fathers, especially those of European descent, don't have that. Instead, they've spent their adult lives chasing jobs and fleeing their relatives, and so they must forge new communities virtually from scratch. Many studies have found that Americans are spending more time alone, and 25 percent now say that they have no close friends—twice as many as two decades ago. This loneliness is linked to mental and physical health problems[3]—problems that can be especially serious for frazzled, sleep-deprived stay-at-home parents.

Dads might want to see themselves as more tough and self-reliant than moms, but they are not immune to the effects of isolation. In fact, many studies find that new fathers are plagued by feelings of depression and anxiety,[4] and at least one recent study finds that stay-at-home dads are especially susceptible to stress-related illnesses.[5] That's why in 2002 Andy Ferguson founded a social network and playgroup called Kansas City Dads, which now claims seventy members.

Before moving to Kansas City with his wife, a bank executive, Andy had participated in a dads' group in Delaware (just one in a series of states and Canadian provinces they've lived in)—something he found highly valuable. "As much as you have fun with your little one, you go berserk talking at that level all day," he says. At the Delaware dads' group, he found adult male company and an "incredible exchange of information, especially when you first start out and everybody else has kids that are older than yours." And, of course, "it's awesome for the kids" and helps "get them socialized."

While Andy—a thoughtful, articulate guy who has a graduate degree from Stanford University—has never been uncomfortable with his role, he did meet several men through the dads' group who were. "I think it's really valuable for them to be with a group of men doing the same thing that they're doing," he says. "It's validation that what they're doing is OK. They're with a mix of other guys. Some are uncertain about it, and it's probably good for them to see that and know that not everybody is completely gung ho about stay-at-home fatherhood. It's also good for them to be with the guys who are naturally comfortable with the role, so they can see that it *is* possible."

When Andy's wife was transferred to Kansas City, he sought out a new group to join—and discovered that there wasn't one. And so he started his own. "My wife had a colleague whose husband stayed home, so I had one immediate connection, and I quickly found another guy who had been toying with starting a dad's group in Kansas City but had never gotten it off the ground," recalls Andy. "I had the drive and the marketing to make it happen."

It turns out that marketing is key because starting a group for dads in a place like Kansas City is much more difficult than starting one for moms. "One main difference is that moms have traditionally always had the support of neighborhood mom groups," says Andy. "And the reason those work so well is that they all live in the same neighborhood, they're similar, and that's why they live where they do. The stay-at-home dads don't have that. So we have to cast a wider net, which means that we are going to catch a more diverse group of personalities."

One of the first steps Andy took was to get a write-up in the

Kansas City Star about the dads' group, which attracted many new members and helped institutionalize the network. "That's what I always tell people who are asking how to get a group started," he says. "Call the editor of the lifestyle section of your local paper and have them do a feature on you. You know, they love that. That's the kind of feel-good filler stuff they're always looking for. And that really expanded the group."

In fact, Kansas City Dads is now one of the largest stay-at-home dads' groups in the country—which is one reason that the annual stay-at-home dads' convention moved from Chicago to Kansas City shortly after the group was founded. Andy says that the dads who show up are looking for a social connection but are also looking for ways to become better parents. However, Andy points out, many stay-at-home fathers will not seek out a group to join, primarily because of manly pride. Their wives often understand the value of parental social connection better than they do. "We get e-mail from guys' wives constantly," Andy says with a laugh. "And I know if the initial contact is from the wife—I even got a contact from a guy's mother—if the initial contact does not come from him, he's never going to show up. Because he's not interested. It's the wife trying to organize him into it. It's the wife who thinks it will be good for him. She's right. It would be good for him. But he hasn't bought into it. He's not going to do it."

One of the men who did join Kansas City Dads and attend the convention is Gus Heise, a thirty-seven-year-old Oklahoma native and full-time father of two children. Gus hails Andy as "the driving force behind the convention, getting it here in Kansas City and making it a success." In the group and at the convention, Gus (who, like Chien, is also religious and Catholic) has found a combination of practical and emotional support. "I'll go to dads' night out and inevitably conversation turns to potty training," he says. "And I don't know what these waitresses think. Here's a bunch of guys, and all we're talking about is potty training and things like that. I get a lot of good advice."

But the group didn't provide community only to Gus—his wife also found support. "Gina got some advice, like dealing with the guilt and not having the contact with the children," recalls Gus. "They don't run to her when they're scared or hurt, which worried Gina. So we e-mailed the group, and the guys said, 'Oh, don't worry. My wife went through the same thing and it'll pass.'" In many respects, groups like Kansas City Dads form the organizational backbone of a kind of parental counterculture, which validates the choices of its members, helps perpetuate their ethos and aspirations, and provides a place for members to share lessons, and thus learn and evolve.

Andy Ferguson says that stay-at-home dads—and their wives—must have a sense of community if their numbers are to grow. "I think community is critical," he says. "Stay-at-home dads face the same issues that affect at-home parents regardless of gender—you know, isolation, depression, being stuck at home with a sick two-year-old for three days in a row, not even talking to anybody else at all. I think community is important for all parents, but I think it is particularly important for at-home dads because they are slightly different and still on the margins."

Andy's insight is backed up by the small amount of research that has been done into the social lives of stay-at-home dads: Fathers who take daily care of kids need support and friendship just as much as moms, if not more. When the University of Texas researcher Aaron Rochlen and his team studied 214 stay-at-home fathers, they found that social support was the most important factor that predicted the psychological well-being and relationship satisfaction of these dads. "Social support seemed important in several different contexts—with their partner, friends, and family," writes Rochlen. "Conversely, those who had low social support in these areas seemed to be struggling more in their relationships and in life."[6]

It's a result echoed in the Canadian sociologist Andrea Doucet's study of 114 stay-at-home fathers. She also discovered "the appearance of self-reliance was important to many men," even as they lamented their sense of social isolation. For men, one of the fathers told her, strength is "the absence of weakness," and weakness, he said, is often equated with "the willingness to share." This father argues that women's openness to sharing springs from the historical experience of raising children and relying on others for help—an experience that has changed his own views on cooperation and self-disclosure. "In order to survive we need to share," concludes this dad.

And, in fact, Doucet does find that it is the fathers who get over fears of disclosure and feel "tightly embraced by the community" who thrive as people and as parents.[7] This correlates with a great deal of other research into the family, which shows that social connections are essential to mental health and well-being.

"Friends are the secret weapon," says Bella DePaulo, a social psychologist at the University of California in Santa Barbara. "When couples have kids, they tend to look inward and focus completely on each other and the baby. You can see the temptation of doing that, and yet that's not the only way to deal with that transition. Some couples do [build] connections to friends and extended family, and the couples who do that are less likely to experience the depression that sometimes happens when people transition to being parents."

Foreign Languages

Chien Nguyen has never joined Kansas City Dads. He says that he is content with his family and small circle of friends, which includes one other stay-at-home dad, Alan Wang, with whom he visits every few weeks. This doesn't mean that Chien doesn't struggle. He describes flashes of anger and frustration. He also paints stay-at-home fatherhood as a series of transitions and obstacles that he had to fight to surmount, and he's sheepishly, perhaps uncharacteristically, proud of his progress. "I met those transitions, and I passed every step," he says. "You can never be comfortable; because once you start getting comfortable then the next step starts."

For him, taking care of the one girl was easy, but the second child threw him for a loop. "You have to start all over again," he says. "It's not double the work. It's four times the work!"

He's also had to struggle to learn how to juggle child-care tasks and take on cooking and housework, so that everything would get done. "One thing I learned to do better is baking," he says earnestly. "Baking is one of my weak points. I could not bake for the life of me, but I've been practicing that, and I've been doing OK. I still can't make waffles!"

His mother has come to tolerate his role, and his siblings have been supportive, but he confronts a growing cultural divide with his older daughter, who now faces the culture of the American schoolyard. "Every time I ask her something in Vietnamese, she'll answer in English," he says. "'How dare you?' I say. 'Speak Vietnamese. You know it's not hard.' And there's a certain way, a polite way, to answer in Vietnamese, and she's answering the informal way," he says. "Like in English you would say, 'Yes,' versus 'Yes, ma'am' or 'Yes, sir.' In Vietnamese, just saying 'yes' to dad is rude. It has to be, 'Yes, Father,' something like that. So that's something she has to learn. I want them to remember the language throughout the course of their life."

Postscript:
Everything Solid Melts into Air

After our interview I wander out of the store. While we were inside talking, the clouds cleared and now the sun is shining. I look around at the glittering pedestrian mall, watching the families stroll by licking ice cream cones, multicolored shopping bags clustering around them like gaudy children. Whereas Kansas City seemed somewhat segregated in the morning, now I see black, white, Latino, and a handful of Asian families walking alongside each other, a bargain-hunting beloved community right here in Country Club Plaza.

This is where Chien's American-born daughters will grow up, in an amusement park where improvisation is vastly more important than tradition and everything solid is always melting into air. Will they remember the language of their father? I consider my own parents and grandparents, and the journeys our family has made—none of them as large as Chien's voyage from bombed-out Saigon to placid, prosperous Kansas City. I certainly don't speak Quebecois; my wife, whose grandparents fled another communist

90

revolution in China, doesn't speak Mandarin. And so I doubt very much that Chien's daughters will remember Vietnamese. Their amnesia will likely leave them gloriously free and unbearably alienated, a condition that seems distinctly, inescapably American.

Time for more coffee!

I find a café, order espresso, and sit down to write. I don't think of Chien. Instead I think about his daughters and my son, and I think about the distances between us. Suddenly—the feeling hits me like a lightning strike—I miss Liko so badly my breath stops and my gut sinks. With each day I am here in this faraway city, he is growing older. A woman sits nearby, whispering into a cell phone; a man stares out the window.

What am I doing here?

I want to jump up from the table and run as fast as I can back to San Francisco.

5

Interlude
Now You See It, Now You Don't

"Unfortunately, nature is very much a now-you-see-it, now-you-don't affair," writes Annie Dillard in *Pilgrim at Tinker Creek*. This is equally true of life in cities. It is also true of parenting. All three are intricate worlds unto themselves, containers of consciousness, definers of perception; but we are never quite able to hold them in our senses. As soon as we wrap our minds around nature, cities, and children, they exceed the limits we think we've set for them.

When Liko was fourteen months old—after I had been taking care of him for two months—San Francisco seemed to shift constantly in and out of focus, and so did my son, as he scrambled up the ladder of a baby's developmental stages, and I scrambled to follow him. The babble from Liko's mouth sharpened into words, the syllables flashing like sunlight on windows. We'd cross the street and on the other side, he'd seem suddenly older. Pushing the stroller or hauling him in the baby backpack, I took him to parks and streets in all parts of the city, and to each we showed a different face.

In the Mission, Latina moms eyed me curiously and approached me cautiously, and one wondered aloud why I wasn't at work. Every month or so, we'd take the F train downtown to the Museum of Modern Art, where once Liko demonstrated new speed and mobility by racing across the gallery and knocking over a six-foot sculpture of a paper airplane—which I caught just before it hit the floor. Summoning as much dignity as possible before a score of shocked museum patrons—who doubtless saw me as the very epitome of the bumbling Mr. Mom—I set the giant paper airplane back on its dais, took Liko by the hand, and walked at a stately pace into the next gallery.

On cool, sunny afternoons I'd put Liko in his backpack, and together we'd hike to the top of Twin Peaks, the mammarian mountain that swells at the center of San Francisco. Sitting on a rock, he'd survey the city like a wide-eyed prince, and each time he seemed to understand a little more of what he was seeing. "Clouds," he said, pointing up. "Bridge," he said later, peering at the fog-touched Golden Gate Bridge. I had feared that he'd never start talking. Now, I felt a little tremor of excitement with each new word.

Through these urban adventures I struggled to understand what the hell I wanted out of life. My desire to take care of Liko warred with a drive—augmented by financial need—to claw my way to the next stage of my career. I had wandered off the beaten career path, babe in arms, and I wasn't sure how to find it again, or if I even wanted to. I could feel myself changing, and the change was uncomfortable as I moved further and further away from my old life and closer to a new one that was not so safe or well defined. I was no longer the nonprofit manager I had been—it made me nervous to feel the skills and instincts slipping away—but I didn't plan to go back to that kind of work, which took too much time and emotional energy away from my family.

On playgrounds, I seldom spoke with other parents, because I didn't feel like one of them. I certainly didn't call myself a "stay-at-home dad" or anything like that. In fact, I passively resisted every category and could hardly bring myself to describe to strangers who I was or what I did. I was alone with Liko on a mountain, looking down at everything, and at that point I didn't want to come down. Never had my daily life been brighter; never had my imagination been darker. The contrast was puzzling and intolerable. In the middle of anxiously sleepless nights, I envisioned us homeless, forced to live with relatives. My wife's job was not fully supporting the three of us, and so I rented an office in downtown San Francisco and ramped up my consulting with nonprofit organizations, as well as my freelance writing, which I increasingly saw as my future. I'd wake up before the sun rose, rush out the door at six in the morning, work as fast as I could for three or four hours, then run home just as my wife was leaving for her job.

Communication between Olli and me was limited to reports on meals, naps, and diaper changes before one of us headed out the door. When she came home at seven, I'd cook dinner while she played with Liko. When we finally sat down to eat, she and I were both exhausted. A baby-sized hole had been blown in our relationship, and we hadn't yet figured out how to relate to each other as parents.

Post and Beam

I found myself doing a funny thing—"found myself," meaning that thought followed action. I gave away money to anyone who asked for it: $5 to a beggar, $150 to a canvasser for California Peace Action, $1 to the barista who made my $1.75 espresso. Once I found a $10 bill on the Castro Street sidewalk; without thinking, I turned and gave it to the man behind me. ("Uh, thanks," he said and hustled away, maybe worried that I'd change my mind.)

Why did I do that? It seems crazy, given the uncertainty we were facing. I did not see myself as generous, and I didn't tell anyone about my random acts of kindness. My wife did hear about the donation to Peace Action; at the time, she gave me a look that I interpreted as pained and disappointed. I mumbled something about wanting to stop the Iraq War, which sounded pathetic even to me. In context, my behavior seemed foolish and even self-destructive. I hid them the way an alcoholic hides a bottle.

The comparison with alcoholism might be warranted. I was addicted to giving away money, each donation like a hit of some drug that alleviated my burdens. In the instant I handed over the money, my anxiety over money vanished. I felt as if I was floating, free, above it all. Of course, in a minute, I'd fall back to earth, but that just made me want another hit.

Obviously, these acts of giving were not motivated by spiritual love for humankind. I told myself at times that I was just looking for good karma; on a semiconscious level, I believed that helping others would somehow make people more inclined to help my family and me. I felt that the world was accumulating some kind of debt to me, quite without its consent, and that when I needed to, I could go to the world and ask to be repaid.

There's a phrase for this kind of behavior: magical thinking. Maybe the magic worked. I got plenty of work as a freelancer and consultant, grinding away on those bleak mornings, more than I could handle given my responsibilities as a dad, and over time our financial worries largely subsided. At the same time, the accumulation of daily caregiving tasks—which I'd gotten better and better at managing—pushed me to see myself more and more as Liko's caregiver.

When Liko was twenty-one months old, my wife went away for a week and left the two of us on our own. That night—our first alone together—Liko curled up into the crook of my arm as we lay in bed, his small back rising and falling with each breath. I held him, feeling like the bed was a raft and we were drifting along some dark river. In a flash I felt totally responsible for Liko and totally capable of caring for him, day or night, in a way that I hadn't felt before.

With embarrassment, I recalled a small incident that occurred when Liko was two weeks old. The three of us were in bed. I was reading a novel, Michael Chabon's *The Amazing Adventures of Kavalier and Clay*. My wife was nursing the baby, who was slipping off to sleep. Outside, the Castro bus rolled up the hill like surf, and we heard the faint voices of people walking on the sidewalk below.

Suddenly Liko vomited all over the bed. Then he started wailing his little lungs out. What was my reaction to this pedestrian minicrisis (the likes of which we went through, oh, maybe four hundred more times in the year that followed)? I was annoyed.

Really annoyed—with both the baby and my wife, as if it were somehow her fault that the baby had thrown up all over everything. How could they be so rude as to interrupt the adventures of Kavalier and Clay?

At that time, as a new dad, I didn't see myself as the one most responsible for the baby. I actually still thought that I was entitled to time to myself, to novels and movies and solitude. Today I am entitled to time alone—as my wife has always been—but back then, I now realize, I hadn't yet *earned* the time. My wife was the one who had given birth, struggled with breastfeeding, and dealt with hormonal chaos; and though it is still difficult for me to imagine, her sleep had been even more interrupted than my own. At that point, I saw myself as a supportive bystander, nothing more.

There's a scene in the Alice Munro short story "Post and Beam" that reminds me of me as I was in the weeks after Liko was born: "Later she asked Brendan to stop so that she could lay the baby down on the front seat and change his diaper. Brendan walked at a distance while she did this, smoking a cigarette. Diaper ceremonies always affronted him a little." I wish I could say that I don't understand Brendan. Unfortunately, I do. Munro describes the mechanism fathers use to foist daily child care onto moms: they lump the baby and mom together and position themselves as above it—like a kind of shop-floor supervisor, sitting in a glass-walled office, watching rows of women sew T-shirts. The supervisor says, or thinks: *You're doing this wrong; you're not doing it fast enough; snap out of it; can't you see the baby's hungry?* I remember my grandfather's words: "She worked for me," he said of his wife. "I always said, *You work for me.*"

Taking care of Liko on a daily basis made me see how foolish and self-absorbed I had been at times during his first year of life, and I felt ashamed. But when my wife left us alone that first night and I held him in my arms, the new feeling of responsibility and capability that washed over me gave me a concomitant feeling of confidence and power; not "power" in the traditionally masculine sense of physical force or strength, but as in the ability to do what has to be done. In that moment—that very moment, like flicking a switch—"father" did not feel like a role that I was adopting but like something intrinsic to my identity. It didn't feel "like" anything, really; it was its own thing, my thing, like my arms or my legs—and so was Liko, who I knew would now always be a part of me and who I am.

I reckon that most fathers pass through such a moment; maybe for some it comes naturally and all at once on the day of birth; for others it might come in increments over years and years. To judge from news stories and the behavior of some dads I've known, there are, of course, men who never learn to think of themselves as responsible for their own—or anybody else's—children. But when I woke up the morning after my night alone with Liko, I knew that I was a dad, and I would be for the rest of my life. As a result, I felt happier than I'd felt in two years, and strangely free.

Are We Not Men?

Confident in my new identity—and pushed by Liko's growing sociability—I began to notice other parents on the neighborhood playgrounds, and I started to spot the other dads who were regulars there. I discovered that each worked for pay, but not as much as his wife. There was Jerry, a tattooed private chef; Nick, a bookish contract archeologist; the playful, redheaded Stefano, a former teacher getting his real estate license—and a dozen others I never got to know well. In fact, now that I was looking, I realized that there were dads everywhere on daytime playgrounds. I reflexively identify them by their vocations—for are we not men?—but in truth I found them to be as disheveled and discombobulated and underemployed as the moms. The moms, however, seemed to readily bond, like soldiers in the trenches, over the conditions of daily life with babies, while I think it's safe to say that the guys were not yet sure of how to relate to one another—or, for the matter, the moms—as caregivers.

Yet there were signs of evolution: I was evolving emotionally, as an individual, but on those playgrounds I could also see a snapshot of men evolving as a group. This was the second time around for Nick; his daughters were then two and seven years old. "There are definitely more dads on the playgrounds now than there were five years ago," he told me, gesturing around him. Stefano was the first father I met who seemed happy to embrace the label "stay-at-home dad," which encouraged me to do the same. In some ways, the label felt insufficient, since we all worked part-time or were preparing to return to work—the term "primary caregiver" seemed more accurate, but also more sterile and meaningless, like a job title.

But when people asked me what I did for a living, I started telling them that I mostly took care of my son, which felt far more solid and consumed much more time than did my shifting and slippery career. For the first time, saying so felt comfortable, even pleasurable. My life revolved around care, not work, and I had reached a place where I was happy with that. (Without thinking much about it, I stopped leaving large tips and making donations to anyone who asked; my emotional and social gain was a loss for the canvassers, buskers, and baristas of San Francisco.)

We men tried to form a manly playgroup, but conflicting nap schedules meant that no more than two kids usually showed up at a time, which is hardly a "playgroup." And so I plucked up my courage, and I set about finding mothers who could join us. I met Beth and her daughter Anna Priya at a music class. I met Karen and her boy Argus, and Jackie and her son Ezra, at the neighborhood playground. I met others at the new neighborhood farmer's market, which became a fixture on our social calendar. I asked them for e-mail addresses; and, after a moment's hesitation, they handed them over. Soon, our playgroup was a going concern, and it formed the nucleus of a social life for me as well as for Liko.

Rebel Dads

In early March of 2005—after eight months of taking care of Liko—I was in my office. I had just finished a big project, and I was debating about what to do next. In an effort to procrastinate, I clicked on my Internet browser and the Google page, my homepage, popped up. A novel idea came into my head: to search for information about stay-at-home dads. I typed the words into the search box, and I was surprised to see thousands of hits.

I clicked around and discovered a number of blogs by and for stay-at-home dads. The first one I read was called Rebeldad, written by a former journalist named Brian Reid. "When I first quit my working-world job to stay home," he writes on the "About" page, "I went excitedly looking for information about at-home fathers. I searched the web, browsed my way through my local bookstore, kept a close eye on my local paper and flipped through the magazines at the newsstand, all in hopes of getting some insight into the new fraternity I had joined. It was a frustrating search. There seemed to be little written about us, even less written for us. I couldn't even find a reliable statistic for how many at-home dads there were."

Brian cited one statistic that I hadn't known: the official census count of stay-at-home dads had risen from 90,000 in 1998 to 147,000 in 2005, the year in which I first encountered Rebeldad. Like him, I found the overall trend—a 60 percent increase—exciting, but the absolute number unlikely: if so many men were primary caregivers in one little playground in San Francisco, how could there be so few—less than 2 percent of caregivers—nationwide? Part of the answer, I discovered, lay in how the Census Bureau got its numbers. If the primary caregiver does any paid work at all, the census doesn't count him as a stay-at-home dad. Because most caregiving dads, in my then still limited experience, appeared to do at least some casual work, this number seemed to miss a broad swath of fathers. In fact, it didn't include me or anybody whom I knew at the time. Later I discovered Bureau of Labor Statistics data that revealed the actual number of caregiving dads to be at least two million.[1]

It didn't take long for me to decide to start my own blog about fatherhood. I had resisted writing about my life as a dad, as several friends urged me to do, because I had struggled so mightily with my new role: I didn't feel that I had anything to brag about, and, indeed, I felt ashamed of the wild fluctuations in how I felt about becoming a father and taking care of my son. But discovering the overall numbers and the existence of an online community, combined with having found so many dads in my daily life, encouraged me to try to get some of my experience down, on the premise that it was a relatively new social phenomenon and thus worth documenting. I called the blog Daddy Dialectic (because much of my fatherly life seemed like a dialogic collision of opposites), and through it I met hundreds of fathers and mothers who were debating and thinking out loud about what made a good parent in the twenty-first century.

I didn't give much thought to how this blog might affect the rest of my life. One day, however, I received e-mail from a female relative—and so did my parents and my wife's parents. A father's responsibility, she wrote to all of us, was to work as hard as possible so that his wife could stay home with the children. By serving as Liko's primary caregiver, she argued, I was behaving irresponsibly and selfishly.

How did this make me feel? I knew that we had gained much from my staying home with Liko and learning to take care of him, but at that moment I realized that few people—even our closest relatives—would be able to see from the outside what changes had taken place. A chasm seemed to open between us and the rest of the world. I filled that gap with anger.

And then another message popped into my e-mail in box. It was a reply from my father. "You love Liko with all you have and that's a really good start," he wrote. "What is good for the family is usually going to be good for Liko. If you and Olli are in agreement that this is the way it should be then that's the way it should be." He wrote many other things, too, but they all boiled down to one message: *You're doing the right thing, and I support you.*

I never felt closer to my father. My anger turned to happiness.

A Duck, a House, a Boy

One day, Stefano and I were playing with our boys at the park. A blonde girl named Amanda, seven or eight years old, joined our games. After thirty minutes or so, she looked seriously at Stefano, pointed at his three-year-old son, and asked, "Do you take care of him all the time?"

"Yep," he said. "My wife is a lawyer, and she earns the money. I take care of him. Jeremy"—he nodded his head in my direction—"also takes care of Liko."

"That's weird," Amanda said.

"Not that weird," said Stefano, grinning. "There's two dads right here."

"Aren't moms supposed to take care of babies?"

"Dads can do it, too," said Stefano. "And moms can go to work."

"I didn't know that," she said thoughtfully. "Huh."

Amanda was really seeing us—dads on the playground—for the first time. One could see the miniature wheels turning in her head, altering the way she saw the grown-up world. "Nature does reveal as well as conceal: now-you-don't-see-it, now-you-do," writes Annie Dillard. "Nature is like one of those line drawings of a tree that are puzzles for children: Can you find hidden in the leaves a duck, a house, a boy . . . ?"

When we do find the images that our expectations concealed, it changes the whole picture and reveals previously unseen possibilities. We can see, for example, fathers taking care of children. And if we look closely enough, we can see our children carefully watching us, calibrating their ideas and expectations, laying the foundation of a social order that will be as comfortable and familiar to our grandchildren as the patriarchal nuclear family was to our grandmothers and grandfathers.

Part II

The Dads of Tomorrow

6

Returning to Glory
Ta-Nehisi's Story

Ta-Nehisi Coates was born in 1975 and raised in working-class west Baltimore. "I didn't grow up in poverty or anything like that, but this was the crack era," he recalls. "You know, people being shot on the streets. Teen pregnancy is out of control. Virtually none of my friends had fathers." Statistics reflect his personal experience: as Ta-Nehisi reached adolescence in the 1980s, single moms headed 43 percent of all black families, compared to 13 percent of white families.[1]

But that wasn't true for Ta-Nehisi. His dad had seven children by four women, but William Paul Coates was deeply involved in raising all of them, and worked hard to knit the mothers and siblings together into a kind of extended family. For a time, Coates, a Vietnam veteran and former Black Panther, even served as Ta-Nehisi's primary caregiver.

"My mother was the breadwinner for many, many years," says Ta-Nehisi. "My dad stayed home with me when I was young. I don't think my parents would characterize themselves as feminist, but there was this sort of applied feminism going on."

The image of a male breadwinner and female homemaker has never been particularly relevant to his family, says Ta-Nehisi. His grandparents and many of his relatives were dual-income families or working single moms, family types he saw all around him in Baltimore's black neighborhoods.

This also reflects the historical experience of the black family. "Attempts to establish a traditional family structure among the masses of blacks were doomed virtually from the beginning," writes Paula Giddings in her landmark study of black women's history. "For when women stayed home, the economy suffered." For example, when the cotton crop of 1867–68 failed, a report from a group of Boston cotton brokers concluded the "growing numbers of Negro women" devoting "their time to their homes and children" led to a labor shortage that prevented the crop from getting out. "You will never see three million bales of cotton raised in the South again until the labor system is improved," said one Georgian planter.[2]

The American economy needed the labor of black women, but so did individual black families. In an era when discrimination was legal and encouraged, black fathers were seldom paid a wage large enough to support a family. A study of the Pattersons, a black family of five in late nineteenth-century Virginia, reveals that the father made $144 a year crafting plow handles, while his wife worked as a stemmer in a tobacco factory for $120 a year. With additional income from one working child, their income totaled $294 a year. Their total minimum living expenses, however, amounted to $273. Clearly, homemaking was never an option for Mrs. Patterson—who, by the way, had been raised by her father after her mother died when she was two. "When I was little," she recalls, "my father used to carry me to the field with him and put me in a basket and sit me under a tree while he worked."[3]

By 1940 women made up half of black urban workers, far above the employment rate of white women.[4] By 1950 black women represented 58 percent of all black professional workers, while white women comprised 35 percent of all white professional workers[5]– a pattern that continues to the present day, when black women are far more likely than black men to graduate from college and obtain professional jobs. (As discussed earlier, today white women are also more likely than white men to graduate from college.)

In the twenty-first century, 84 percent of college-educated black mothers work for pay, compared to 74 percent of their white counterparts. Black women have more parity in wages with black men (ninety-one cents to every black man's dollar) than do white women with white men (seventy-eight cents to every white man's dollar).[6] And according to a 2007 Pew Research Center survey, black mothers are more likely than white moms to say full-time work is ideal.[7]

"I got [the message] loud and clear [that] I was not going to be dependent on a man," recalls one contemporary black mother of her upbringing. Her mother stressed to her, "You're going to marry for love because you're not going to need the money. And why? Because you're going to have your own."[8] Note the irony: though black mothers have been vilified as "welfare queens,"[9] in fact, throughout American history, they have always held more paying jobs than their white counterparts.

But the jobs aren't always good ones; indeed, black women are more than twice as likely as white women to live below the federal poverty level.[10] Black women have had to struggle for what they have, and sometimes that struggle has been waged in the face of both racism and sexism. Giddings argues that female breadwinning existed side by side with patriarchy in the black community, and black women's relative success in the workforce has even seemed to fuel calls for female submission. "The responsibilities of black women did not diminish their men's demand for dominance—often the demand was heightened," she writes.[11] In 1897, W. J. Gaines, a bishop in the African Methodist Episcopal Church, wrote of black women: "It is often the case that by failing to be a 'keeper at home,' and to preserve herself chaste and pure, she forfeits the love and respect of her husband, and this renders the marriage distasteful and repulsive."[12]

Some commentators have used this history to explain the surge of misogynist lyrics in today's hip-hop music during an era when black women outnumber men in college and on the job. But "those moral failings are often just a reflection of how the larger society and black communities think about black women," writes cultural critic Mark Anthony Neal. "Many criticisms of hip-hop simply deflect attention from equally disturbing practices within more traditional and acceptable black institutions."[13]

Ta-Nehisi acknowledges these unresolved tensions through the lens of his personal experience. "People always talk about an increased level of machismo and sexism and misogyny in the black community," he says. "I don't know about that. But I do know that economic circumstance creates certain things, things that don't fit that macho image. If you need your woman to work, that's just it. The conversation's dead. There's not much more to be said after that. Ya'll is gonna starve if she don't work."

"There were probably gendered roles in my house," Ta-Nehisi says. "I'm sure there were, and I'm sure my mother would tell you that there were. I'm speaking from a child's perspective, though. It wasn't how I saw it."

Natural Father

Ta-Nehisi's father gave his children an informal Black Nationalist education, while his mother stressed schooling. "My parents are responsible for my being a writer when I was young," says Ta-Nehisi. "I used to get in trouble, and my mother used to make me write essays about why I was wrong and what I had done. My dad always would assign reading stuff—Booker T. Washington, Malcolm X, *Tale of Two Cities.* My parents were just relentless."

Even so, Ta-Nehisi's vibrant, phantasmagorical inner life apparently didn't leave much room for school. He played video games, obsessed over X-Men comics and fantasy epics like *The Chronicles of Narnia,* and mooned over professional wrestlers and basketball players. Despite his parents' heroic efforts—Ta-Nehisi's mom checked on his homework every night, and his father later got a job at Howard University so that Ta-Nehisi and his siblings could one day attend the school tuition-free—he did poorly in high school, earning a 1.8 grade point average early in his senior year.

He still made it into Howard. "My mother visited the admissions office every week, and she pulled strings," he says. There he met Kenyatta Matthews, the woman who would become his partner and the mother of his child. She graduated and he dropped out, and together they moved to Harlem in New York. Their son Samori was born when Ta-Nehisi was twenty-four years old—younger than any other dad I interviewed for this book, most of whom became parents in their mid- to late thirties. "You know, that didn't strike me as young," he says. "I didn't understand. What I knew of the world, coming from west Baltimore, is that people had kids at that age. That's what I knew."

To him, fatherhood was an intensely meaningful rite of passage, personally, culturally, and politically. "I was very eager to be a father," he says. "I defined fatherhood as part of manhood." And growing up during a time and in a place when so many fathers seemed to be abandoning their children made Ta-Nehisi acutely conscious of his responsibilities as a dad.

"It's funny today, when I talk to a lot of my friends who grew up a little differently, and they have a strong sense of themselves as individuals," he says. "I don't think I had that. I was very much about the idea that there was some sort of responsibility to African-Americans to have children, to father children, to be an involved father, to be a good father. To, you know, produce soldiers"—that is to say, a mature, responsible, socially conscious man, a trustworthy member of Ta-Nehisi's community. "That's how I thought about it. I guess to some extent I still think about it that way."

To Ta-Nehisi fatherhood is a form of activism that will allow him to help reverse decades of social damage, which he says he "processed as a fall from glory"—that glory being a stable family unit firmly embedded in a confident and culturally coherent black community. Fatherhood represented an opportunity to restore that glory, if only in his own home. "I just thought, it was the ultimate service to black people if I can be a great father. It was almost a nationalist, Afrocentric way of seeing it."

It's a sentiment echoed in many memoirs by black fathers. For instance, in his book *The Pursuit of Happyness* (2006), Chris

Gardner recounts how being raised without a father drove him to be the best father he could be. "Everybody else knew who their daddy was," he writes of his boyhood. "My long-term plan had already been formulated, starting with the solemn promise I made to myself that when I grew up and had a son of my own, he would always know who I was and I would never disappear from his life."

On the day his son Chris Jr. is born, Gardner imagines the baby saying to him, "All right, Poppa, I'm counting on you." Later, Gardner is tested in a way that few Americans fathers are. His wife deserts him and his son, and together they are plunged into homelessness. His story becomes a grueling account of survival, as Gardner describes in vivid, painful detail his day-to-day struggles to secure food, shelter, income, and day care. But over time, father and son develop a profound attachment to each other.

When Gardner does locate a day-care provider, his son cries hysterically as he is dropped off. "That killed me," writes Gardner. "He could probably feel my reluctance to leave him with strangers, but I had no choice. All I could do was reassure him, 'I'll be back. I'll be back.' Backing out, practically in tears myself, I kept repeating, 'I'll be back.'" And he did come back, every day.

The absence of Gardner's father created a hole in his life that Gardner fought to fill by "always coming back," no matter what hardships they faced. Like Gardner, Ta-Nehisi was galvanized (and politicized) by fatherlessness in his community, but he was also inspired by the example his own father provided. "I felt I was the product of a great, *great* father and that I had a responsibility to go forward and try to live that out as best I could."

Kenyatta has always—"except for maybe one or two years we've been together"—made more money than he has. Thus when they became parents, it seemed "natural" for Kenyatta to become the breadwinner and for Ta-Nehisi to become the caregiver. Neither was troubled by the role reversal. By Ta-Nehisi's account, they didn't even see it as a reversal: their family structure arose organically from their respective backgrounds, and the two individuals interlocked as a complementary pair.

"My dad stayed home with me when I was young, so I don't see taking care of Samori as this alternative thing," he says. "It wasn't really an alien idea."

Nonetheless, Ta-Nehisi wanted to succeed as a writer, and he is not, perhaps, quite so immune to traditional gender roles as he initially leads us to think. Ta-Nehisi worked full-time stints as a staff writer for the *Village Voice* and later for *Time* magazine, which briefly allowed him to make more than his partner, but he was laid off from both jobs. "I took great pleasure in actually being able to take care of my family," he says, meaning that it pleased him to serve as the primary breadwinner. "I took great, great pleasure in that, and losing it was hard to take. I don't know how much is being a dude and how much of that is that nobody likes being poor."

After he was laid off from *Time* in 2007, he says, "I went back to being a stay-at-home dad." Today Samori is in second grade, and Ta-Nehisi sees himself as the parent most responsible for managing his son's life, a situation he enjoys. "You know, getting laid off is always a difficult thing, but it gave me back time with my son. I mean, that's just absolutely huge. I take him to school and then pick him up at the bus stop after school. He played little league football this summer, so I would take him to practice. I make doctor's appointments and make sure he does his homework. I cook lots of meals; I'm kind of a foodie.

"And to me, it's just natural."

Million Man March

Today 28 percent of white kids, 39 percent of Latino kids, and almost 70 percent of black kids live without biological fathers in the home.[14] The numbers are stark, and so are some of the images we see on TV and movie screens. It's not an exaggeration to claim that in American mainstream culture, black fathers have been historically portrayed as sociopathic demons.[15]

This narrative has its roots in stone-cold racial prejudice that characterizes black men as lazy, irresponsible, and sexually predatory, but in the early twentieth century this image developed a male supremacist bent and mutated into something more purportedly "scientific." In the late 1930s, the scholars John Dollard (a white psychologist) and E. Franklin Frazier (a black sociologist) published two separate books with similar theses: both argued that a sexually promiscuous matriarchal culture, shaped by slavery and sharecropping, had undermined the authority and confidence of black men. One solution flowed from these twin analyses: put black fathers at the head of the family and community.

Dollard and Frazier's influential arguments had astonishingly long legs. In 1965 the assistant secretary of labor in John F. Kennedy's administration, Daniel Patrick Moynihan (drawing heavily upon Frazier's work), famously called the black family a "tangle of pathologies" and forcefully argued that a matriarchal structure "seriously retards the progress of the group as a whole and imposes a crushing burden on the Negro male."[16] American society "presumes male leadership in private and public affairs," he wrote. "The arrangements of society facilitate such leadership and reward it. A subculture, such as that of the Negro American, in which this is not the pattern, is placed at a distinct disadvantage."[17]

In short, black women were too strong and independent. For the race to progress, black women had to go back to the kitchen. It was a sentiment repeated over and over by black and white politicians, preachers, pundits, and some scholars in the decades that followed, who blamed mother-led homes on every trouble that afflicted poor and working-class black communities. "The problem is that inner-city children are trapped in criminogenic homes, schools and neighborhoods where high numbers of teenagers and adults are no more likely to nurture, teach, and care for children than they are to expose them to neglect, abuse, and violence," opined one Princeton professor.[18]

Certainly, Ta-Nehisi describes west Baltimore as a perilous place, where fights were constant, shootings were commonplace, and fathers were frequently absent. Black activists, journalists, and leaders from Bill Cosby to Barack Obama to the *New York Times* columnist Bob Herbert have rhetorically battled against violence and fatherlessness in America's black communities. "We, as men, must atone for the abuse of our women and girls," wrote the Nation of Islam leader Louis Farrakhan in advance of 1995's Million

Man March. "We must atone for the destruction that is going on within our communities."[19]

As the range of these examples suggest, however, neither the "black community" nor "black fatherhood" is monolithic—to the extent that these categories have limited usefulness. After all, if we speak of "white fatherhood," what are we talking about? Who is the archetypal white father? Ozzie Nelson? Jack Butler in *Mr. Mom*? Homer Simpson or Al Bundy? What are the differences between Irish Catholic fatherhood and German Protestant fatherhood? Are we talking about my grandfather, my father, me? Can we characterize white fathers according to the behavior of the most violent and irresponsible among them? And if we elevate the worst fathers to representative archetypes, what would that do to white fathers as a whole? As is the case with European Americans, when we speak of African Americans we are using a cultural umbrella that shelters myriad, sometimes clashing, traditions. "Those Africans who were enslaved and transported to the New World [cannot] be said to have a shared a *culture*," wrote Sidney W. Mintz and Richard Price in 1967 in their pioneering and controversial anthropological study *The Birth of African-American Culture*.[20]

Slaves were taken from many parts of Africa, and they faced a range of circumstances in the Americas, from parts of the Caribbean where nuclear families were allowed to stay together to the vicious deracinations of the American South, where owners broke up families thinking it would help them control their slaves. And after Emancipation former slaves and their sons and daughters fanned out across the country seeking work, facing conditions that created new behaviors, new cultural forms, and new traditions. Mintz and Price cite a dizzying array of family structures arising within the African diaspora, from communal kin-based cultures in the Caribbean and South America to the circumscribed mother and child families of the United States. Of course some black Africans did not arrive in America as slaves but came freely prior to the Civil War, just as today waves of African immigrants (such as Barack Obama's Kenyan father) are becoming the newest African Americans.

And of course, as we have seen several times in this book, individuals can and do rebel against their cultures and try to forge something new that simultaneously reflects their inner ideals and helps them to survive. Some of these rebellions prove to be successful adaptations, and they are mainstreamed by others. In almost every American community today, stay-at-home dads are rebels whose numbers are proliferating.

In short, it is time to dispense with the absurd notion that there is one kind of black father, or white father for that matter. There is not. Absentee and abusive black fathers are a fact of life (as they are in other communities) that has powerfully influenced dads like Ta-Nehisi and Chris Gardner. Yet as their stories illustrate, the absentee father is not the only model of fatherhood available to young black men. Ta-Nehisi drew inspiration from his own rebellious father, who briefly served as a stay-at-home dad, even as he felt the sting of disapproval for serving as his son's primary caregiver.

In a 2002 essay for the *Washington Monthly,* "Confessions of a Black Mr. Mom," Ta-Nehisi writes, "In more than a few sectors of America, there are highly technical terms for unemployed college dropouts who are supported by their pregnant girlfriends—bum and freeloader the most common ones. But in the black community, where there is an involuntary tradition of working moms and unemployed dads, the nomenclature is even more defined: no-good-nigga being the current label of choice."

He reports getting a hard time from family members and people he encounters on the street. "Yet through it all, I was never sorry for the choice I had made," he writes. "And eventually, I found my community more supportive than I had imagined. . . . It's very hard to equal the high of pushing a stroller up Brooklyn's Flatbush Avenue and seeing a black woman about your mother's age shoot you a smile that says, 'You done right, boy.' "[21] Ta-Nehisi is tapping a strain of involved, caregiving, egalitarian fatherhood that might, contrary to stereotype, be more prevalent in the black community than elsewhere.

In one study, for example, sociologists John F. Toth and Xiaohe

Xu examined data from the National Survey of Families and Households, and discovered that African American fathers were far more likely to participate in their children's activities than white fathers. Even black fathers who expressed a strong belief in gendered divisions of labor were more consistently involved in the day-to-day lives of their children than their Euro-American counterparts. Qualitative studies and informal testimonials also reveal an intense ethic of involvement among black fathers.[22] As these results illustrate, white fathers might be more likely to be employed and present in the house, and yet, historically, they are more often emotionally absent.

It also turns out that black husbands are, on average, more likely to do housework. In a time-use study using 1994 data, the sociologist Bart Landry discovered that middle-class black husbands spent two more hours a week on household tasks than their white cohorts, while working-class black husbands spent over four more hours a week on housework than their white counterparts. Overall, black middle-class husbands performed one-third of traditionally female tasks in their households, while white men took on about one-fourth of the tasks. Unsurprisingly, Landry also found that 80.2 percent of black husbands agreed that men and women should both contribute to household income, compared to only 47 percent of white fathers.[23] Landry's finding has been supported by other studies.[24]

Thus it seems that while many black children are indeed growing up without fathers, those who do have fathers at home are seeing them take on more care and housework than white kids see. Moreover, the raw numbers of fatherlessness might be misleading. Just because biological fathers are absent doesn't mean that other men are. Demographic trends "tend to conceal the variety of ways black men participate in the father experience, although they may not be legally part of the nuclear family," write Michael E. Connor and Joseph L. White. "Because of high rates of divorce, out-of-wedlock births, separation, dissociation, and reconstruction of families, more men are assuming father-like roles to children who are not their biological offspring."[25]

This view does not dismiss the importance of responsible biological fatherhood nor let men off the hook for abandoning families; the authors' point is that "fatherless" black children often *do* have father figures in their lives, and those figures can step into the breech and provide role models, especially for boys. It creates a model of "social fatherhood" that is not necessarily antithetical to other kinds; in many places around the world, cultures combine the two kinds of fatherhood, and children have many adults, male and female, watching over them, and they are better for it. (This topic will be discussed further in the next chapter.)

"In Afro-America the 'household' unit need by no means correspond to 'the family,' however defined," write Mintz and Price. "It is, for example, common for domestic groups (those which pool economic resources, share responsibility for socializing children, etc.) to span several households."[26] This describes Ta-Nehisi's extended family perfectly, with its multiple mothers and half-siblings taking responsibility for each other and migrating between each other's houses.

Many people, of course, both inside and outside the black community, call this the undesirable product of a history of oppression, one that cries out for a solution. This goes for mainstream leaders like Bill Cosby as well as radicals like Louis Farrakhan, who repeatedly has called for black fathers to provide for their families and for black mothers to return to the home and allow the men to assume leadership of the community. As his speeches make clear, he sees this reassertion of patriarchal authority as one necessary step in the healing and normalization of the black community.

Farrakhan has white doppelgangers, most notably conservative preachers like Pat Robertson and the late Jerry Falwell. In both communities, calls for the father-led family are framed as a solution to problems like crime, poverty, and divorce. And yet the empirical evidence suggests that it is the American economy, not young men's souls, which must be saved if stable families are to stand a chance.

"The marriage rates of all native-born young males and young black males (22–32 years old) in the U.S. are strongly correlated

with the annual earnings of these young men," writes Andrew
Sum, director of the Center for Labor Market Studies. "The
higher their annual earnings, the more likely they are to be married. Among native-born black males, those men with earnings
over $60,000 were four times more likely to be married than their
peers with annual earnings under $20,000." He continues:

> Unfortunately, the mean annual earnings of young men
> without four-year college degrees have plummeted sub-
> stantially over the past 30 years, and declined again over the
> 2000–2007 period. Declining economic fortunes of young
> men without college degrees underlie the rise in out-of-
> wedlock child-bearing, and they are creating a new demo-
> graphic nightmare for the nation.[27]

In the face of such hard facts, we might reframe the debate.
"Black men who are unable to find work often think that they
aren't good fathers because the only model of fatherhood they
know is one where black men are, above all else, providers," writes
Mark Anthony Neal in his 2005 book *New Black Man*. "We need
black men to be there for their children, not just financially, but
physically and emotionally. So it is crucial that we establish new
rules of fatherhood that allow black men to be good fathers regardless of their temporary economic status."[28]

As Neal, Landry, and others argue, the historical raw materi-
als of those "new rules of fatherhood" are there, for anyone with
the imagination to look for them and apply them to their lives. It's
a hope echoed by Ta-Nehisi, who sees stay-at-home fatherhood
as a solution, not a problem, for fatherlessness in the black community:

> Farrakhan was right in calling on men to return to the fam-
> ily, but his insistence that they assume the traditional role
> of provider, while women submit to them, was highly mis-
> guided. After all, no black woman was going to take that
> submissive stuff seriously, and given the realities of the econ-

omy, a lot of dads, especially young ones, aren't going to become venture capitalists before their kids reach draft age.

Perhaps, instead of focusing so much on the check-writing aspect of fatherhood or trying to marry off unwilling partners for the children's sake, it's time for a political movement that seeks to transform "no-good niggas" into an army of Mr. Moms. Since no one has figured out how to make black men much richer, or married, for that matter, why not at least take advantage of the one asset we have in abundance: our time. . . .

Not only would the children be better off, but their fathers might actually discover what I already know: that fatherhood is fun, and that it really is the noble calling that I had envisioned, despite the crappy diapers.[29]

Postscript:
We Are Culture

But it's not just black families that might benefit from adopting Ta-Nehisi's perspective; in an economy where lifelong male employment is a thing of the past, other families could as well. "Culture and tradition are part of our flexibility, and we can, therefore, change the dictates of culture because we *are* culture," writes the anthropologist Meredith Small. "This is why cultures not only evolve, they can also be forced to change, can be revolutionized."[30]

I once asked an anthropologist friend how cultural change happens. He replied without hesitation, "Most anthropologists would say that cultural contact is what changes cultures," and he proceeded to give me a list of examples from every continent on Earth. Many of these were unpleasant: islanders encounter Europeans and their age-old religious order disintegrates; one tribe wars on another and adopts the battle tactics and weapons of their enemies; and so on.

As we delved more deeply into the topic, however, it emerged that cultures can and do often change without violence. For instance, white America has learned jazz, rock and roll, funk, disco, hip-hop, and a great deal of slang, among other things, from black America—and the transmission has been, by and large, peaceful, even joyful. Today the cultural points at which white and black America intersect might be the most genuinely *American* cultural forms we have. This might apply to parenting as well as to music and the arts. Culture, argues Meredith Small, should be a facilitator, not a dictator: in surveying parenting practices around the world, we can pick and choose "those elements that we feel are most useful and germane to the modern parenting situation and *decide* to parent with this or that element."[31]

Drawing on decades of research and theory, Bart Landry writes, "Black middle-class families were the pioneers of the American family revolution, a revolution that has ushered in a new and more egalitarian era of spousal relationships."[32] More specifically, we can find America's original dual-income and reverse-traditional families in black communities; they have already solved some problems that other families have only started grappling with. By demonizing black fathers and mothers, white America may well have missed some vital lessons about how men and women can live as equals, and how they can raise children in that context.

Ta-Nehisi's story suggests something else as well: as stay-at-home dads like his father raise more and more boys, those boys might, like Ta-Nehisi, be more likely to grow up to become primary caregivers themselves. "I guess not making much money would trouble me, if I felt like I wasn't a very good father," says Ta-Nehisi. "If I didn't have anything else to bring to the relationship, then, yes, it would trouble me. If you are a man who thinks that what you bring to a relationship is economic power and that's it, then I guess that would trouble you. What else is your claim to the relationship? I'm just glad I wasn't raised that way."

7

The Astonishing Science of Fatherhood, or Three More Myths about Male Caregiving

Jackie Adams and Jessica Mass met ten years ago. "I think we were destined to be parents," says Jackie. "We would stay home, we would watch movies, then we moved in together. It was always about creating this home. We always talked about having a kid."

It didn't take long for Jackie and Jessica to locate a sperm donor or for Jackie to get pregnant. After a twenty-eight-hour labor, Ezra ("the only name we could agree on") was born. Both parents are women and thus, some might think, both are biologically programmed for motherhood and intrinsically predisposed to understand each other's experiences. But though Jessica had read dozens of books on birth, nothing prepared her for the reality of the labor —or the demands her new role as breadwinning, nonbiological parent placed on her.

"I remember during the labor feeling really useless," she says. "After we got home, we had this situation where she was in bed with him and I was on the couch. I was like, 'Are you OK, can I get you anything?' That surprised me. Because I think culturally we're trained to assume that that's what the father does. In the movies, the mother does stuff and the father runs around looking silly and saying, 'Are you OK?'

"I did feel silly," continues Jessica, "but I definitely didn't feel like a father, because I'd grown up learning to be a mother. I think anyone who gives birth has this instinctual knowledge of what that baby needs, but I didn't know how to make myself a part of the nourishing of this little person."

Gopal Dayaneni knows exactly what Jessica is talking about. Gopal, a former preschool teacher and stay-at-home father of two kids, had always wanted to be a parent. "I entered into parenting with way more confidence than was appropriate," says Gopal. "Because I'm a preschool teacher, people think I'm an expert with kids; they assume I must be a great parent. And *I* just assumed that I knew what I was doing." It turned out that he was wrong. Being a parent and being a teacher, he discovered, "are two fundamentally different things." He enjoyed a special, but highly complex, connection to his children—and that connection raised basic questions about his identity.

"The first time we gave her a bottle, that was something," he recalls of his daughter Ila. "She was six or seven weeks old. I sat down with her in a rocking chair, and I gave her the bottle. She totally took the bottle, right up against my body, comfortable and warm. She looked up at me and I was so taken with her. And it occurred to me that my entire life, I didn't want to be a father. I actually wanted to be a mother, and I would never have that. I started crying. I was happy, but I wanted that relationship with my child that I will never have."

This story has a punch line: "After that, she never took a bottle again," says Gopal. "She screamed her head off every time I tried." And as infants and toddlers, both of Gopal's children cried when their mom, Martha, left for work as a teacher, cried when she came back, and talked about her all day in between. This made for some very difficult days.

"They just love their mother more," says Gopal ruefully.

Physical Laws, Cultural Outlaws

Jackie and Jessica are friends of ours. So are Gopal and Martha. Our Bay Area social circle is surrounded (and our families are permeated) by evidence that the traditional ideology of biology is not destiny. Fathers care for children, while mothers run off to work, and some of the dads wish they could be mothers. Lesbian couples form families, and one of them will fulfill many of the traditional functions of fatherhood and even struggle with many of the same issues biological fathers do. Some of those lesbian moms are calling themselves "lesbian dads," a taxonomy that embraces "dad" as a socially constructed role instead of a biological function.[1] As we see in the examples of Jessica and Gopal, these nontraditional parents often face exceptional challenges in learning how to care for kids.

To some, our families appear "unnatural," a word that my desk dictionary defines as "contrary to the physical laws of nature" and my thesaurus says is synonymous with "abnormal," "aberrant," and "perverted." When a mom like Jessica founders or the children of a caregiving dad like Gopal cry out for their mother, many people would smirkingly submit their stories as evidence in defense of what they call the "traditional family." This, they say, is what happens when you mess with the natural order of things.

For decades right-wing activists and politicians have used precisely this language to oppose gay and lesbian marriage and other nontraditional family arrangements.[2] Even some scientists have invoked "the physical laws of nature" to justify traditional gender roles. "Having descended from a long line of mothers who nursed, fed, cleaned, carried, comforted, and defended their young," writes famed primatologist Frans B. M. de Waal, "we should not be surprised by gender differences in human empathy."[3] Working mothers are struggling against "the natural wiring of our female brains and biological reality," writes neuropsychiatrist Louann Brizendine, throwing rhetorical caution to the winds.[4] "Understanding our innate biology empowers us to better plan our future."[5] A man, meanwhile, "can't seem to spot an emotion unless someone cries or threatens bodily harm."[6]

Brizendine's book, *The Female Brain,* sat on best-seller lists for months after it appeared in 2006. The notion that the biology of mothers and fathers and of reproduction predetermines our domestic divisions of labor is not just a curiosity: it forms the finger-wagging thrust of public arguments against working mothers and stay-at-home fathers, not to mention gay and lesbian families. In the public sphere, the two issues—working mothers, on the one hand, and gay and lesbian families on the other—are intimately linked. Attacks on one kind of family go hand in hand with attacks on the other—and similar kinds of "science" are invoked in both cases.[7]

"Behavioral biology is a magnet for those with an ax to grind," writes Robert M. Sapolsky, a professor of biology and neuroscience at Stanford University. Small discoveries, cautiously offered by conscientious scientists, are seized upon by ideologues of all stripes and inflated to be indisputable proof of their righteousness.[8] In the process, complicated truths are swept aside.

Sapolsky's cautionary note goes for me as well as everyone else, and so in this chapter I will try to avoid the pitfalls of cherry-picking research to prove my point, which is that men have the necessary biological tools and behavioral capacity for taking care of children. Science is an evolving dialogue, in which new conclusions are constantly modifying old ones. If you, dear reader, scan the endnotes for this chapter, you'll see that I've drawn almost exclusively upon research published in the ten years prior to this book's publication, with a heavy concentration on 2006–08. But in trying to present the cutting-edge science on the subjects of sexual difference and fatherhood, I am mindful that future research will modify and extend earlier work and that conclusions will evolve.

When the Harvard researchers Irven DeVore and Robert Trivers launched the field of sociobiology in the 1970s—which sought to find biological bases for human behavior—critics quite rightly raised the specters of social Darwinism and Nazi eugenics, both of which invoked biological science as justification for policies that ranged from abandonment of the poor, denying rights to women and many other people, forced sterilization, and systematic genocide.

But as sociobiology branched off into evolutionary psychology and behavioral ecology, researchers discovered some things about human beings that directly contradicted the self-serving assumptions of the social Darwinists as well as of gender fundamentalists who would put men and women into neat "Mars and Venus" boxes. Scientists like Jonathan Haidt, Leda Cosmides, Marc D. Hauser, and many others have found that human beings appear to be designed and/or naturally selected for compassion, altruism, cooperation, and so on—this goes for men as well as women, for the differences between the two sexes are actually quite small. As I will argue in the pages to come, we all have the capacity to care for children and for one another. Compassion and empathy are skills, not fixed traits, that can be developed.

That capacity is something that every new parent discovers in their children: They usually turn out to be tough, adaptable little monkeys who demonstrate a remarkable ability to learn and grow. But this goes for adults as well. "You take that hoary old dichotomy between nature and nurture," writes Sapolsky, "and, the vast majority of the time, regardless of which behavior you are thinking about and what underlying biology you are studying, the dichotomy is a sham. No biology. No environment. Just the interaction between the two."[9]

And that is what this chapter is about: the interaction between biology and environment, and specifically how that interaction shapes the caregiving behavior of men. To paraphrase Sapolsky again, the facts behind the myths of male caregiving are relatively simple, but the implications are not. As we explore three more myths about male caregiving, we step onto rough terrain.

Myth No. 1:
Fathers are not biologically
fit to care for children.[10]

Men Are from Mars, Women Are from Venus—that's the title of John Gray's best-selling 1992 magnum opus, which purports to show how men and women are alien creatures who come from two different planets. And a big part of that popular myth—which has a highbrow academic counterpart—is that men are not suited for activities that demand care, empathy, and compassion.

Before demolishing this misguided shibboleth and showing the degree to which primate males like me are adapted for caregiving, I would like to concede one thing: men and women differ in both biology and behavior. But one can change the other. Moreover, averages are not absolutes, and there are bigger differences within the sexes (especially among men) than there are between them. Of course, there are the obvious, visible dissimilarities between men and women: the size of hips and mammary glands, distinctive genitalia, and so on. Gay or straight, we can be grateful for those differences; we are built to gain pleasure from them.

But our brains are somewhat different as well: a woman's prefrontal cortex, which figures out high-level problems like the best way to ask for a raise or which drapes go with the couch or how to combine general relativity with quantum theory, is thicker than a man's. The hippocampus, a banana-shaped music box where memories shimmy and emotions harmonize, is bigger in a woman than a man. Women have larger structures in the parts of the brain related to language.[11]

On average, men and women do equally well on IQ tests, but there are fewer average men, and they appear more likely to fall on either the smart or the not-so-smart ends of the spectrum.[12] They are also more prone to extremes of behavior and accomplishment. One big, obvious example: at this writing, men head all but twelve of the Fortune 500 companies; meanwhile, men outnumber women in federal and state prisons by a ratio of ten to one.[13]

"Stereotypes are sustained by confirmation bias," says Florida State University psychologist Roy Baumeister. "Want to think men are better than women? Then look at the top, the heroes, the inventors, the philanthropists, and so on. Want to think women are better than men? Then look at the bottom, the criminals, the junkies, the losers. In an important sense, men really are better *and* worse than women."[14]

In a speech to the American Psychological Association, Baumeister argues that men and women are different but equal. "Women specialize in the narrow sphere of intimate relationships," Baumeister says, and that has encouraged the development of skills like cooperation and empathy. Meanwhile, he says, "Men specialize in the larger group. If you make a list of activities that are done in large groups, you are likely to have a list of things that men do and enjoy more than women: team sports, politics, large corporations, economic networks, and so forth." This encourages traits like aggressiveness.

Baumeister finds some support in a large amount of research: at first glance, our respective bodies appear to have been built for these two different kinds of socializing. Many laboratory experiments have found that women are much more likely to involuntarily imitate other people's emotional expressions than are men—a behavior that is considered a mark of empathy and, writes the neuroscientist Emiliana R. Simon-Thomas, is "thought to reflect increased activity of 'mirror neurons,' cells in the brain that activate both when someone performs an action *and* when he or she sees someone else perform the same action." She points to one study that shows average women truly *feel* emotions that they witness other people experiencing, while brain activity in men shows that most of them just identify and analyze the emotions they observe.[15]

There's more. When the Dutch neuroscientist Erno Jan Hermans and his colleagues injected twenty female test subjects with testosterone in a 2006 experiment, they found that the women's ability to recognize and mimic facial expressions declined measurably[16]—a result echoed in another study the following year.[17]

None of these results is a good argument for male caregiving, since men's brains are comparatively drenched in testosterone. How can you take care of a baby if you can't even read her face?

And we haven't even talked about the link between testosterone and aggression. We will get to that in a moment.

This evidence does indeed seem to support the contention that the females of our species have evolved to specialize in intimate spheres, while men have evolved to operate in larger, hierarchical social groups. This, in turn, seems to support the notion that men and women should naturally fall into traditional family roles: men ought to go out into the world to work; women should stay home and raise babies.

There's just one problem with this argument, and it's a big one: if these ways of socializing are shaped by human evolution and rooted in biology—and therefore, the thinking goes, fixed and everlasting—how is it that the patterns have fluctuated so much over time and across cultures? In places as diverse as southwestern China, central Africa, and Kansas City, USA, for example, we find groups of men taking care of kids. As sex discrimination has lifted over the past half century, women have moved in huge numbers into "team sports, politics, large corporations, economic networks, and so forth." If men are better than women at rising to the heights, as Baumeister contends, how is it that women now outnumber men in higher education?[18] If women are inept at competing in hierarchies, how could it be the case that twentysomething women in many cities are now earning *more* than men of their generation?[19]

To explain that seeming contradiction, we need to take a look at the degree to which environment shapes biology. Now it's time to discuss testosterone and aggression.

Testosterone is a part of a cluster of hormones collectively known as androgens or anabolic steroids, which give both male and female bodies characteristics that we call "masculine." Women who take extra anabolic steroids grow beards and stronger muscles, and men who take them are more likely to act like insensitive jerks. Testosterone is indeed associated with higher levels of aggression—there's no question about that—and men do have more testosterone. This fact might make empathic behavior more of an uphill struggle for the average man.[20]

But here's the thing: our testosterone levels vary a great deal, within individual bodies as well as between groups. What causes testosterone levels to rise and fall? Research shows that it doesn't happen at random. Men on losing sports teams lose testosterone, but it spikes when men witness or contemplate violence. In other words, testosterone is a tool our bodies use in response to specific circumstances. It does not use us, not when we are normal and healthy.

"Study after study has shown that when you examine testosterone levels when males are first placed together in a social group, testosterone levels predict nothing about who is going to be aggressive," writes Robert Sapolsky. "The subsequent behavioral differences drive the hormonal changes, rather than the other way around."[21] To put it a different way, you can't blame men's behavior on hormones. If he is free of mental and physical illness or disability, a man is responsible for the choices he makes, especially the ones that result in violence. That also goes for women, of course. No woman is a slave to her hormones.

There's another circumstance in which testosterone falls dramatically: when a child is born. Studies by biologist Katherine Wynne-Edwards and others show that pregnancy, childbirth, and fatherhood trigger a range of hormonal shifts in the male body— but only if the father is in contact with the baby and the baby's mother, a crucial point to which we will later return. New fathers don't just lose testosterone, they also *gain* prolactin, the hormone associated with lactation, as well as cortisol, the stress hormone that spikes in mothers after childbirth and helps them pay attention to the baby's needs.[22]

In many ways, then, male and female bodies converge as the two become parents; for some men, the process is so intense that they will end up involuntarily mimicking signs of childbirth, a strange but widely documented phenomenon called *couvade*. The convergence starts to end for the male only if he is separated from his family. Interestingly, the hormonal shifts don't diminish with second children; instead, they increase.[23] Our bodies learn fatherhood, and fatherhood appears to be very much like learning to ride a bike.

It's not just our hormones that are changing but the very structure of our brains. Mothers and fathers literally build new brain cells and neural connections as they become parents, a process that I can personally attest is somewhat painful. (See chapter 5; you can practically hear the dwarfs in my head knocking neurons together.)

To understand the impact of fatherhood on the brain, a team of Princeton University researchers compared the brains of daddy marmoset monkeys to their childfree fellows. Why marmosets? Because their males are the stay-at-home dads of the animal kingdom, who carry babies 70 percent of the time and give them to mothers only for nursing. The researchers discovered that the fathers developed better neural connections in the prefrontal cortex —which, you will recall, is thicker in females. In other words, marmoset dads' brains become more like those of the females.[24] The same group of researchers found that fatherhood generates new cells and connections in the hippocampus in mice,[25] the memory-processing center that is also somewhat bigger in the average human female.

You can't apply this directly to humans, of course: marmosets are a different kind of primate and mice have tails and whiskers. These results suggest new directions for research, nothing more. But plenty of other studies have demonstrated the degree to which human parenting stimulates brain activity in both males and females, as well as how experiences can change the very shape of our brains.

According to a series of studies by University of Wisconsin neuroscientist Richard Davidson and colleagues, the brain makes about ten thousand new cells every day. Those cells are not generated randomly, but in response to changes in environment. They go to where the brain needs them, and each cell makes around ten thousand connections to other brain cells.[26] Whatever parts of our brains we use when soothing a crying baby, those parts physically grow every time we do it. More research by New York University's Joseph LeDoux shows that when adults bring to mind a strong emotional memory, it gets chemically recoded in the brain.[27] And it turns out that brain structures that support positive emotions are extraordinarily susceptible to environmental input.[28] If we are loved, we learn to love. The memory of love changes our brains down to the chemical level.

In short, our brains program themselves to cope with new experiences or a new set of challenges—like the ones associated with having a child, for example. One can't just look at one woman's brain and compare that to one man's brain, and then conclude that whatever strengths and weaknesses one observes are fixed and everlasting; in fact, our brains will physically evolve in response to experience.

Don't have empathy? No problem. Even in adulthood, you can build it. Even if you're a guy!

At this point, I would like to hazard a modification to Roy Baumeister's proposition. Instead of saying that men and women are different but equal, it seems more accurate to say that they are different, equal, *and changeable*—that is to say, they can be more or less different and more or less equal, depending on the interaction between biology and environment.

This leads us to the next problem with the argument that men are from Mars, women are from Venus: there are bigger differences within each sex than there are between the two, and these differences are driven by a bewildering array of factors. We have already discussed how men tend to fall at extremes of biology and behavior, but recent studies have mapped the degree to which individual men and women vary on both biological and behavioral levels.

For example, a 2008 study (at this writing, the largest and most authoritative of its kind) methodically compared the brains of a hundred men and a hundred women. The researchers found that sex accounted for no more than 1 to 5 percent of the variation between the two groups. Many other factors had much stronger roles in shaping individual brains, some of them highly technical. "The optimal relation between neurons, glia, and axons may depend more on surface area and speed of transmission than on sex hormones or chromosomal sex," write the authors of the study.[29]

Sentences like that one put lay people to sleep, but the bottom line isn't hard to understand: men and women are much more alike than different. These neuroanatomical findings are echoed in many other scientific disciplines. "In contrast to the media focus on gender differences, a new consensus challenging this view is emerging from the research literature," says a 2007 report from the Council on Contemporary Families. It continues:

> Many well-designed studies find no significant gender differences with respect to such cognitive and social behaviors as nurturance, sexuality, aggression, self-esteem, and math and verbal abilities. The big story is that there is far greater within-gender variability on such behaviors than there is between-gender difference. For example, when young boys act up and get physical we are accustomed to hearing their behavior explained away by their high levels of testosterone. In fact, boys' and girls' testosterone levels are virtually identical during the preschool years when rough-and-tumble play is at its peak.[30]

So much for Mars and Venus, unless you want to write a book called *Some Men Are from Mars, Some Men Are from Venus, but Lots of Guys Live on Earth.*

Of course, none of these studies proves that men and women are exactly the same. The studies I cite do indeed find differences between the brains and behavior of men and women, but most of the differences are not hardwired, as they would be in two kinds of circuit boards. Instead, they're *soft*wired; the brain is more akin to an organic lump of clay than to a computer. In both the long run (say, over millions of years of evolution) for the entire species and the short run (since this morning) for individuals, the human brain grows (or dies) only by contact with its environment, as clay can be shaped by hands.

In the end, it is more correct to stress individual variance, not group conformity. "Perhaps the only definitive conclusion we can draw," writes Emiliana R. Simon-Thomas, is that "almost all humans, regardless of sex, have the basic ability to cultivate empathy"[31]—and cultivation is a social activity. And so, if we want a more thorough explanation of differences between men and women, fathers and mothers, we must look beyond biology and neuroscience.

Myth No. 2:
Fathers are incompetent caregivers.

How *can* we explain differences in behavior? How can we reconcile the existence of fathers who really *can't* be trusted to hold a baby with the stay-at-home dads who are profiled in this book? In short, how can we account for such diversity?

The answer is actually pretty obvious, given what we know so far: First of all, individuals are different from one another. If one man does something, it doesn't follow that all men will robotically adopt the same behavior. Secondly, culture is crucial to shaping both behavior and biology, and culture never stops changing in response to changes in the environment.

Robert Sapolsky's studies of savanna baboons in Kenya reveal how the culture of even a seemingly violent, hierarchical species like baboons can become more peaceful, benign, and egalitarian in response to a change in circumstances. When Sapolsky saw one baboon troop lose its most violent male members to disease, he found that the troop slowly but surely developed a "low aggression/ high affiliation" way of life, with a looser, less bellicose social structure. It's a unique baboon culture that persists to this day, more than twenty years later, as adolescent baboon males who join the troop from outside "wind up *adopting* the unique behavioral style of the resident males"—for example, by grooming each other more and engaging in more egalitarian sexual behavior.[32]

Sapolsky's other studies of baboons reveal that changing social circumstances can affect the collective physiological condition of a troop: if the violently hierarchal atmosphere stabilizes or shifts in a peaceful direction, stress-related hormones and illnesses go down, and health improves.[33] They still attack each other, mind you; just not as often. The males of Sapolsky's troop became more feminine, the females more masculine, but they were still shit-throwing baboons.

That should be reassuring to those who fear less polarized, more egalitarian gender roles will somehow rob us of our humanity. The sort of cultural evolution that Sapolsky observed in his troop frequently occurs in human cultures—for example, the anthropologist Douglas P. Fry has documented the persistence of nonwarring societies all around the world and has traced the progression of many cultures (e.g., Iceland, Sweden, and Costa Rica) from more violent to more peaceful.[34] However, as Fry's analysis reveals, human beings are far more complicated and diverse than other primates. In particular, this principle of diversity applies to how we humans take care of our kids.

Males exhibit some form of care in 40 percent of primate species, but "there is more variation in fathering styles across human cultures than among all other species of primates combined," report Harvard anthropologists Sarah Blaffer Hrdy and Mary Batten.[35] Not just "styles" but the very structures in which we rear children. Take, for example, the Na people of southwestern China: they don't get married, don't have a concept of marriage, and don't have a traditional concept of fatherhood. Men and women openly rendezvous for reproductive purposes, but they do not shack up together. Instead, brothers, sisters, and extended family are the ones who live together and rear children. Lineage is traced through mothers and the culture is matriarchal.[36] Despite the absence of fathers, however, male caregiving is reportedly much more common than elsewhere in China or the world. According to University of Michigan anthropologist Erik Mueggler, even today it is commonplace throughout the region to see men (brothers, uncles, grandfathers) taking care of kids while women work.[37]

It's hard to imagine a family structure more foreign to contemporary Americans than the Na's. And yet even within the boundaries of the United States, today we see a dizzying range of fatherhoods—yes, that's plural—from stay-at-home dads (pioneered by those marmosets with the thick prefrontal cortices) to polygamous patriarchy (common throughout human history and still being practiced among Mormon-derived sects) to sperm donors who serve as more than uncles but less than full-fledged dads to the children of female-headed families.[38] Oh, and there are breadwinning dads. Of course, they also fall into different buckets: married, never married, divorced, and more. Each kind of fatherhood generates a different set of behaviors.

Thanks in part to this diversity, there is a lot we don't understand about the process of making fathers and fatherhoods, and we only recently started to study how dads develop and behave. In the past, says Scott Coltrane, researchers looked only at whether the father was present and married to the mother. They might also have looked at demographic or economic information about the fathers. But they did not study how fathers interacted with their children or what impact fathers had on children's development. Until the 1970s, it was (unconsciously?) assumed that mothers were solely responsible for child outcomes.

But, says Coltrane, "in the late seventies researchers started saying, 'Wait a minute, why don't we measure what the fathers are actually doing? How do they parent?'" He continues:

Today scholars tend to include father variables in their studies, so we are doing a better job of tracking the father participation that is occurring. And we are considering that men might be doing housework beyond taking out the trash and mowing the lawn. And because women are more likely to be employed and earn good wages, more families are sharing more of the family work, so when we look we see shifts.

Applying the same measures to mothers and fathers, says Coltrane, is still "relatively novel, as simple an idea as that is."

During the past twenty years, researchers have made a number of discoveries about how critical father involvement is to child development, and how it can be cultivated. "It's still very much the case that a mother's role is considered mandatory, but a father's role is discretionary," says Ross Parke, which suggests that fathering needs more social reinforcement than mothering. He and his colleagues have developed a "systems view" that attempts to describe all the factors that influence a father's involvement with his children. They include many forces that the fathers I interviewed have already identified, each in his own idiosyncratic way: cultural beliefs about the role of mothers and fathers (see Ta-Nehisi's story); relationships with his own parents (Ed spoke of this); timing of entry into the parental role (this shows up in Chien's story); informal support systems such as playgroups and friendships (see the comments from Alan Ferguson and Gus Heise); the stress and complexity of his job, if he has one (this is a recurring dilemma in Vince Janowski's life); and the quality of the relationship with the mother (which runs as a subtext throughout this book).[39]

But here's another thing they've discovered about father involvement: the gender ideology of the mother matters quite a bit in shaping a father's caregiving activities. By and large in our culture today, mothers are still the "gatekeepers"—that is, they control access to, and management of, children. Mothers can discourage fathers' involvement by holding them to unrealistically high or rigid standards, not giving them chances to learn from failures, redoing tasks, ridiculing efforts to help or participate, overseeing their child care in a critical, supervisory manner, and more.

This finding doesn't apply to every couple, of course—it didn't come up as a significant issue for *any* of the couples I interviewed for this book, and it doesn't apply to my own family—but the finding is documented and replicated in the research literature.[40] Of course, gatekeeping behavior is not evenly distributed throughout womankind; it depends heavily on cultural values and beliefs about the bodies of mother and fathers. "If the mother believes that moms are more biologically suited for rearing children, gatekeeping goes up," says Parke.

When some people hear this, they think we are "blaming the victim"—that is, blaming mothers for the disproportionate share of child rearing that they do. But this assumes that most mothers see child care primarily as a burden or see themselves as victims. In fact, they tend to see mothering as valuable and desirable and intrinsic to their identity,[41] though it goes without saying that child care can indeed be a heavy weight to carry alone. Many studies have shown that relationship satisfaction falls catastrophically when the father doesn't hold up his end,[42] as well it should.

Parke's insight about the relationship between gender stereotyping and gatekeeping behavior—that beliefs about gender can alter the very way gender plays out—feeds into a tremendous amount of research about the social impact of how gender is framed. For example, one University of British Columbia study in 2006 found that simply telling women before they take a test that women in general have less natural aptitude for math causes their individual test scores to decline.

"The findings suggest that people tend to accept genetic explanations as if they're more powerful or irrevocable, which can lead to self-fulfilling prophecies," says investigator Steven Heine, echoing Parke.[43] This phenomenon—which psychologist Claude Steele and colleagues call "stereotype threat"—has been widely duplicated in other lab experiments and has been found to affect racial minorities as well.

"Lift this stereotype threat, and group differences in performance disappear," says Rodolfo Mendoza-Denton, a psychologist at the University of California at Berkeley. "Whether one is an older person learning how to operate a computer, a woman learning a new scientific procedure, or a father learning to feed a baby, negative stereotypes can hurt performance in ways that seem to confirm these very stereotypes."

Mendoza-Denton's own research has shown that "notions about innate ability don't just hinder the performance of negatively stereotyped groups—it's worse than that. They actually *boost* the performance of positively stereotyped groups." So while belief that abilities are determined by biological identity can increase anxiety among negatively stereotyped groups, Mendoza-Denton argues, "it reduces anxiety among positively stereotyped groups by reassuring them that their group membership guarantees high ability. So stereotypic views of fixed ability not only perpetuate achievement gaps—they exacerbate them."[44]

In his 2003 book *The Essential Difference*, psychiatrist Simon Baron-Cohen makes a very convincing case that empathizing defines what he chooses to call "the female brain" and systemizing defines "the male brain." But Baron-Cohen cautions against misapplying his argument: he is not talking about all men and all women, "just about the average female, compared to the average male."[45]

We've already discussed how difficult it is to apply group comparisons to individual male-female comparisons—again, averages don't tell us much about living, breathing persons—but Baron-Cohen's case faces a real problem: Research by Mendoza-Denton and others reveals that his samples are spoiled by deeply held stereotypes, positive and negative, that affect performance—not only stereotypes, but differences in power between groups that are related to differences in education, income, and wealth. This is also one of the difficulties with Roy Baumeister's argument, or that of anyone who relies on comparative measurements of "the average male" and "the average female"—or, for the that matter, "the average black guy" versus "the average white guy."

Does that mean there are *no* differences between men and women? No. But we are a long way from having an accurate picture of the roots, or the meaning, of those differences. It is entirely possible that we will never accurately identify those differences until we have first eliminated inequality.

Neither Mendoza-Denton nor I know of a study that specifically tests for stereotype threat against stay-at-home dads, but, based on interviews with the dads themselves, there can be little question that such stereotypes affect men's caregiving behavior.

"Fathers face the stereotype of being cavemen when it comes to children," says Mendoza-Denton. "The problem for dads is that, given negative stereotypes, whichever strategy they choose is likely to be more easily labeled as wrong precisely because it is dad who is doing it, and those who disagree with the strategy may feel more justified expressing disapproval because of dad's gender."

We are much too accustomed to thinking of women as the victims, but when it comes to taking care of children, it is men who are entering a female domain and confronting stereotypes that can hinder them in sneaky ways. Obviously something can be gained from positively stereotyping women as great caregivers—but in the twenty-first century, can anything be gained by stereotyping fathers as incompetent caregivers?

Myth No. 3:
The children of stay-at-home dads
are at risk of dysfunction.

We might have something to gain in negatively stereotyping fathers if it turns out that men, in fact, are incompetent at caring for kids. So are they? Do involved fathers and stay-at-home dads actually harm their children's health and development in some way?

I looked and I found one study that says yes, so let's get that one out of the way. A right-wing think tank in the United Kingdom, the Centre for Market Research and Organisation, did a study that shows the sons—but not the daughters—of stay-at-home dads do marginally worse in school than sons raised by mothers. "Our analysis points strongly towards the idea that fathers do not, on average, provide the same degree of cognitive stimulation to sons that mothers provide," says the study.[46] But does it also indicate that stay-at-home fathers might be good for daughters? That implication isn't, needless to say, explored. This result will need to be replicated before it can be taken seriously, and I look forward to seeing more studies along these lines.

Other than this one study, the limited research that's been done into both involved fathers and stay-at-home dads shows nothing but positive effects, for children as well as for mothers, society, and the fathers themselves. From a scientific standpoint, it turns out that male caregiving is in everyone's best interest:

- fathers are just as responsive to the needs of young children as mothers, and talk to them almost as often;[47]
- fathers universally provide forms of play and stimulation that mothers do not do as much of, such as unpredictable, emotionally arousing, non-toy-mediated physical play, all of which are essential to a child's development;[48]
- numerous comparisons of children raised by single dads and by single moms reveal few differences in the children's development;[49]
- mothers tend to be happier and more sexually interested in men who show that they are able to care for kids (and do housework);[50]
- father involvement leads to better social adjustment for adolescents;[51]
- and, finally, father involvement contributes to children's lifelong educational attainment.[52]

Researchers continue to make new discoveries about father involvement: For example, a report published in 2007 by the Equality and Human Rights Commission in the United Kingdom, based on research tracking nineteen thousand children born in 2000 and 2001, found that emotional and behavioral problems were "more common by the time youngsters reached the age of three if their fathers had not taken time off work when they were born, or had not used flexible working to have a more positive role in their upbringing."[53] In short, nothing is to be gained from discouraging father involvement. As the UK study suggests, just being there can make a difference for children.

Please note, however, that none of this research about the importance of fathers constitutes an argument against lesbian-headed families. Ross Parke, a pioneer who made many of these discoveries about the benefits of father involvement, is quick to point out that new longitudinal research shows that lesbian families are producing children who are as healthy and functional as those who come from heterosexual parents.[54] These findings change the terms of the debate: today, Parke argues, we need to shift the focus from the gender of the parent to the style of his or her parenting. Children, it seems, need playful variety, not rigid gender roles.

Stay-at-home dads are still too new a social phenomenon for social scientists to have studied their long-term impact on children, but some preliminary research has been done. When the Yale University psychiatrist Kyle Pruett interviewed kids raised by stay-at-home dads, he found that they were normal, healthy, and well adjusted. As the children approached adolescence, however, Pruett found one key difference: they didn't seem to care all that much about fixed gender roles. "Gender polarization seemed a marginal, rather than central, issue for these youngsters on the threshold of their adolescence," Pruett writes. "Their equanimity concerning gender issues in their peer relations was striking because of the usual anxiety and conflict at this stage." The kids were drawn to peers who shared their views on gender roles. "None of my girlfriends want to be housewives," says one girl. "None of my guy friends want nothing to do with their kids—they think kids are cool."[55]

It's a challenging notion: kids raised by fathers might spend their lives crossing gendered boundaries without even knowing they are there. This could be a liability in some contexts and an advantage in others. When I was growing up in places like Michigan and Florida in the late twentieth century, boys who demonstrated too lively an interest in girl things were teased and beaten up, and that could go for boyish girls, as well.

Today in places like San Francisco—which has a very high concentration of dual-income, reverse-traditional, and gay and lesbian families—that's not entirely true. When I've quizzed junior high school kids about the kind of teasing they get in San Francisco schools, none have mentioned being called a "faggot" or a "dyke" or the like in a threatening way, and they generally felt that their fellow students were tolerant of gender border crossing. (The biggest thing they *do* get teased about? Clashing fashion sensibilities, apparently.) Nontraditional families are placing bets, whether they are conscious of it or not, on the possibility that border-crossing children will be better adapted to thrive in the twenty-first century: girls are changing to succeed in public settings while boys are learning to operate in intimate spheres.

Win, lose, or draw, time will tell.

Child psychologist Robert Frank and colleagues conducted the only other studies I have found at this writing on the impact of reverse-traditional arrangements on children. In one study, they directly compared traditional to reverse-traditional households in order to understand parent-child bonds. The result: women who worked full-time still formed strong connections with children, but that wasn't usually true of the fathers who worked full-time. They also found that domestic tasks and child care were more fairly distributed when the at-home parent was a male.[56]

"The child of an at-home-dad family has both a strong father influence and a strong mother influence," says Frank. "Both parents play an important role in the child's development. This is in contrast to the at-home-mother family, in which a child has a strong mother influence but little influence from the father."[57]

Bending the Twig

Many of the parents I have interviewed would not be surprised by that conclusion. Remember Gus Heise, the Kansas City stay-at-home dad we met in chapter 4? His breadwinning wife Gina has some opinions that echo Frank's findings.

"Family is more important to a woman than to a man," she says.

There's more of a connection. And maybe it's because of the fact that women carry a baby for nine months, and so they're already into the deal as soon as the baby appears. When she comes home she wants to be with the kids, she wants to help out, she's involved. And I don't think a guy would do that. He hasn't been dealing with the kids, and so it's harder to make that connection, whereas I think a woman just has that nine-month head start on a guy.

Her husband agrees: "I think a guy wouldn't necessarily feel the pull to have to get home from the office. Whereas she's like, 'It's five o'clock. I gotta get home to my kids.'"

This might sound like stereotypical thinking, but consider: differences in the brains and minds of men and women might be small, but as groups, we still play very different roles in reproduction, separate and unequal. Men don't bear children and they don't breastfeed. As Gopal Dayaneni discovered, we can't argue with these facts (and they affect lesbian couples like Jessica and Jackie, as well, when one bears children and the other does not). Those experiences are unique to females who become biological mothers. They shape a mother's entire existence and provide a deep, mysterious, broad bond with her children. Men and women's respective roles in reproduction can create an enormous gap between fathers and mothers, not to mention fathers and children—but *only if the gap is permitted to grow.*

To Gina, who embraces her breadwinning role, the persistence of the gap is an argument in favor of stay-at-home fatherhood. "The world would be a better place if more fathers stayed home and took care of their children," she says. "I think they would have better relationships with their children. I think they would be more respectful towards mothers. I think they would have better relationships with their wives. There's just more partnership when a man stays home, and I think a man becomes more aware of other social issues."

When discussing the first myth of male caregiving, above, I mention that a father's body changed (diminishing testosterone plus rising prolactin and cortisol) only if he was present in the life of the mother and newborn. Feelings of attachment grow in a cultural context that can squash the attachment or allow it to flourish. Aside from a strong argument in favor of paternity leave, findings like these suggest that Gina might have a point. If biology does indeed create stronger attachment for biological mothers, it might make more sense for males to serve as caregivers (at least for a time) so that connection with their children can be reinforced. In this way, we are managing the environment to provide a counterweight to the reproductive division of labor, and to maximize the entire family's investment in a child's welfare.

It's an argument with interesting and tricky implications.

Pregnancy, childbirth, and breastfeeding—and a man's distinct reproductive drives, such as the constant production of sperm— are brute biological facts. Our bodies *are* different, and so are our roles in reproduction. But how human cultures and human individuals react to those facts is all-important. We've already met the Na people of China, a society in which men are free to sow their seed while still being expected to take responsibility for children. That's one response. Or consider the Aka pygmies of Central Africa, whose fathers hold their infants more than 20 percent of the time and remain "within arm's reach of the baby an unheard-of 50 percent of the time."[58]

If those cultures are too strange or archaic for your tastes, take a tour around the modern globe. We've mentioned the diversity of fatherhoods in the United States and we've seen a patchwork of laws and public policy, from how divorce settlements are crafted to the amount of paternity leave we offer, which have had the effect (if not the intent) of discouraging paternal involvement. Meanwhile, governments in northern Europe have provided public support for both sexes to stay home with children, without regard to marriage status. This seems to have facilitated greater father involvement.[59]

Anthropologists argue about why cultures develop the way they do, even as we argue about the direction our culture should take. One thing is for certain: biology might, in a sense, mark the frontiers of the country in which we must live, but we are not its prisoners. Within the ambit our bodies provide, we are confronted by a mazelike world of choices. "What magnifies small differences into major divisions of labor?" asks Sarah Blaffer Hrdy.

The simplest answer is that *people* do, by following the path of least resistance. As [biologist E. O.] Wilson put it, "At birth the twig is already bent a little bit." Where natural inclinations lead depends on how much effort is expended bending them back. Among humans, conscious effort can minimize preexisting differences. More often, small differences in responsiveness are exaggerated by life experiences and then blown out of all proportion by cultural customs and norms.[60]

As Hrdy describes, it is all too easy for the new father to tell himself that he does not want to intrude upon the special mother-child bond, and it is always easier for the exhausted mother to simply give a crying infant her breast instead of the father's arms. Likewise, it's easier for the father to bow to the power of the breast. When his wife Martha wasn't present, Gopal recalls feeling a sense of panic as his infant daughter cried. "If Ila was crying because she wasn't taking a bottle and I called Martha and she didn't walk through the door three seconds later, I would work myself into a frenzy," he says. "In my head, I was thinking, 'Where the hell are you?'" (This issue has also come up for lesbian couples I have interviewed.)

Yet neither Gopal nor Martha would do things differently. "Having a partner who stays home helps tremendously," says Martha. "It's easy to play the game of the overworked mother, but I'm not an overworked mother, because Gopal takes on so much care." For his part, Gopal loves taking care of his two children, even with all the challenges he faces. It satisfies a primal drive he feels, to fulfill a role that traditionally falls to mothers.

I also know what Hrdy is talking about. It happened in my family during the first year of my son's life, when I lumped him with his mother and set myself outside of their little dyad. We were simply following the path of least resistance, the one that seemed most natural. But when it fell to me to care for him every day, I realized what we had lost when we followed that easy path, and I discovered what could be gained by taking the rougher one:

Liko and I learned how to sleep, eat, grow, and play together, and fatherhood was grafted (forever, I think) onto my sense of self. My life and perceptions broadened, and I would like to think my family's horizons did as well. This is a strength we will carry with us through whatever vicissitudes we face.

And sometimes, as we'll see in the next chapter, a family must summon all the strength it has in order for its members to survive.

8

Searching for Heroism
Kent and Misun's Story

For years, Kent Hoffman worked in a square, gray, windowless room. In that room he fixed harps for a living. This is more complicated than it might sound to the uninitiated. "The harp is a very intricate mechanical beast," Kent explains to me, "with maybe a thousand moving parts in it."

Each of the forty-seven strings has two disks to fret the strings and modify the pitch, and seven pedals corresponding to seven notes on the scale. Kent would tune the strings and ferret out the sources of odd echoes and stray jangles that most people can't even hear. It was isolated, precise, demanding work—and I imagine Kent in his tiny room, testing the strings and making small, beautiful sounds, each hanging like an icicle, glittering but artless.

In those days Kent was part of a specialized club of "harp regulators" that seldom numbers more than twenty in the United States at any one time. He'd spent years acquiring the necessary and variegated mix of mechanical and musical skills. He could never have guessed that he might one day apply the mechanical skills and solitary habits of mind to nursing a child through a life-threatening disability.

"I never thought about parenthood," Kent says. "In fact, I was adamant; I was never going to have children. I was very self-centered. I wanted to live my life and do what I wanted to do. I didn't feel that children were a necessary part of that."

We are talking on his screened-in back porch on a lazy, warm April afternoon in an affluent Chicago suburb. In the backyard Kent's wife Misun sets up a hydrogen rocket with their two children: Clinton, eight years old, and his sister Louise, who is four. Clinton walks in graceful arcs that seem to follow the unnatural curve of his body, his abnormally small chin tilted high as he peers through glasses whose lenses are wide and thick as pop bottles. As Kent talks, he watches his family through the screen door, his pale eyes expressionless. The rocket goes off, rises eight or nine feet in the air, sputters in a circle, and then falls over the fence and into the neighbor's yard.

"Fortunately," says Kent, his voice dry and ironic, "my mom has not reminded me of the fact that I once didn't want children."

Kent grew up in Oswego, Illinois, which at that time was a sleepy farm community of eighteen hundred people, fifty miles west of Chicago. "Oswego was very conservative, but my father was from Brooklyn and my mom was from Massachusetts, and they were a lot more liberal than the community." They were a traditional family with a breadwinning father and stay-at-home mother, but both parents raised theirs sons in nontraditional ways. "My mom believed that boys should learn how to cook and sew and do laundry and know how to take care of themselves," says Kent. "I think she planted the seed in my mind that men and women should do the same work."

And Kent's father was a highly involved dad, when he was home from his job as an electrician. "He read us stories, and he let me bang on wood and nails out in our barn," says Kent. "He taught me how to use tools. There was nothing formal about it, but he would be puttering around, and I would putter around with him, and I picked up what he knew.

"The thing I got from my father which I really value, is he paid attention to us. He liked doing stuff with us. When he was home, he definitely involved his kids in his life. There wasn't a thing where he'd come home and read the newspaper and we kids didn't exist. Most of my friends didn't have dads like that."

From an early age Kent was fascinated by tools as well as music. After college, he worked as a theater technician, setting up lights and sound systems; then he got a job in the harp factory, living a life that sounds solitary but fulfilling. But in 1997 he met Misun, when they both were thirty-three years old.

Misun had a PhD in finance and economics from the University of Chicago and had embarked upon a career as a financial consultant. Misun says her parents, both physicians, were "very involved in our schoolwork and our lives. They would emphasize for us that playing was work, we were learning through playing, and they wanted to know what we were learning about. They were really hoping that we would become doctors, win a Nobel Prize, save the world, and, of course, have kids, too."

Driven by her parents' high expectations, as well as her talent and ambition, Misun raced through an elite education and came to specialize in the intersection of litigation and finance. It never occurred to her that work and family might conflict. "I had seen my mother doing it, and I knew that it would never be a problem," she says. "Balancing work and motherhood, not that hard. Worst case scenario, we'd have a nanny."

She never imagined herself supporting a family, but other people apparently saw that she might one day. "At one point when I was in graduate school," she says bemusedly, "a woman turned to me and she said, 'We've got to find Misun a guy who would be a good stay-at-home dad. That would be perfect for her.' And I was like, 'Are you kidding? You're crazy, no way.'"

At the time she met Kent, Misun was already making good money; she stood to make quite a bit more as her career advanced. Kent's prospects, on the other hand, were more limited. An introverted and thoughtful personality who enjoyed the technical details of his work, Kent had little interest in pursuing a management job.

"I liked the relationship, and the only way that it was going to go forward was if we had children," says Kent. "One thing that scared me was I didn't feel I'd do a good job raising children. I tend to be focused on my own stuff, and you need to spend a lot of time and effort on children—you need to be focused on them, not yourself—and that comes back to my parents, and the time they spent with us."

Misun would never give up her work and Kent, inspired by his parents' example, could not stand the idea of other people raising their children. They were at an impasse in their courtship, until Kent made a fateful decision. "What basically changed things is that I said, at one point early in the relationship, 'OK, if you want to have children, I'm going to stay home with them. I'm not going to work. I don't care if I have to cook and clean and take care of everything else, I want to take care of the kids.'"

Helpless

No one gets a medal for the sacrifices we make as parents. We give up hours that no one will ever count, sleep that no one else loses, peace of mind that few people notice is gone. Our troubles and triumphs are private ones, only sometimes shared with another parent.

Some parents sacrifice more than others.

Clinton Hoffman was born with an abnormally small jaw. This one defect catalyzed a dozen others, all of them serious. Since Clinton could not get enough air through his pinched trachea, his organs didn't get enough oxygen, which triggered a series of system failures in the newborn's body. Kent held him for fifteen minutes before he was placed in the intensive care unit.

When the baby came home after three weeks in the ICU, Kent's life as he had known it—the solitary hours with his hobbies and harps—was over. For the next two months, Kent's entire life revolved around one tiny baby whose life hung on a thread. Nurses taught Kent how to insert a feeding tube and nasal gas drip, and he stayed by his son constantly, gradually settling into a routine of meticulous care.

At two months, Clinton turned blue and Kent rushed him to the hospital.

"We did a sleep study, and they discovered that he had critically low oxygen," recalls Kent. "He wasn't gaining weight, which triggered other problems. We had to trache him at two months"—that is to say, insert a tube into the baby's windpipe so that he could breathe. Clinton could not babble or even cry. He could not utter a sound.

"When that happened, it changed life even more," says Kent. "From then on, we either had to have a trained, registered nurse taking care of him, or one of us had to learn how to do all these medical procedures. So we had nursing help at night, and I took care of him during the day."

Instead of the gray room of the harp factory, Kent sat alone in a bright nursery, watching over a silent, motionless, underweight newborn; instead of fretting strings, Kent applied his technical skills to monitoring a miniature factory whose sole product was Clinton's continuing life: the tube in the stomach through which Clinton got formula; the heat-moisture transfer device that kept moisture in Clinton's lungs; the compressor that moisturized the trache; an apnea monitor; and the pulse oximetry machine, which measured Clinton's blood-oxygen level.

Kent's days narrowed to a grinding routine of care.

Meanwhile, in a perverse twist of fate, Misun's career was kicking into high gear. Within months of Clinton's birth, she was putting in seventy-hour weeks and traveling two or three times a month for a big project in Texas, one that would ultimately establish her reputation in her field.

"It was very hard," she recalls. "I remember for several weeks I would cry when I got on the plane." But she still got on the plane. She knew Kent was at home taking care of Clinton, doing what had to be done. She also did what she had to do, providing for the family. She never doubted her choice for a moment, and she tells me that she has no regrets. To her, making money was part of mothering.

Chatterbox

I've heard many parents, especially mothers caring for newborns, describe moments when they "broke" or "surrendered," overcome by sleep deprivation and repetitious daily routine; in those broken places they grew new identities as parents. But Kent never describes such a moment to me. Instead I have a sense of basic continuity between his professional life as harp regulator and the tasks he faced as caregiver to a disabled child. Only the self-centeredness vanished, pushed aside by his son's life-or-death struggle.

I think of Kent when I occasionally hear people cast aspersions on the masculinity of stay-at-home dads. Kent is not manly in the sense that we might see a heavyweight boxer or pro ball player as manly. He's not effeminate, either. He just lacks big muscles and aggressiveness. He does, however, embody a quality that might be the only thing worth preserving of the traditional masculine ideal: stoic heroism.

Is that overstating the case? Was he simply doing something that any parent would do, when confronted with a threat to the life of an offspring? In that sense, is Kent unexceptional? Should he get special credit for doing something which women have been expected to do for centuries?

In a 2006 essay, "The Banality of Heroism," psychologists Philip Zimbardo (famed for the Stanford Prison Experiment) and Zeno Franco argue that "the decision to act heroically is a choice that many of us will be called upon to make at some point in time. By conceiving of heroism as a universal attribute of human nature, not as a rare feature of the few 'heroic elect,' heroism becomes something that seems in the range of possibilities for every person."[1]

We think of "the hero" as male and conceive "heroism" as some form of physical risk. This bias, which is reflected in Zimbardo and Franco's essay, holds up the warriors of the *Iliad* and *Beowolf* as heroic archetypes. Their attempt to democratize heroism—and validate its banality—still appears to exclude the female experience.

Certainly women are capable of physically brave acts (child-birth comes to mind)—and yet it seems to me that their greatest historical forms of heroism have been rendered invisible: caring for aging relatives, sacrificing their desires for the sake of their families, or, at the most public end of the spectrum, volunteering at the front lines of nonviolent social change. Far from being exalted, these heroic acts are often denigrated.

Male participation in traditionally female realms provides a contrast and thus reveals the meaning and heroism that have always been there and that sexism has deliberately concealed. And so it is the very ordinariness of Kent's heroism that makes it noteworthy—and the fact that he provides a new heroic role model that could be followed by all men. Kent's commitment was extraordinary, but his caregiving was something that everybody, including any man, is capable of. His example says to men that there are more ways to be a hero than rescuing a kitten from a burning building or fighting in a war.

Even so, Kent's heroism remains masculine in how it expresses and defines itself: He attacks his caregiving as a series of problems, solutions, and goals, and he remains uncomfortable with revealing his own pain or vulnerability. When I ask him how he withstood the isolation and demands, he mumbles something I can't quite hear and then falls silent. As I prompt him, I realize that he is embarrassed by my question.

"I didn't think about it, I just did it," he finally says. "It was tremendously horrible, but I had to learn all this stuff and go forward and become an advocate and learn and keep going. I worked to get rid of the feeding tube. Just getting him to learn how to use the bottle was a big thing. It was a fight." He says this without self-pity or pride; it's just a statement of fact.

The problems multiplied, but so did solutions. Since Clinton could hardly move in his crib, his muscles failed to develop, and so they started on physical therapy. He lost much of his hearing, and he still couldn't vocalize—"because he couldn't get air across his vocal chords"—so they started speech and developmental therapies and to teach him signs. In all this time, Clinton never cried or whimpered. He couldn't. The only sounds Kent heard in the nursery were the hums and beeps of machines.

By the time Clinton was six months old, the crisis point passed. He would live. "One of my happiest days was when I fired the nursing agency," says Kent. "They were glad to go, too."

Clinton grew and thrived—though his mental and physical health still required intense management and advocacy—and Misun and Kent aggressively pushed their son into wider human society. At age two they sent him to a preschool for hearing-impaired children. Though hearing loss was not his primary disability, he would at least be able to communicate with others through hand signs. At age four, he finally gained the ability to speak.

"I set two goals for him," says Kent. "One, I wanted him to go to a normal public school in kindergarten. Two, eventually, I want to get him into college. He can do what he wants there, but I want him to go to college."

When I see Clinton, age eight, he is just finishing kindergarten. I watch him play with my own son, who came along for the interview, and they bounce around in the living room creating glorious little-boy chaos and destruction. (At one point while we're talking in the kitchen, I hear a terrible crash and turn to run into the living room, concerned that my son is destroying their house. Kent stops me. "That's nothing," he says. "Don't worry about it." I learn that this is typical of Kent's laid-back parenting style.)

Later Kent shares the family photo albums with me, and Clinton sits beside us providing a running commentary on the pictures. ("Look, Daddy, I'm naked!") Clinton, it turns out, is a chatterbox, perhaps making up for lost time. I look at his smiling face, and a realization hits me: *This is a really happy kid.* He might have died; in previous eras, he would have. Against all odds, despite all those years of silence and isolation, he's alive and happy and very sociable.

The boys also play with Clinton's little sister Louise, who was born healthy—"luck of the draw," says Kent. "It was a big relief. Louise changed our lives, because here was this healthy child who was screaming her head off. We realized all of the things that we had missed." As he says this, we hear Louise shriek with laughter.

Today, the family lives something resembling a normal life. Clinton will always need special help and attention, but Kent is careful to give his kids space to play on their own and take childhood risks—and Kent is committed to preserving his own private space, puttering in his basement workshop and remodeling parts of the house, a never-ending project. "At this stage when they're both going to preschool, I get a few hours in the morning," he says. "I let them occupy themselves. I take them out, I do stuff, but I'm not Supermom. I'm not doing crafts with them all the time."

Misun still puts in sixty hours a week at the office. "I like my work," she says. "I love solving the problems. I love working with the people. I'm very glad that I didn't stay at home."

Things don't always happen at home in exactly the way she'd like: An intense and methodical person, Misun has a more structured, hands-on style with the children. "I have a lot of confidence in Kent as a parent," she cracks, "but if he was a nanny I'm not sure I would have hired him!" Even so, she believes that Kent's arms-length style is right for Clinton and Louise. "I think my kids are actually benefiting from the fact that they don't have me doing more. I think a little neglect is actually a good thing for children. It gives them freedom to figure out what they're going to do."

Kent does not see their relationship as unequal: He sees it as a partnership in which each has a role to play. "Her career got a major boost as a result of me staying at home," says Kent. "When she goes away, she doesn't have to worry about the kids or juggling anything. She's been able to do what it takes and focus on her job."

But what if the couple broke up—where would that leave Kent? Kent did not seem concerned about that possibility. For her part, Misun tells me, "I see myself supporting Kent and my family for the rest of my life."

The Parent Paradox

Kent and Misun defy many gender stereotypes. To some, Misun Hoffman—note that she took her husband's name, an unexpectedly traditional gesture in a reverse-traditional home—might present an uncomfortable paradox: a woman who was determined to be a mother, but who had no intention of sacrificing her career or taking primary care of her children. Moreover, she seems to have been psychologically prepared to be the primary breadwinner, a role she relishes—and for her this is as much a part of parenthood as playing with the kids, a feeling not shared by many mothers who see work as taking time away from mothering. According to traditional gender expectations, Misun is a terrible, even immoral mother, who abandoned her son during his hour of need.

But she did not really abandon her son, did she? She left him in the care of her husband and co-parent. For his part Kent demonstrated a level of care that men are not stereotypically capable of. However, Kent does not parent exactly like a stereotypical mother: He allows his children to take risks that many mothers would not. He focuses more on remodeling the house than on cleaning it, which is true of many stay-at-home dads.[2] His care work is often explicitly goal-oriented and his discipline with the kids, both parents tell me, tends to be strict. (This doesn't contradict his hands-off approach: he prefers to set rigid boundaries and then let the kids run wild within them.) After years of intense sacrifice caring for Clinton, he now appears determined to preserve a private space for his hobbies. In one light, he might be judged a bad father, who should be working so that his wife could spend time with the kids. In another light, he might be judged a bad mother, incapable of giving every ounce of his being over to caregiving.

But both Kent and Misun reject those standards as the wrong ones. Indeed, can we judge men by old-fashioned feminine standards that were largely set by a patriarchal social order that demanded women give up personal aspirations and submit themselves to the men in their lives? Can we judge breadwinning moms by traditional masculine standards?

As we discussed in the previous chapter, men's caregiving behavior was first studied in the late 1970s, after their involvement with children started to increase. These studies did indeed show differences in caregiving behavior for mothers and fathers: for example, dads tend to play with infants and toddlers in idiosyncratic "staccato bursts" while mothers engaged in more "soft, repetitive, imitative" kinds of play. Mothers were more likely to hold infants, but home observations showed that both parents could be equally responsive to infant needs—in fact, investigators found that factors like age and social status, not gender, most determined levels of responsiveness and interaction with children.[3] These differences are surely the result of a complex interplay of biology and environment.

Caregiving fathers, and their female partners, often capitalize on these differences in order to reinforce the dads' masculine identity. When Andrea Doucet studied one hundred (mostly heterosexual) stay-at-home fathers and fourteen reverse-traditional couples in the early twenty-first century, she found that the dads "were quite adamant to distinguish themselves as men, as heterosexual, and as fathers—*not* as mothers." Indeed, many of the stay-at-home fathers I have encountered resent being called "Mr. Mom"—in other words, they dislike being told that they are doing the mother's job. "Just as young boys don't want to be called 'sissies,'" observes Doucet, "men do not want to equate their care work as 'women's work.'"[4]

The Canadian men whom Doucet interviewed were careful to list the ways in which their parenting differed from a mother's:

First, the overwhelming majority of fathers spoke about their efforts to impart a more "masculine quality" to their family care through promoting their children's physical and outdoor activities, independence, risk taking, and the fun and playful aspects of care. Second, given that domestic space, the home, is metaphorically configured as a maternal space with feminine connotations of comfort and care, many fathers more readily identified with the house, as something to build and rebuild. Thus many stay-at-home fathers spoke about work they were doing on the house, landscaping, carpentry, woodworking or repairing cars.

This is echoed in my own interviews: Kent, for example, describes to me how he is remodeling their spacious house and how he built from scratch many of his children's toys. After our interview, he takes me upstairs to see the Rube Goldberg train set he created for his son. It wraps itself around the room on a shelf about three feet off the floor: the tracks are lined with hand-carved trees and houses, small people pushing strollers and driving trucks, stray wires snaking around the buildings. In earlier chapters, we heard Ed describe letting Juno take greater risks than his wife did; Chien told us of transmitting his cultural heritage to his daughters— which is the father's role in many cultures—even as he struggles to learn to bake; and Ta-Nehisi mentioned in our interview that he spends a lot of time playing football with his son.

And caregiving fathers seem to strive to distinguish themselves from mothers in another way: each cultivates a private place apart from the children, in the form of hobbies or part-time paid work, often in the equivalent of a clubhouse—a basement or shed or office that is their domain alone. "The secret to perfect male happiness is a well-equipped clubhouse," writes Michael Chabon in his 1995 novel *Wonder Boys.* That seems true enough: Kent spends his free time building furniture and toys, tinkering with house electronics, remodeling parts of the house. He enjoys it; he does not apologize for it the way I've heard mothers seem ashamed of their hobbies and interests apart from children.[5]

Motherhood is usually conceived as all consuming and "antithetical to self," writes Daphne de Marneffe. This is often a modern woman's greatest fear about motherhood, that she will lose her identity and come to experience life only through her child. From this perspective, motherhood seems like a void. As de Marneffe points out, "politically motivated descriptions of 'stay-at-home motherhood,' so devoid of imaginative reach and moral nuance, seem to support the notion that when a mother is home with her children, 'nothing' is going on."

De Marneffe argues that "this stubborn self-effacement" conceals "the pleasures, the self-expression, and the moral fulfillment mothering can afford."[6] In my research I hear echoes of this truth in the stories of stay-at-home dads—but I also hear a great deal about the private space that stay-at-home dads cultivate apart from fatherhood. During my own time as a primary caregiver, I very much lived in two worlds: one bright and playful and messy and consumed entirely by a child's needs, the other cerebral and observant and curious and inward-looking. In morning and late-night hours, I plotted the next stage of my shifting career, and I wrote about my new experiences, the way I've heard other dads describe turning to woodworking or sports or part-time jobs.

To be sure, many mothers experience life the same way, and "a room of one's own" is among feminism's most fundamental demands, but at this point in history, the double existence I am describing does not seem to define mothers' lives the way it does the lives of stay-at-home dads. It may well be true that men, even when they are primary caregivers, are simply not as absorbed as mothers in the emotional and visceral minutiae of parenthood.

Of course, men's feelings and behavior are diverse: all of the guys I interviewed have different styles for expressing emotion, and they occupy themselves in different ways. In contrasting fathering with mothering, we speak of averages, not absolutes, and we must always keep in mind that individuals are not statistics. Culture, biology, and environment push against each other to make each one of us unique—and, despite having mapped the human genome, we still have not found a gene for washing dishes. Meanwhile, social science has certainly identified the ideological structures that influence behavior, from the all-consuming cult of motherhood to the ideal of a male worker unencumbered by family responsibilities.

Whatever the cause, to some people this is evidence that men are unfit to be primary caregivers. And yet think of Kent's example: can anyone in his or her right mind argue that Kent was not up to the job of caring for his son? Andrea Doucet argues that we cannot judge stay-at-home dads through a maternal lens. "When that happens," she says, "other ways of nurturing are pushed into the shadows and obscured." Instead of looking at what men *don't* do when compared to mothers, says Doucet, we ought to look at what they *do:*

> For example, a maternal lens misses the ways in which fathers promote children's independence and risk-taking, while their fun and playfulness, physicality and outdoors approach to caring of young children are viewed only as second-best, or invisible, ways of caring. Similarly, a maternal lens overlooks the creative ways that fathers are beginning to form parallel community networks, to those that have traditionally existed by and for mothers; many of these networks are set up around their children's sports.

Clinton's total dependence temporarily annihilated Kent's independence—but not his sense of self. And as Clinton has grown healthier and more autonomous, Kent has pushed his son to be independent and acted to carve out more time for himself. By hiring babysitters and sending both kids to preschool as soon as they were able, says Kent, he gets more time to himself and he's in "a much better position to give the children better quality time."

To Doucet this is something to emulate. "I think that men do not face the same fatherload because they do carve out time for themselves, even when they are at home with the kids," she says. "Perhaps there are some interesting things that [women] can learn from men."[7] Misun echoes this sentiment: "I can't imagine fathers competing with each other about fatherhood stuff the way mothers do. They'd rather talk about tools or whatever. That's good." As stay-at-home dads stretch the definition of fatherhood, they also have the potential to reshape full-time caregiving.

In her book *Do Men Mother?* Doucet argues that today men are in the process of creating their own "language of care"—a way of talking about taking care of kids that is specifically masculine but still "embraces qualities of relationality, connections, interdependence, responsiveness, and responsibility." They do not, by and large, sound like mothers, and they do not act exactly like mothers. And yet they do all the things—changing diapers, wiping noses, washing dishes—traditionally imposed on women. As we have seen, fathers still tend to look to moms for guidance in how to take care of children. Though men who care for children are entering a traditionally feminine realm, still men and women appear to want for them to retain some essentially "masculine" quality. Many people want the difference, but today we reject the inequality that seems to come with it.

This can create cognitive dissonance, confusion, and guilt. What strikes me most about the story of Kent and Misun is their guiltlessness. They do not appear to feel they should be doing something that they are not. They are utterly comfortable in their respective roles—a role reversal, by traditional standards. This is why the Hoffmans are the last family profiled in this book: Like Ta-Nehisi Coates, their inner lives—their desires and feelings—appear to be aligned with the economic and social reality in which we all exist. They don't struggle against their roles or desires, in the way, for example, that Ed and Rachelle sometimes seem to, a conflict that has taken its toll on their marriage. Instead, Kent and Misun embrace them.

And shouldn't they? The roles weren't imposed; they were freely chosen, based on the circumstances that flowed from free decisions they made earlier in life. By any standard, their family works. Despite great challenges, its members are healthy and happy. The question is, can our dysfunctional twenty-first century society catch up with this highly functional twenty-first century family, and see them through the right lens? Will we see them as an example to follow—or will they remain invisible?

Postscript:
Who Do You Want to Be?

After I have turned off the recorder, Misun and I sit talking in their dining room, disheveled by one of Kent's running remodeling projects; she is quizzing me about research into the impact of reverse-traditional arrangements on children. Clinton wanders in.

"Hey, Clinton," she says. "Do you think you'd like to be like your daddy when you grow up?"

Clinton smiles his crooked smile. At first I'm not sure he understands the question, but Misun looks at him patiently.

"I want to be like mommy!" he finally says.

Misun winks at me. The wink says: *He's kissing my butt.*

"That's great," she says. "But do you think you might like to take care of your own kids, when you have them?"

"Yes," he says.

"So you want to be more like daddy and stay home while your wife works?"

"I want to be like daddy *and* mommy!" says Clinton.[8]

Can he have it both ways? Maybe in the twenty-first century, he can.

9

Conclusion

Remember the Future

One day when Liko was two years old—at this point I had been taking care of him for almost a year—we were playing with our new friends Karen Curtiss and her son Argus at their apartment. Liko pushed aside a big basket of toys and an oversized Richard Scarry book, and in the corner found—"buried sort of like it was porn," Karen later told me—*Peace Trek: Family Coloring Book,* published in 1986.

Liko and I read it together, he sitting on my lap, the dog-eared, floppy book propped up in front of us. "Why are people in this picture smiling and relaxed?" we read. "They are at peace with themselves and with everyone else in the world. That would make anyone a happy person. We must learn to be at peace with ourselves before we can help bring peace to the world."

The coloring book depicted businesses with names like Soy Foods, Planetary Holistic News, Holistic Health Clinic, Curative Herb Garden, and Peace Academy. This was a wheat-germ future that combined nostalgia for an agricultural past with hope that technology might bind humanity together on a global scale.

"In a world filled with conflict and fights over money and property, many problems are caused," concluded *Peace Trek.* "Many people think that all these problems can only be solved by raising children differently, and with much more love and attention."[1]

Liko got bored with this utopia, jumped up, and grabbed a fire truck out of Argus's hands, but I have never stopped thinking about *Peace Trek* and the act of reading a book like that to my son. I am broadly sympathetic to its vision, but, curiously, I found *Peace Trek* to be cloying, passive-aggressive, and idealistic in a vague and precarious way. Karen's comparison with porn is apt; intended for children, *Peace Trek* read like a masturbatory political fantasy. Whether it's sex or social progress, many people prefer to read about idealized situations instead of going through the trouble of getting the real, messy thing.

And yet I am haunted by the absence of viable utopias at the beginning of the twenty-first century. When our children grasp for ideals—as the best of them inevitably will—will we have anything to give them except disillusionment? In an age of familial fragmentation, what guidelines can we give them for how to raise families of their own? What expectations can we impart to our sons about what makes for a good partner and father? What political and social changes will enable them to meet their ideals? And how can we, as the parents of today, help build a future for our children?

The Conservative Challenge

Of course, there's no shortage of utopias that try to imagine a more perfect family, as well as a more perfect social order. The Shakers and hippies of America, and the kibbutzim of Israel, all imagined family forms that were fundamentally communal. None of these radical experiments caught on beyond hardcore believers, especially when it came to changing the nature of the relationship between parents and children.

Take the kibbutz movement. Early Jewish settlers in Palestine made children a communal responsibility. Babies slept outside the home, side by side in dormitories. "This experiment failed the test of reality," writes Israeli sleep researcher Avi Sadeh. In a study that compared a kibbutz that still kept this "children's house" sleeping arrangement with other kibbutzim in which babies and young children slept in their parents' homes, researchers found that "children who slept in their parents' houses tended to have longer continuous periods of sleep than those in communal sleeping situations on the kibbutz." They also found "that the kibbutz children's sleep improved greatly after moving to family sleeping arrangement." As a result of this dynamic, kibbutz children's houses declined and have almost disappeared.[2]

Despite such failures, explicitly utopian experiments persist today: in a 2006 *New York* magazine article, Annalee Newitz profiles a one-hundred-person commune on Staten Island that sounds like *Peace Trek* in action, warts and all. "Our cars are a perfect example of socialism," says a founder. "Nobody owns them, so we treat them like shit."[3] If children are defined as a collective responsibility, will they be treated like cars on a commune?

This prospect makes conservative, traditional ideas of family and child rearing much more attractive. Indeed, the Christian Right has capitalized on the understandable discomfort many Americans feel with the legacy of '60s-style utopianism, using it as a lever to revive their own conception of utopia, which pushes forward the father-led family as a showcase for the world they want to live in. "These homes are the source of ordered liberty, the fountain of real democracy, the seedbed of virtue," write conservative evangelical activists Allan C. Carlson and Paul T. Mero in *The Natural Family: A Manifesto*.[4] Their vision of the Christian Right home is unashamedly patriarchal and manifestly unequal, and contains an unmistakable appeal to fathers searching for an ideology that puts them back at the head of the family. "We do believe wholeheartedly in women's rights," claim Carlson and Mero. "Above all, we believe in rights that recognize women's unique gifts of pregnancy, childbirth, and breastfeeding."[5]

The Christian Right commitment to inequality is not merely rhetorical. One study by University of Virginia sociologist W. Bradford Wilcox found that "evangelical Protestant husbands do an hour less housework per week than other American husbands." And he notes additional research that has "shown that women raised in evangelical Protestant families . . . marry earlier, bear children earlier, and work less [outside the home] than other women in the United States."

Wilcox concludes, "It is true that evangelical Protestantism—but not mainline Protestantism, Reform Judaism, and Roman Catholicism—appears to steer men (and women) toward gender inequality." But Wilcox's study also reveals that evangelical Protestant belief shapes men's behavior in positive ways, helping them to manage anger and stay committed to family relationships.[6] The conservative vision of the family isn't *just* about male domination; it also teaches men how to fulfill their responsibilities.

The Christian Right and evangelical Christians are not one in the same—"Survey research shows that 70 percent of evangelicals don't identify with the Religious Right," reports Rice University sociologist Michael Lindsay.[7] However, conservative evangelicals form the social base for the Christian Right, which has actively tried to shape its institutions—prefiguring plans for American society as a whole—to reflect its conception of gender roles. Starting with the fall 2007 semester, for example, the Southwestern Baptist Theological Seminary in Texas introduced a new major in homemaking—available only to women. "We are moving against the tide in order to establish family and gender roles as described in God's word for the home and family," says seminary president Paige Patterson. "If we do not do something to salvage the future of the home, both our denomination and our nation will be destroyed."[8]

The Natural Family describes a comprehensive range of public policies that flow from making the patriarchal family the basic building block of society. In the authors' view, families, not government, should care for the sick and the vulnerable, thereby making welfare, universal health care, and Social Security irrelevant and even anti-Christian; mothers should take care of young children instead of federally subsidized day-care providers (or, for that matter, fathers); older children should be educated at home, not in public schools; and so on. In this way the Christian Right philosophy of the home roughly converges with antitax, antigovernment sentiment, except when it comes to legally enforcing the movement's vision of how families should be structured. Their views have powerfully influenced the platform of the Republican Party and shaped public policy for over a generation.

The example of the Christian Right campaign for "family values" points to one simple conclusion: ideals matter. Our personal expectations and grander utopian aspirations shape our behavior as well as our institutions. But ideals have limits, for they must push against economic, technological, and social forces that no individual can control. Ideals rise and fall based on the degree to which they help adherents thrive in their environment. As dishwashers, washing machines, and cheap clothing have made housework less time-consuming and economically essential, a skilled domestic specialist is less and less necessary to families. People are living longer and have access to birth control, and today the average woman spends less than a quarter of her life with young children.

And evangelical homes must confront the same problems as their nonevangelical counterparts: the erosion of real wages, the rising costs of necessities like health care and education, and the declining rights of workers, to name a few. These forces shape the homes of evangelicals as surely as they shape the homes of other sectors of society, which explains why, for example, rates of teen sex and divorce are not significantly lower in these homes. In fact, divorce is especially high in Bible Belt states, due at least in part to higher unemployment.[9]

In *The Natural Family,* Mero and Carlson blame virtually all these social and economic developments on feminism: in their view, it is the "imposition of full gender equality"—not, for example, inflation or globalization—that "destroyed family-wage systems."[10] There's no empirical evidence for this declaration, but that hardly matters: scapegoating claims like this one serve to mobilize Christian Right constituencies for its social agenda of putting heterosexual men back at the head of family and society, a strategy that has seemed to work in electing conservative politicians.

"People have personal standing in a discussion about what a good marriage is and what a bad marriage is," Republican operative Bill Greener told journalist Brian Mann. "They feel comfortable in that dialogue. It's about something they understand, a lot more than about trade policy."[11]

But for all its gains in the political realm, the Christian Right continues to lose the culture war. According to Gallup polls, in 1982 only 34 percent of Americans "believed that homosexuality was an acceptable alternative lifestyle." By 2007 that number had risen to 48 percent.[12] The year before, 61 percent of those polled by People for the American Way supported at least civil unions for gays and lesbians, which shows the degree to which our conversations about family structure have evolved.[13] Meanwhile, heterosexual families are more egalitarian than ever, with more and more men participating in housework and child care, more and more mothers working, and their relationships increasingly voluntary and negotiable—all of which requires higher levels of empathy, compromise, and interpersonal equality.[14] Divorce has declined slightly in recent years but still spells the end for almost half of all marriages.

I would argue that the Christian Right, today's leading champion of the so-called traditional family, is losing the culture war because economic developments are not on their side. "So is marriage doomed?" write economists Betsey Stevenson and Justin Wolfers. "Marriage in which one person specializes in the home while the other person specializes in the market is indeed doomed. The opportunity cost of having women stay out of the labor force is likely to continue to rise—particularly as young women are surpassing men in education attainment and higher education is becoming more important for market success."[15] In the twenty-first century, in most cases, both parents will keep a hand in the labor force, but one of them will likely take some time off to care for children when they are young. For a growing number of couples, that parent is a father.

The families I profile in this book are not a collection of left-wing radicals. Many are religious and conservative in their personal inclinations, if not necessarily politics; even among the mothers, few self-consciously described themselves as feminist and several couples even rejected the label outright. There might have been a time when becoming a "Mr. Mom" required some high degree of ideological commitment, but research shows that this is no longer the case. The changes of the past half century have altered the landscape and rules of discourse in ways that appear to be long lasting. The daddy shift—my term for the movement of fatherhood from solely breadwinning to both breadwinning and caregiving—affects everyone, regardless of political orientation.

W. Bradford Wilcox urges that we distinguish "between what elite evangelicals [like James Dobson] say and what average people are doing." While elites may rail against the social and economic changes of recent decades, Wilcox says that "your average evangelical takes all that with a grain of salt." That's in part because most evangelical wives work. "Part of that is a class issue," Wilcox says. "Evangelicals are more working class, than, for example, mainline Protestants, [and] they have less economic flexibility. And so the reality on the ground, with gender issues, is more flexible than some might expect." As a result, claims Wilcox, "many evangelicals are walking Left, talking Right." Their marriages are still measurably less equal in the way housework and child care is divided, but more equal than Christian Right rhetoric suggests.

In other words, the more their behavior compromises with reality, the shriller the rhetoric can be. This cognitive dissonance—that is, the clashing of our idea of the way things ought to be with the way they really are—permeates conservative conversations about gender and the family. It also illustrates the degree to which flexible gender roles have infiltrated even the parts of our society that are supposedly most resistant to change.

For example, in a 2007 segment of Rush Limbaugh's right-wing radio talk show, he grumbles against fathers cooking for their families and parents buying toy kitchens for boys. "This is not men reshaping and rethinking their roles," says Limbaugh. "That's being done for them with various sorts of pressure being applied if the behavioral model that is demanded isn't met." And the pressure, he argues, echoing Carlson and Mero, is coming from "feminazis"—his term for feminists.

This kind of talk, filled with petty resentment and misdirected rage, is common in right-wing media and among conservative leaders. But on this particular day, Limbaugh got a surprise when the calls started coming in from listeners. Here's the first:

RUSH: To the phones, to Fort Wayne, Indiana. This is Steve. Nice to have you on the program, sir.
CALLER: Mega dittos, Rush. I absolutely love you.
RUSH: Thank you.
CALLER: I'm a stay-at-home dad. I run a small business out of my home, and my boys—I got two boys—are great cooks. Now, I haven't bought 'em a kitchen set, and it's not on my short list of toys to buy, but they can make a mean batch of cookies, but they're in wrestling, and they'll kick somebody's tail with a sword—playing swords with them—and I wouldn't have a problem with them cooking at all. That's not a . . . I cook every meal in our house.
RUSH: How old did you say that these two boys are?
CALLER: My boys are eight and five.
RUSH: Eight and five, and they bake cookies?
CALLER: They do. They buy a brand-name mixer and . . . [16]

And so on. As he listens, Limbaugh is obviously confused. It's hilarious, ironic—and a perfect illustration of Wilcox's research. It's also a measure of the degree to which conservative ideologues like Limbaugh are being left in the dust by their followers, who must, after all, live in the same twenty-first century as the rest of us. Nothing gives me more hope that gender egalitarianism is the wave of the future.

For those who self-consciously commit themselves to traditional values while adopting a reverse-traditional family form, conservative ideology becomes, at best, a comfort and, at worst, a liability, in a twenty-first-century environment. Wilcox (a serious social scientist who works from a conservative perspective) argues that the strength of the evangelical narrative is that it explains why, for example, women still do twice as much housework as men—it's their God-given inclination. But that can be turned around: The evangelical narrative can't explain the fathers and mothers who are profiled in this book. It can't (yet) account for the stay-at-home father who calls into Limbaugh's show.

This creates an unhappy gap between ideal and reality, the place in which average right-wing evangelicals must live. And stubbornly adhering to the narrative creates another gap, between their utopian homes and the homes of everyone around them. In the face of social change, individual homes might preserve their purity. But in the end, they will sacrifice their ability to communicate with neighbors—or, I believe, to thrive in the twenty-first century.

Today, the fathers who listen to Rush Limbaugh are not, perhaps, so different from the fathers who took women's studies classes in college. Their experience is generational and so resists neat political categories. We're not living the future that many feminists of the 1960s hoped for—it's a good deal stranger and more complicated—but it does represent a transitional step toward the egalitarian society that many of them were trying to create. Stay-at-home dads are not necessarily antisexist men—note how quickly and awkwardly Limbaugh's caller inserts that bit about his boys kicking "somebody's tail with a sword"—but their choices still help chip away at the sexual division of labor. Stay-at-home dads have their activists, but most of them are best viewed as the quiet results of historical and economic processes, not militants in a mass movement.

Indeed, I don't think the daddy shift can be called a social movement at all; parenting is not the same thing as activism. If I had to pick an analogy, I would compare the daddy shift to the progress of a glacier: large, slow, and, if current conditions prevail in the future, inexorable. In other words, the daddy shift is an evolution, not a revolution.

Even so, the emergence of modern stay-at-home dads has powerful political implications. It creates a constituency of fathers who are more likely to care about issues—from paid leave to legal protections for caregivers—historically championed by mothers. Their personal decisions might not be linked to a policy agenda, but nonetheless, policy changes could support their personal decisions. The more fathers and mothers see that link between personal and political the better.

Now is the time for a new vision of a good family and a good father, one that is more consistent with the realities of the time and place in which we live.

The Twenty-first-century Family

In this book, I have tried to explore what reverse-traditional couples can tell us about successful twenty-first-century families. This is what I have discovered.

- Their stories reveal that men and women do not have to fall into a pattern in which one dominates and the other submits, even when one is working for pay and the other is taking care of children. Reverse-traditional families cannot directly challenge structural inequalities between men and women—that's not their job; their job is to raise children—but their existence does create a parental counterculture that asks all parents to reconsider their work and care arrangements.

- Similarly, they show us how family roles as caregivers and breadwinners can be negotiated instead of imposed by gender expectations. Their stories reveal that men *can* take care of children and women *can* support families—and that those roles can evolve over time, in response to the demands and desires of the moment. We have also seen the degree to which this flexibility and interchangeability can help some couples to survive their private boom-and-bust cycles, economic and emotional.

- The "mommy wars" books of the early twenty-first century[17] have tried to force women to pick either career or home, but most stay-at-home dads would call this a false dichotomy. They demonstrate (as many mothers have) that homemaking can be a life stage instead of a life-consuming career. Some of the dads I interviewed are career homemakers—this describes Kent Hoffman and Andy Ferguson, for example. But most of the others—from Ed Moon, who designs Web sites on the side, to Ta-Nehisi Coates, who has a successful writing career—combine primary parenting with some degree of paid work, minus the anxiety many moms seem to feel.[18] Even fathers who are full-time, career homemakers are often skilled in cultivating private spaces where they can regain their sanity and maintain a connection to a wider community.

· Stay-at-home parents of both sexes can form new communities together. While gender apartheid still characterizes playgroups and social networks, I have discovered, through my own experience and in interviews, that dads and moms and their kids *can* hang out together, cultivate platonic friendships, and forge cross-gender social networks. This enriches and diversifies neighborhood life and gives young children new male role models.

· Last but not least, these stories reveal the ways in which caregiving triggers broad and deep emotional and behavioral changes in fathers, strengthening their attachment to children and their ability to care for them. This is the clearest, most important lesson we can learn from reverse-traditional families—one that is applicable to other types of families. All fathers should take time off to care for their children.

However, every progressive social change creates new problems that must be addressed. For example, if both parents want time with children but someone must still bring home the bacon, they must each surrender part of what they want. One breadwinning, nonbiological lesbian mommy friend of mine describes her relationship with her partner as a constant negotiation. "The problem is that we both want to be the mom," she says. This is her way of saying that both of them value time with their two boys: caregiving is something for them to compete for, not avoid. One parent may have given birth to the child and the other may work every day to support the family, but both want to be as involved as possible in raising children—a pattern often seen in lesbian families.[19]

A similar pattern also turns up in two-daddy families. When Michael Mendez and his partner Mike set out to adopt their son Christopher, he says, "We had always talked about one of us staying home. We're very family-oriented. We value each other's families. Given all the work you have to go through to adopt, whether you're gay or straight, for us it didn't feel right to send the child off to day care after a month or two of family leave. Mike made a little bit more than I did, and so financially, even though we did well as a couple, it made more sense for him to work and me to stay home."

Even so, "I know that Mike feels guilty that he's not the primary caregiver," says Michael, who lives in Oakland, California. "Once he comes home, Mike takes over, and he's primary caregiver from that point on. They spend time playing, take a bath, they have this whole bedtime routine. And on weekends, Mike takes over. Part of it is that he wants to give me a break but he also wants that time with Christopher."

Michael sounds remarkably healthy, confident, and practical when compared to the neurotic self-doubt and ideological tension I've encountered in many new straight parents, including myself. Studies by psychologists Sondra E. Solomon, Robert W. Levinson, and others have found that same-sex couples tend to share housework and child care far more equally than straight ones, fight more fairly when they disagree, and bounce back more quickly from arguments.

"The findings suggest that heterosexual couples need to work harder to seek perspective," reports the *New York Times*. "The ability to see the other person's point of view appears to be more automatic in same-sex couples, but research shows that heterosexuals who can relate to their partner's concerns and who are skilled at defusing arguments also have stronger relationships."[20]

Just as the black family I profiled in chapter 6 has something to teach other kinds of families, so gay and lesbian parents have something to teach straight ones about how to think and behave in a way that assumes the partners are equal. Ironically, the secret to success might lie in accurately recognizing each other's differences. "One source of value in a marriage, as in every negotiation, is that the partners are different," writes Rhona Mahony. "No one marries his or her identical twin." Of course, couples often share similar educational levels, religions, and so on, but even so, personal traits and desires can vary widely even among couples who share similar social, cultural, and economic backgrounds—and, in the case of gay and lesbian couples, the same sex. Indeed, Mike and Michael might seem very similar, right down to their names, but their work and care decisions are based on differences that have nothing to do with gender.

Mahony argues that while these differences can cause friction, they can also create value in a relationship. "Rachel wants to climb to the top of her profession; Don wants to be a good person and put energy into his personal relationships," writes Mahony, who spends much of her book *Kidding Ourselves* describing how women can finesse negotiations in marriage. "Couples who respect that difference find that they complement each other, as in a traditional marriage."[21]

This is the first trick of a successful twenty-first-century parental partnership: to identify what you want and find a partner who knows what he or she wants, bargain openly for roles as changes like parenthood loom, and clearly identify what strengths each partner brings to the table. We saw this principle in action with Misun and Kent Hoffman. Misun made it clear at the outset that she wanted children but that she also wanted to pursue her career, and Kent responded that he wanted to raise the children himself if she would support him. If the couple had not been able to arrive at this arrangement, says Kent, the relationship would not have gotten to the next stage.

Romantically, this can be a bitter pill to swallow. On a practical level, however, and for the future emotional health of the family, it is a discussion that every modern couple must have. If the sexual division of labor is indeed in the early stages of dissolving and gender roles are up for grabs, couples must put their respective assumptions and innermost desires on the table. When they do not do this, the silence can become a liability in their marriages. Misun and Kent did, and it became a source of strength. And after the children were born, Kent was grateful for his wife's success as a provider, and Misun expressed appreciation for her husband's unique contributions as a caregiver.

This is also true of Gopal and Martha, whom we met in chapter 7. "I've always wanted to be a father, since I was a teenager," says Gopal. "There was definitely an understanding that we would share parenting. I always knew that I wanted to stay home and she always knew that." This combination of self-knowledge and honesty created the basis for a successful reverse-traditional partnership.

In recent decades we have tended to stress romance in marriage, but perhaps that has gone too far. As the daddy shift continues, we may (ironically enough?) need to see a revival of hardheaded negotiation in marriage contracts, both formal and informal. But the dynamic has changed: instead of women seeking to "marry up" to a man with earning potential and a man seeking a woman who will raise his children and clean his house, today the marriage contract is about establishing a division of labor consistent with the individual needs, goals, and yearnings of both parties.

In *Maternal Desire,* psychotherapist Daphne de Marneffe tries to imagine the psychology of family life in which men and women equally value child care. "Like a gestalt drawing that looks like a rabbit or a duck, depending on our perspective, whether we see the typical woman's or typical man's predicament as preferable depends on what we focus on." She continues:

I think that has to do with what Arlie Hochschild brilliantly characterized as "the economy of gratitude" in marriage. A couple's satisfaction with their division of labor is deeply tied to what counts as "a gift" in their relationship. "When couples struggle," Hochschild wrote, "it is seldom simply over who does what. Far more often, it is over the giving and receiving of gratitude." In our marriage, our division of labor worked in part because we agreed on the nature of "the gift." My husband and I both felt that caring for the children was a good to be prized.

"A good to be prized" is a phrase that sticks with me, for it is exactly how my wife and I see it. At times I have given Olli the prize of taking care of Liko; at other times, she has given it to me. We have also given each other opportunities to pursue our career goals. She and Liko gave me the time to write this book; for that I am grateful. We struggle—and I must constantly remind myself how lucky I am and how much I owe to her—but somehow we keep stumbling forward. This is the next trick of the successful twenty-first-century couple: to prize time with children and to feel grateful for each other's contributions and sacrifices, whatever they may be.

There are those who cannot conceive of a world without a sex-based division of labor. They see it as grimly androgynous, and thus not sexy. The freedom frightens them. But consider: for thousands of years, a person's station in life was fixed at birth and shaped by social class, caste, race, and order of birth, as well as sex. Societies were hierarchically structured, and social status determined the courses of people's lives, from the food they ate to the clothes they were allowed to wear to the work they'd do as adults. As Mahony notes, "Caste still rules the lives of millions of people in India in that way."[22]

But for millions of others, the Industrial Revolution swept that traditional way of life away—and indeed, today in fast-developing India, caste is in steep decline. For us in the United States, the American Revolution enshrined the pursuit of individual choice and happiness as something to which every one of us is entitled. As a culture, we Americans do not believe that a child's social and economic fate should be determined by birth.

Instead, we believe in mobility, ambition, and yearning. We wouldn't dream of restricting an individual's right to apply for different kinds of jobs; why should we consign men or women to one kind of role in the family? Today we face a range of choices that would dismay and even derange the slaves and citizens of the ancient world, and yet somehow we muddle through, and the world is better for it.

If systems like caste and royal birthright can be swept into the dustbin of history and if their absence can actually permit societies to rise to the next level of development, we can do the same with the sexual division of labor. Sex and sexiness will not disappear, though they will evolve, as indeed they have evolved. Women today can be both powerful and sexy, when once that was very rare; men today pay more attention to their appearance, for better and for worse. When more fathers stay home, children will not suffer; thanks to early pioneers and early research, we now know that involved fathers bestow tremendous benefits on children, families, and society.

Gender Convergence

Today the question is, will the number of stay-at-home dads continue to grow? Will the number of hours men spend on child care increase? Will women's economic opportunities keep expanding?

The truthful answer is that no one knows. No outcome is assured, but historical momentum *is* on the side of equality and freedom: The number of stay-at-home dads has increased almost every year since the census started counting them, and the percentages of men saying they'd be willing to consider full-time fatherhood has also steadily risen. Inequalities persist, but fathers *are* doing more housework and child care. In the meantime, more and more women have gone to college, gone to work, and increased their earning power.

As a result, equality is spreading. Studies from the 1970s found *no* examples of dual-income families in which parents shared unpaid family work. Wives were often grateful if the husband did any housework or child care at all. In the 1980s, researchers did start spotting a small number of couples consciously committed to equality, even if time-use studies revealed a gap between ideal and reality. By the 1990s, however, studies were finding more and more couples that seemed genuinely to share family work—and yet, by all accounts, they were not nearly as ideologically driven as egalitarian families from the '80s. In fact, many of the couples were quite ordinary. [23]

Today, this long-term trend toward casual egalitarianism is intensifying. "The evidence overwhelmingly shows an ongoing shift toward what we call 'gender convergence,' an ever-increasing similarity in how men and women live and what they want from their lives," write the sociologists Molly Monahan Lang and Barbara J. Risman in 2007, surveying decades of studies.

"It is not just behaviors but also women's and men's attitudes that are changing," they continue. "Women consistently hold more egalitarian attitudes than do men, but the general trend has been upwards for both sexes. Research shows that since the 1970s Americans have become increasingly more accepting of women contributing to family decisions, holding a job, and sharing the care-taking of children with others."[24]

This does not imply that we are inevitably marching off to a golden future of equality between men and women. Women's economic power shows every sign of continuing to grow—it's hard to argue with so many college degrees—but men's gains in child care and housework are much more tenuous. What will encourage the growth and health of families in which fathers act as caregivers to children? The research we have covered strongly suggests that dads need more positive role models in the form of other men who are willing to speak about their experience with caregiving and parenting. This only makes sense.

Reverse-traditional moms and dads also need community: stay-at-home dads and breadwinning moms must form their own respective networks. At the same time, however, breadwinning moms have much to gain from building personal, professional, and political bridges with breadwinning dads. Likewise, stay-at-home parents of both sexes face many of the same joys and dilemmas, emotional and social, and have natural grounds for solidarity.

In order for their numbers to grow, caregiving dads also need the support of the women in their lives, who must open the gates and let men into worlds that were once the exclusive domain of mothers. For many women, this is easier said than done, and it raises more questions than answers. Still, it must be done, not for the sake of some abstract ideological commitment, but for the sake of our families. "Paradoxical as it sounds," writes Daphne de Marneffe, "coming to a place of parental sharing with one's mate is intimately timed to awareness of one's maternal desire. Only in fully experiencing that desire, as well as our ambivalence and fears, can we open ourselves to the importance of similar feelings in men." This, she argues, facilitates tighter and more egalitarian family bonds.[25]

Breadwinning moms need positive role models as well: As media coverage of stay-at-home dads has expanded, their female partners have remained comparatively invisible. As full-time dads have founded their own playgroups, networks, and conventions, breadwinning moms are still relatively isolated from each other. And just as we are raising boys to be able to take care of children, girls must be prepared for the possibility that they might one day take financial responsibility for their partners and children. Female breadwinning should be valorized, as it has long been in parts of America's black community, alongside male caregiving.

But the problem goes beyond role models and interpersonal relationships. When motherhood shifted to include breadwinning, it changed society. As fatherhood shifts to encompass child care, society and workplaces must continue to evolve in accepting caregiving as an essential part of human life, a process that can be helped along only if more and more men have a stake in the issues traditionally championed by mothers and their allies. It is not enough for us to change as individuals—for men to, for example, become more empathic and involved and for women to focus more on career goals.

Society and public policy must change as well.

No Excuses

"In making excuses for our neglect of the world's children," writes the economist Jody Heymann, "people often claim that no one knows what can be done to help. In fact, there is extensive evidence regarding what would make a difference in the health, development, and education of the hundreds of millions of children growing up in working families." Drawing on decades of social scientific studies, she writes:

> We know that providing paid maternity and paternity leave at the birth or adoption of a child is crucial for children and parents. We know that ensuring that children four to five years old have access to high-quality early education will make an enormous difference to their later educational and developmental outcomes. There is no doubt that providing an affordable level of short-term paid leave for parents to meet the health needs of their children would improve children's access to preventive care when they are healthy and to adequate diagnosis and treatment when they are sick.[26]

Heymann is not talking here about utopia, a Greek pun that simultaneously means "no place" and "perfect place." She is talking about real social policies enacted by actual political entities such as Canada and the nations of the European Union, as well as in some Latin American, Asian, and African countries. The success of these programs has been tested and measured, and there is no doubt as to their efficacy. According to at least one study, the societies that have embraced them are among the happiest in the world.[27]

We know these policies have worked to facilitate more father involvement, and we now know that fathers can and must be involved in the care of children if the kids are to thrive in the twenty-first century. In this new context, a good father does many things. He sets limits, metes out incentives and rewards, provides love and hugs, climbs jungle gyms, stays on top of the child's health care and schooling, and supports the mother as a person and parent, whether they live together or not.

Today, a good father is also willing to take on primary care of his children and support his partner's career ambitions, if that is what circumstances dictate. He is willing and able to discuss and cooperate, not lay down the law. Fathers who attempt to force their wives to do their bidding, a relationship acceptable for thousands of years and sanctioned by law, are today not good fathers at all. It is no longer manly to diminish the strength of our female partners. In fact, it demeans all men, as well as women. I don't believe that I am unique or idiosyncratic in my conception of a good father; research, including my own, shows that many men today share my ideals. Not everyone, but enough so that it might make a difference.

But today we fathers must do more than rear a child and respect the mother: we must also fight in a public arena for what we want. For decades women and mothers have mobilized to change our society so that their ambitions and contributions are recognized and so that they can pursue whatever opportunities are available to them. They have heroically tried, and often succeeded, in changing workplace culture, public policy, and laws to support their roles as mothers. As I write, organizations like MomsRising and Mothers are Women are leading the good fight for health care, parental leave, and more—and many individual mothers are waging lonely struggles in their offices for respect of their role as parents.

The same cannot be said of fathers. Too often, we as a group have docilely accepted the "ideal worker" model, which pretends our families don't exist. Too often, we have allowed ourselves to be bullied into accepting the rules of a game that shortchanges our children and pushes us into roles that contradict our common sense and innermost feelings. There is nothing manly about having a seventy-hour working week shoved down your throat. To paraphrase one father I heard interviewed on NBC news, there's nothing masculine about sitting at a computer in a fluorescent-lit office instead of coaching your daughter's softball team. When work and family are out of balance, we as men are enervated and emasculated, not empowered. As a group, we have complained privately but remained silent in public. This is understandable, but also inexcusable.

In this book, we have seen how individual fathers have bravely embraced new roles, often in the face of isolation and relentless disapproval from extended family and society at large. But today, fathers as a group must start advocating for changes in society, public policy, and the workplace that will allow them to be the fathers that they want to be. We as dads must love our kids enough to work for a more just and sustainable society, a place where all children can grow up free, fed, and cared for.

Priority number one for fathers must be paid, gender-neutral parental leave along the lines of what is now offered in places like Germany and Sweden: at least six weeks, preferably twelve, of paid time off, followed by the option of taking at least a year off to care for a child. The second and third priorities must be a minimum number of paid sick days for all American workers as well as flex-time, which together will allow parents to stay home with their children when they are ill or take them to the doctor or pick them up from school.

We also need a greater diversity of career tracks, so that it is recognized as normal for parents to cut back on hours or tempo-rarily drop out of the workforce when kids are young. We need policies for part-time workers that prorate their pay and benefits instead of cutting them off altogether.

And it can't stop there: we must join with mothers in win-ning antidiscrimination policies, universal health care, subsidized day care, high-quality early childhood and public education—all the policies Jody Heymann lists as necessary for children and their parents to flourish.[28] As we saw in chapter 3, studies have shown that many policies also seem to fuel higher levels of male caregiv-ing. And gay dads and lesbian moms are parents too: they deserve rights of marriage and adoption, as well as protection against dis-crimination.

These are cultural battles, not just political ones. As we press for public policies that support our role as fathers, we have to speak of our love for our children and assert our right to spend time with them: stories of caregiving fatherhood must take their place alongside tales of motherhood, and everyone, from our fellow fathers to our in-laws to talk-radio listeners, must hear them. In short, we have to make fatherhood an issue and put it front and center in our society. If we don't do that, change will be something that happens to us, instead of something we create.

Imagining the Family

Remember *Peace Trek,* the utopian coloring book? Later I discussed it with Karen Curtiss, Argus's mom. Her husband Mark, she said, was the one who brought the book home. "Mark takes things at face value and does not devolve into worst-case scenario," said Karen, who sees herself as the cynical one in the family. "Mark thinks not only that the world can be good, but that essentially it *is* good."

When Liko and I looked at *Peace Trek,* Karen both avowed and disavowed it in the same breath, "saying I was too cynical for that kind of thing, but admitting—no, gushing—about how cute it was when Mark read it to Argus." And I must confess that, as skeptical as I feel about *Peace Trek,* I also love the image of Mark sharing with his son its utopian vision. Because I think we have to do that, even if we as adults are too corrupted by our experience to believe fully in visions of a better future. It's a balancing act: we work to realize a vision of a good life and good society even as we try to train our kids always to question that vision, to modify and improve upon it as life and history go on.

In truth, it is something we do automatically, creating stories of the future. Even those who reject extremist ideals, from left to right, hold in our minds an ideal of the perfect family; we all work to realize that ideal in daily life; all of us fail and suffer disappointment in not reaching that ideal. We try to forge a good life for our kids, inside and outside of standard gender roles: dad stays home; mom stays home; mom and dad split it all down the middle of a pie chart they post on the refrigerator; kids have two dads or two moms; we move to be closer to relatives or we flee from them; and we tinker with disciplinary regimes, trying to balance freedom against restraint. In that sense, every home tries to be a utopia, and thus all of us inevitably live in that unhappy gap between ideal and reality.

"There's got to be a utopian strand, there's gotta be positive stories," the science-fiction novelist and former stay-at-home dad Kim Stanley Robinson once told me. "You can criticize over and over again, but it also helps to have some vision of what should happen. It means there are wishes still in existence for a better and more just world, and it means people want to escape, like prisoners, the current reality. All to the good!"[29]

There is one final argument for trying to imagine a more ideal future: The past is very different from today, and we have every reason to believe that the future will be equally strange, if not more so. In the first chapter of this book, we saw how much families have changed in just a few decades; some of the changes have been so incremental that our society has hardly noticed. But family life today is radically different than it was fifty years ago, when trends were just emerging that would support involved fathers and breadwinning moms. Even twenty years ago, the number of stay-at-home dads was barely worth counting. And so it is only natural to ask what family life might look like fifty years from now if current trends continue.

Fifty years ago, workplace discrimination was legal and commonplace. Today, it is often illegal and furtive. Thus fifty years from now, the government could very well provide support and protection for gender-neutral parenting.

Fifty years ago, the vast majority of mothers didn't work. Today, 80 percent of them work, and the number of stay-at-home dads is growing steadily. Fifty years from now, perhaps the majority of fathers will put in at least some time as primary caregivers, and women will have reached economic and political parity with men.

Fifty years ago, the heterosexual, same-race, sole-male-breadwinner, female-homemaker family was considered the only healthy norm, against which all others were measured. Today, new family forms are proliferating, and social science is discovering that they do just as good a job of raising children as the 1950s-style family. Fifty years from now, we may be utterly comfortable with our diversity and the choices we face.

Viewed in this light, it is exciting to think about how our society will continue to evolve. And it is worth thinking about, because it suggests new ways of life and new directions for advocacy. We must remember that there is a future—there is always a future, with or without our participation—one that we will help to shape and that our children will live in.

Let's add up the pieces we have collected, and see what picture emerges. Not a fantasy, I hope, but one that builds upon the best of how we live today.

Beyond the Daddy Shift

In my ideal world, one parent, rich or poor, will be able to take at least the first year of his or her child's life off of work. Affluent parents will have their professional jobs held for them. Lower income parents will receive state support. Breadwinning parents will receive a minimum of six weeks paid leave, and most employers will be legally required to offer them the opportunity to cut down their work-hours for the first year of the child's life. These policies will apply to all new parents, male and female, gay and straight.

Biological mothers will be the ones most likely to take advantage of the first year off. But at the end of the first year, it will be dad's turn. The transition will be marked with a rite of passage. There will be a party at the office; that night the dad's buddies will throw him a celebration that very much resembles a bachelor party. Beer and liquor will flow and ribald jokes will be told.

The next morning, dad will wake up to a new life. His partner will go back to work, and he will be alone with the baby. His life will be hard at first; no utopia can ease the passage to full-time parenthood. He'll struggle with juggling a hundred tasks and losing time for himself. He'll start out as an incompetent slob, like most new parents, but he will learn. At first the emotional tools he has at hand might prove inadequate, but he will grow and develop emotional muscles where he didn't know he had them.

In this utopia, he won't be lonely. The playgrounds will have at least as many dads as moms. There will be playgroups, support groups, and places for him to go if he really needs help. Relatives will provide what support they can, and no one will give him a hard time: In fact, his caregiving stage of life will be validated and valorized.

In this egalitarian utopia, parents might still sort themselves according to gender. Some moms will prefer to hang with moms, some dads will want male company, but there will also be mixed-gender groups of parents who aren't that hung up on sexual differences—groups that will almost certainly include many gay and lesbian parents. There will be flirting: sex and sexual difference will not disappear, only inequality based on differences. People will have to deal with it, as they always have.

As dad learns to take care of children, mom will also get the support she needs as new breadwinner. She'll be welcomed back to the office with a reverse rite of passage, and there will be procedures in place to help her get up to speed. Just as her partner is struggling with his new role, she will probably struggle with feelings of guilt and separation. Her need for flexibility will be informally understood by colleagues and formally supported by a combination of workplace and government policy. Violations will occur, but in this utopia, the state will be on the side of parents, not employers.

Leave and flextime policies will be gender-neutral and will be defined by an understanding that both parents will serve as caregivers at some point and that the working parent ought to make time for children and provide support to partners who are currently caregiving. Again, these policies will apply as much to gay and lesbian parents as to straight ones.

Of course, many couples will prefer to split paid work and child care fifty-fifty from the beginning. Others will prefer more traditional and reverse-traditional arrangements where one parent specializes, especially when they have more than one child. Some dads and moms will both work and send their children to subsidized, high-quality, universal preschools. Choice and bargaining will define a world where the division of labor is not based on sex and the welfare of children is considered a national responsibility.

No utopia can guarantee a happy partnership. Some relationships will decline and dissolve. But in this world, fathers will rarely abandon their children, because they will have developed a deep attachment during the year or two in which they served as primary caregivers. Mothers will not be condemned to poverty by divorce. In a context of gender equality, the postdivorce couple will be better able to build a new, cooperative relationship as coparents. New families will form and be understood as a kind of extended family.

Girls will be raised to serve someday as breadwinners as well as caregivers. Boys will be psychologically and practically prepared to take care of children. Even so, individual preferences and proclivities will emerge. As these girls and boys grow up and start dating and contemplate parenthood, the division of labor will be discussed, not taken for granted. It is my dearest hope that all children will indeed get the love and attention they need, and this will help create a world, as *Peace Trek* promises, in which everyone feels a responsibility to everyone else and to the earth.

What do you think? Would you want to live in this world?

If your answer is yes, roll up your sleeves. If we want to live in this world, we're going to have to build it first.

Epilogue

Another Fatherhood Is Possible

I have been told that we write the books we would like to read. This is certainly true of me and *The Daddy Shift*.

When I became a father, I knew nothing—absolutely *nothing* —about parenthood in America. I had no idea about how to change a diaper or bathe a baby. I didn't know anything about parental leave. I didn't know anything about the cost of child care and preschool or how economic forces would shape our caregiving arrangements. I hadn't thought about how parenthood would affect our household division of labor. I had no big ideas about what might make for a good father.

And when I started to take care of Liko every day, I didn't see myself in any way that was positive. At first I saw only the negative aspects: no regular work, no free time, no adult companionship, no respect. I certainly didn't see myself as a pioneer or rebel or anything of the sort, as some called me, and in many ways I wasn't: This was not a role I embraced self-consciously. Like almost all the fathers I interviewed for this book, I wasn't trying to undermine an age-old sexist social order. I wasn't trying to make the world a better place. We were just trying to take care of our kid, going day to day, and we had bad days as well as good ones. In other words, we were normal, and we still are.

I spent the first six months of caregiving acting and thinking as though we were taking a short trip on a little raft, crossing from one side of a lake to another. It didn't occur to me that the experience might change the way I thought about myself, my family, and the world. But slowly, my view broadened. I reflected on my feelings and experiences. I talked to my wife. I talked to other parents. I started to read. I delved into the history, economics, and science of male caregiving—trying to understand why the older generation reacted the way it did to our arrangement, and why people of our generation didn't seem to think it special or unusual—I discovered that our family had a significance that went beyond our internal emotional dynamic.

Our choices were made possible by social changes that preceded us. At the same time, our choices have consequences. History isn't something you just read about in books; it isn't made only by presidents and generals, moving pieces on a giant chessboard. It's something that all of us make every day, through an accumulation of little decisions and reactions.

In *The Daddy Shift,* I have tried to write the book that I wish someone had given me before I became a father. I have tried to write a book that can help thoughtful new parents see the social context in which they make their decisions, in hopes that they can make each one more confidently.

Fathers are often made to feel—and they make themselves feel—that they are losers for wanting to spend more time with kids and less time at work. Meanwhile, mothers are often made to feel—and they make themselves feel—that they are losers for wanting to spend more time at work and less time with kids. As a result of following traditional gender roles, both parents can feel guilt, anger, and anxiety. Both feel like losers.

The reverse can also be true: Mothers inclined to feminist ideals beat themselves up for wanting to stay home with kids. Fathers who were raised with high expectations of involvement, but who remain dedicated to their jobs, feel like they fall short as fathers . . . and sometimes they do. Both moms and dads struggle to adjust their self-images and strike a balance, and little in our culture or economy helps them in any positive way.

As I hope the stories in *The Daddy Shift* reveal, it doesn't have to be this way. There are alternatives. Another fatherhood is possible. And there are many reasons why more male caregiving and more female breadwinning make sense: to give young children the attention and care they need; to allow both mothers and fathers to pursue their desires and opportunities; to strengthen a father's bond with his child; and more.

I also hope that the relatives and friends of stay-at-home dads and breadwinning moms might read this book and come away with a better understanding of reverse-traditional families in their midst. Not only that, but come to embrace twenty-first-century families in all their diversity, from gay and lesbian families to different kinds of immigrant families to stepfamilies.

However, this book should not be construed as an argument against traditional families. As I said in the introduction, over the years my own family has ranged from traditional to reverse-traditional to dual-income. There are times when a mother needs to care for a child and times when a father needs to. My point is that both should have the opportunity and tools (emotional and practical) to do so.

Or perhaps that understates my case. In fact, I do think all fathers ought to take time off to care for young children, for two months, two years, a lifetime—whatever is possible. To dads, I say that you will never regret it, and it will transform your relationship with your child. To moms I say, you will discover a side of the dad that you have never seen before, and new possibilities will emerge for you and your family.

I remember Liko's first day of preschool, which was also the first day of my new job at *Greater Good* magazine. We woke and made breakfast and battled to get his clothes on and pack lunch. My wife gave each of us a peck on the cheek and we rushed out the door. We waited in the bus shelter, Liko on my lap, the air white with fog. He stroked my beard slowly, thoughtfully. It was just the two of us, and the bus shelter felt like an island.

On the bus I read books to him and he looked out the window for excavators, dump trucks, skid steer loaders. I felt happy. But when the bus stopped near his school, my stomach suddenly clenched. The fog had burned off and the sun was shining, but I hardly noticed.

Inside, little-kid chaos and cheerful hallways. Hello to the teachers, hello to the parents. Liko looked more and more worried and panic rose up inside both of us. *This is it,* we both thought. *This is really it.* When it came time for parents to leave, distress zipped around the bright, brittle classroom and touched each child. Liko's eyes darted around the classroom, and he wrapped his arms around my leg. "No, Daddy," he said. "Don't go. Please, Daddy. Don't go." He started to cry.

I felt sick, but the teachers leaned forward as if to remind me about the routine everyone discussed at the orientation, the one where parents are supposed to pretend like this is a jolly good time. I felt like a child myself, but I put on the adult mask of a smile. "Have fun," I said to my son. "Mommy will pick you up."

On the way to work I felt as though someone had kicked me in the stomach. My head throbbed. Ridiculously, I was even short of breath. *It's such a small, normal thing,* I told myself. *Going to school. No big deal.* But as the day went on, I only felt worse. And in the weeks to come I found myself craving the feel of Liko's fingertips on my face.

It was a melodramatically agonizing moment, and yet, in retrospect, it also symbolizes the degree to which my relationship with my son had been transformed. I was no longer the bystander I had been during the first year; separating from him felt like cutting off an arm. Of course, even many full-time working parents feel this kind of bond without having had the benefit of staying home with their child. We can each take many paths to the same destination.

This was my path, and this is the book I wanted to read.

Acknowledgments

I express the most profound gratitude to the couples that allowed me into their lives and provided the interviews that form the heart of this book. Thank you to my mother, father, and grandfather, who patiently tried to answer my questions. Thanks also to my wife, Olli Doo, and to the community of parents that has nurtured and sustained my family.

Thank you to the University of California, Berkeley, Greater Good Science Center and to my colleagues there: Dacher Keltner, Jason Marsh, Christine Carter, and Tom White. I could not have written this book without their help, both individual and organizational. Thanks also to Alex Dixon, who provided transcription services. Alex is a wonderful writer, and he will one day write a book of his own, I have no doubt.

Thank you to Ruthanne Lum McCunn, who prodded me at the right moment and introduced me to Beacon Press; Christine Cipriani, the first editor who championed this project; and Andy Hrycyna, the editor who nurtured and shaped *The Daddy Shift* into its final form.

Sections of *The Daddy Shift*, especially chapters 1, 3, and 7, draw from a range of academic disciplines in which my personal competence is humble at best. I am indebted to the scholars and researchers who generously agreed to critique parts of this book in manuscript form: Jeff Cookston (psychology), Stephanie Coontz (history), Nancy Folbre (economics), Emiliana Simon-Thomas (neuroscience), Elizabeth Lower-Basch (public policy), Rodolfo Mendoza-Denton (psychology), and Erik Mueggler (anthropology). Obviously, none of them is responsible for any mistakes that might appear in this book. They are also not responsible for my interpretation of the facts; indeed, their occasional disagreements with my interpretations sometimes changed my mind and sometimes served to sharpen my arguments.

I thank the writers, activists, scholars, and friends who provided praise, criticism, intellectual guidance, inspiration, and information, sometimes all at once, whether they knew it or not: Philip Cowan, Carolyn Pape Cowan, V. P. Gagnon, Dana Glazer, Lisa Jervis, Claire Light, Miriam Peskowitz, Brian Reid, Shira Tarrant, and my fellow Daddy Dialectic bloggers: Chicago Pop, Chip, Tomas Moniz, and Christopher Pepper.

I am grateful to the magazines and editors who published early fragments of *The Daddy Shift* and helped me to develop some of my ideas: the editors of AlterNet; the editors of *Public Eye,* especially Abby Scher; the editors of *Mothering* magazine; and Sally Smith of the redoubtable *Noe Valley Voice.* I am also very grateful to the readers of my blogs, Daddy Dialectic and Fathering, whose comments contributed much to my knowledge and ideas about the family today.

Thank you to my writing group, Kill Your Darlings: Olivia Boler, Susan Godstone, Fiona Hovenden, and Mark Segelman. As Kurt Vonnegut liked to say, everyone should get themselves a gang.

The Mesa Refuge provided time and the wide, lovely landscape of Point Reyes in which to write first drafts of four of the chapters. Thanks to my fellow Mesa refugee, Ariane Conrad, for the hula-hoop lessons.

Notes

Introduction: Twenty-first-century Dad

1. Families and Work Institute, *Generation and Gender in the Workplace* (Watertown, MA: American Business Collaboration, 2004), 4; Suzanne M. Bianchi et al., *Changing Rhythms of American Family Life* (New York: Russell Sage Foundation, 2006), 113–24; Kimberley Fisher et al., "Gender Convergence in the American Heritage Time Use Study (AHTUS)," *Social Indicators Research* 82, no. 1 (May 2007): 1–33. These results were echoed in a survey of three thousand parents by Reach Advisors, a market research firm that also found that Generation X dads did twice as much child care. Reported in Stephanie Dunnewind, "Gen X Dads: Many Young Fathers More Involved than Baby Boomers before Them," *Seattle Times,* June 17, 2006.

2. U.S. Census Bureau News, "Single-Parent Households Showed Little Variation Since 1994," March 27, 2007, www.census.gov/Press-Release/www/releases/archives/families_households/009842.html (accessed June 27, 2008). For more information on the source of the data and accuracy of the estimates, including standard errors and confidence intervals, go to appendix G of www.census.gov/apsd/techdoc/cps/cpsmar06.pdf.

3. U.S. Census Bureau News, "Nearly Half of Preschoolers Receive Child Care from Relatives," February 28, 2008, www.census.gov/Press-Release/www/releases/archives/children/011574.html (accessed June 27, 2008). For a full report, see U.S. Census Bureau, "Who's Minding the Kids? Child Care Arrangements: Spring 2005," www.census.gov/population/www/socdemo/childcare.html (accessed May 1, 2008).

For additional background, see Lynne M. Casper, "My Daddy Takes Care of Me! Fathers as Care Providers," Current Population Reports, Census Bureau, September 1997.

4. For a quantitative comparison of couples in 2000 and in 1980, see Paul R. Amato et al., *Alone Together: How Marriage in America Is Changing* (Cambridge, MA: Harvard University Press, 2007), passim. Sociologist Barbara J. Risman also found that studies from the early 1970s could not identify *any* genuinely egalitarian couples, as measured by time-use instruments, where husbands and wives shared work equally; by the mid-1990s, however, such couples were appearing more and more often in social scientific studies. See Barbara J. Risman, *Gender Vertigo: American Families in Transition* (New Haven: Yale University Press, 1998), 93–98. This research is discussed more extensively in the final chapter of this book.

5. Bianchi et al., 113–24.

6. Martin H. Malin et al., *Work/Family Conflict, Union Style: Labor Arbitrations Involving Family Care* (Washington, DC: Program on WorkLife Law, 2004).

7. Scott Coltrane, "Fathering: Paradoxes, Contradictions, and Dilemmas," in *Handbook of Contemporary Families: Considering the Past, Contemplating the Future,* ed. Marilyn Coleman and Lawrence H. Ganong (Thousand Oaks, CA: Sage, 2004), 224–43.

8. U.S. Census Bureau News, "Mother's Day: May 13, 2007," March 14, 2007, www.census.gov/Press-Release/www/releases/archives/facts_ for_features_special_editions/009747.html.

9. The National Survey of Families and Households statistics are reported in Lisa Belkin, "When Mom and Dad Share It All," *New York Times,* June 15, 2008. Web accessible source data is available at www .ssc.wisc.edu/nsfh. Also, according to the Bureau of Labor Statistics, married, nonemployed moms spend three hours a day on housework and cooking, while married, nonemployed dads spend half that time on the same tasks. U.S. Bureau of Labor Statistics, "Table 1. Time spent in primary activities (1) and the percent of married mothers and fathers who did the activities on an average day by employment status and age of youngest own household child, average for the combined

years 2003–06," www.bls.gov/news.release/atus2.t01.htm (accessed June 27, 2008). Rather than seeing this as further evidence of inequality, we might ask the question: Are unemployed fathers not doing enough housework—or are unemployed mothers doing too much?

10. U.S. Bureau of Labor Statistics, "Women in the Labor Force: A Databook" (Washington, DC: U.S. Department of Labor, 2007), www.bls.gov/cps/wlf-databook-2007.pdf (accessed June 27, 2008); David Cotter, Paula England, and Joan Hermsen, "Moms and Jobs: Trends in Mothers' Employment and Which Mothers Stay Home," in *American Families: A Multicultural Reader,* 2nd ed., ed. Stephanie Coontz (New York: Routledge, 2008); U.S. Bureau of Labor Statistics, "Wives who earn more than their husbands, 1987–2005," November 30, 2007, http://stats.bls.gov/opub/ted/2007/nov/wk4/art05.htm (accessed June 27, 2008).

11. David Leonhardt, "A Diploma's Worth? Ask Her," *New York Times,* May 21, 2008.

12. Jennifer L. Hook, "Care in Context: Men's Unpaid Work in 20 Countries, 1965–2003," *American Sociological Review* 71, no. 4 (August 2006): 639–60.

13. "The results show that policies that free women from work for child care—for example, parental leaves—depress men's contributions to the home, and that extending parental leave to men increases men's contributions. Although there is reason to suspect that publicly supported child care may decrease men's contributions to the home, the results do not support this." Hook, 656.

14. Rhona Mahony, *Kidding Ourselves: Breadwinning, Babies, and Bargaining Power* (New York: Basic Books, 1995), 4.

15. For example, one gay Bay Area father I interviewed likened becoming a father to a second "coming out." Before parenthood, when he and his husband traveled outside of the Bay Area (e.g., Texas, where one of them had relatives), they could pretend to be platonic friends when it was convenient or necessary to do so; after parenthood, the nature of their partnership could not be concealed—they are both fathers to their child, and hiding that fact is not an option. Not only that, this father told me, also their position relative to the gay community changed. In some ways, he said, they became a minor-

ity group within a minority group who had more in common with straight couples. Even so, the father who stayed home with their child often found himself in the exact same position as the average straight stay-at-home dad—for instance, being the sole male parent in neighborhood playgroups.

16. Geraldine Fabrikant, "Would You Hire Your Husband?" *New York Times,* June 29, 2008. Statistic obtained from the Center for Women's Business Research.

17. James T. Bond with Cindy Thompson, Ellen Galinsky, and David Prottas, *Highlights of the National Study of the Changing Workforce* (New York: Families and Work Institute, 2002), 2–3.

18. Philip A. Cowan and Carolyn Pape Cowan, "New Families: Modern Couples as New Pioneers," in *All Our Families: New Policies for a New Century,* 2nd ed., ed. Mary Ann Mason, Arlene Skolnick, and Stephen D. Sugarman (New York: Oxford University Press, 2003), 196–219. Also see Carolyn Pape Cowan and Philip A. Cowan, *When Partners Become Parents: The Big Life Change for Couples* (New York: Basic Books, 1992), 16–29.

19. Wade F. Horn, "You've Come a Long Way, Daddy," *Policy Review* (July–August 1997): 24–30.

20. Allan C. Carlson and Paul T. Mero, *The Natural Family: A Manifesto* (Dallas: Spence Publishing Company, 2007), 119–20.

21. Ibid., 20.

22. David Popenoe, *Life without Father* (Cambridge, MA: Harvard University Press, 1996), 211.

23. Reader comments on Jeremy Adam Smith, "God vs. Stay-at-Home Dads," Daddy Dialectic, November 15, 2006, http://daddy-dialectic .blogspot.com/2006/11/god-vs-stay-at-home-dads.html.

24. Chip, "Hirshman's 'feminism' as masculinist ideology," Daddy Dialectic, June 21, 2006, http://daddy-dialectic.blogspot.com/search?q= dialectics+of+dad-hood.

25. Nancy Gibbs, "Bring on the Daddy Wars," *Time,* February 27, 2006.

1. A Stay-at-home Dad's History of North America

1. Paraphrase of Robert L. Griswold, *Fatherhood in America: A History* (New York: BasicBooks, 1993), 13. The quote from Stephanie

Coontz is from an e-mail she sent to me and is used with permission. The historical research of both Griswold and Coontz was enormously important to me in shaping this chapter, and I thank Coontz for the feedback and inspiration she generously provided to me.

2. George Lakoff et al., "The Nation as Family," The Rockridge Institute, www.rockridgeinstitute.org/projects/strategic/nationasfamily/nationasfamily (accessed September 17, 2007).

3. This was true in the United States and throughout the Western world. Elizabeth Pleck, *Domestic Tyranny: The Making of American Social Policy against Family Violence from Colonial Times to the Present* (Urbana: University of Illinois Press, 2004); David Peterson, "Wife Beating: An American Tradition," *Journal of Interdisciplinary History* 23, no. 1 (Summer 1992): 97–118; Donald G. Dutton, *The Domestic Assault of Women: Psychological and Criminal Justice Perspectives* (Vancouver, BC: UBC Press, 1995); Richard Gelles and Murray Straus, *Intimate Violence* (New York: Simon & Schuster, 1988); Heather Douglas and Lee Godden, "The Decriminalisation of Domestic Violence: Examining the Interaction between the Criminal Law and Domestic Violence," *Criminal Law Journal* 27, no. 1 (February 2003): 32–43.

4. Arthur D. Colman and Libby Lee Colman, *The Father: Mythologies and Changing Roles* (Wilmette, IL: Chiron Publications, 1988), 3–5.

5. Ralph LaRossa, *The Modernization of Fatherhood: A Social and Political History* (Chicago: University of Chicago Press, 1997), 24.

6. Michael E. Connor and Joseph L. White, "Fatherhood in Contemporary Black America: An Invisible Presence," *Black Scholar* 37, no. 2 (summer/fall 2007): 2–8.

7. Stephen M. Frank, "'Rendering Aid and Comfort': Images of Fatherhood in the Letters of Civil War Soldiers from Massachusetts and Michigan," *Journal of Social History* 26, no. 1 (fall 1992): 5.

8. Quoted in Michael Kimmel, *Manhood in America: A Cultural History* (New York: Free Press, 1996), 86.

9. Neil M. Cowan and Ruth Schwartz Cowan, *Our Parents' Lives: The Americanization of Eastern European Jews* (New York: Basic Books, 1989), 196.

10. Margaret Marsh, "Suburban Men and Masculine Domesticity, 1870–1915," *American Quarterly* 40, no. 2 (June 1988): 165.

11. David Leverenz, *Paternalism Incorporated: Fables of American Fatherhood, 1865–1940* (Ithaca, NY: Cornell University Press, 2003), 23.

12. Mirra Komarovsky, *The Unemployed Man and His Family* (New York: Dryden Press, 1940), 357.

13. Bart Landry, *Black Working Wives: Pioneers of the American Family Revolution* (Berkeley: University of California Press, 2000), 45.

14. Ibid., 49.

15. Ibid., 5.

16. Griswold, 2.

17. Ibid., 41.

18. Ibid., 49.

19. LaRossa, 12.

20. Maxine P. Atkinson and Stephen P. Blackwelder, "Fathering in the 20th Century," *Journal of Marriage and the Family* 55, no. 4 (November 1993): 975–86.

21. LaRossa, 13.

22. Stephanie Coontz, *Marriage, a History: From Obedience to Intimacy, or How Love Conquered Marriage* (New York: Viking, 2005), 218.

23. Kimmel, 87.

24. Carolyne Zinko, "WWII opened doors for many women in Bay Area, but not all," *San Francisco Chronicle,* September 26, 2007. The woman quoted, Maggie Gee, age eighty-four, flew an airplane as a Women's Airforce Service pilot during the war and later become a physicist at Lawrence Livermore National Laboratory.

25. U.S. Department of State, "The American Family, by the Numbers," *U.S. Society & Values* 6, no. 1 (January 2001), http://usinfo.state.gov/journals/itsv/0101/ijse/numbers.htm (accessed December 4, 2007).

26. Stephanie Coontz, *The Way We Really Are: Coming to Terms with America's Changing Families* (New York: Basic Books, 1997), 38.

27. Talcott Parsons, "The American Family: Its Relations to Personality and to the Social Structure," in *Family, Socialization, and Interaction Process,* eds. Talcott Parsons and Robert Freed Bales (Glencoe, IL: Free Press, 1955), 3.

28. This may sound radical, but the contemporary reader should keep in mind that Elder in her theory and definitions, and her interview subjects in the way they spoke about their lives, never ventured out-

side the confines of traditional gender roles. For example, none of the fathers expressed a desire to stay home with the children while their wives worked; I doubt such an idea would have occurred to them. In embracing values Elder labeled "developmental," these men were seeking to change the style, not the structure, of family life, so that it might be kinder and gentler.

29. Rachel Ann Elder, "Traditional and Developmental Conceptions of Fatherhood," *Marriage and Family Living* 11, no. 3 (August 1949), 98–100, 106.

30. J. M. Mogey, "A Century of Declining Paternal Authority," *Marriage and Family Living* 19, no. 3 (August 1957): 234–39.

31. Coontz, *Marriage, A History,* 243.

32. This dialogue is based entirely on my personal recollection of a *Brady Bunch* commercial that ran incessantly during my youth. The enterprising reader is free to dispute my memory.

33. Sara Evans, *Personal Politics: The Roots of Women's Liberation in the Civil Rights Movement and the New Left* (New York: Vintage, 1980), 51.

34. Coontz, *Marriage, a History,* 249.

35. Jane Smiley, "21st Century Family Values," *The Observer,* June 25, 2000.

36. National Organization for Women, "Statement of Purpose," 1966. Full text available online at www.now.org/history/purpos66.html.

37. Arlie R. Hochschild, *The Second Shift* (New York: Viking, 1989).

38. Griswold, 220.

39. Jeremy Adam Smith, "Living in the Gap: The Ideal and the Reality of the Christian Right Family," *Public Eye* 22, no. 4 (winter 2007–08). Also see Stephanie Coontz, "In Search of Men Who Are in Search of Commitment," *Washington Post,* September 7, 1997. Coontz argues that the late twentieth-century Christian Right "men's movement" called the Promise Keepers was a complex phenomenon: "Critics of the Promise Keepers should not fall into the trap of demonizing the men to whom these rallies appeal. Many of the men who attend are searching for an anchor that will keep them committed to their wives in a world where other men are contemptuous of such values. They are looking for alternative models of manhood to those presented by

Rambo or Donald Trump. At the rallies they hear that it is not weak to express emotions, that manliness isn't about power or financial success or domination."

40. Griswold, 224.

41. See, for example, Stallone's 1986 movie *Cobra,* which he wrote.

42. This happens in the 1990 film *Total Recall,* starring Arnold Schwarzenegger.

43. Why should it be the case that positive images were found in science-fiction series and comic books, instead of elsewhere? My pet theory is that it was safest to envision a new kind of fatherhood in fantastic settings, with spaceships and aliens, in the same way that political dissidents in dictatorships often use fantasy and science fiction to make allegorical or satirical points that they cannot make in forums that are taken more seriously by authorities. In American culture, of course, the authority lies with the market, not a president for life.

44. James Robinson, *Starman: Sons of the Father* (New York: DC Comics, 2005), 5–24. Stories originally published in single issues of *Starman,* nos. 75–80.

45. This is actually a recurring pattern in pop cultural depictions of fathering in the 1970s, '80s, and '90s: the mother is erased, usually because she has died or abandoned the family, and only in this circumstance are men shown taking care of young children. In many cases—*Kramer vs. Kramer* comes to mind—the mother's absence gives the father an opportunity to show that he can mother better than any woman. To be sure, such depictions embody a high level of sexism and are a product of their times, but they also took another step in the right direction, as images of masculinity were stretched to encompass caregiving behavior. My perception is that this narrative is starting to disappear today: we are seeing fewer stories along these lines and more in which father and mother are partners in raising their children.

46. Ralph LaRossa et al., "The Changing Culture of Fatherhood in Comic-Strip Families: A Six-Decade Analysis," *Journal of Marriage and the Family* 62, no. 2 (May 2000): 375–87.

47. See endnote 1 of the introduction to this book for evidence of this.

2. Searching for Role Models

1. Rosenfeld said this in an interview I had with him. His research is summarized and explained in Michael J. Rosenfeld, *The Age of Independence: Interracial Unions, Same-Sex Unions, and the Changing American Family* (Cambridge, MA: Harvard University Press, 2007).

2. Philip A. Cowan and Carolyn Pape Cowan, "New Families: Modern Couples as New Pioneers," in *All Our Families: New Policies for a New Century,* 2nd ed., eds. Mary Ann Mason, Arlene Skolnick, and Stephen D. Sugarman (New York: Oxford University Press, 2003), 198.

3. U.S. Bureau of Labor Statistics, "Women in the Labor Force: A Databook," (Washington, DC: U.S. Department of Labor, 2007), www.bls.gov/cps/wlf-databook-2007.pdf (accessed December 20, 2007).

4. David Leonhardt, "A Diploma's Worth? Ask Her," *New York Times,* May 21, 2008.

5. Quoted in Alex Williams, "Putting Money on the Table," *New York Times,* September 23, 2007.

6. M.P. Dunleavey, "A Breadwinner Rethinks Gender Roles," *New York Times,* January 27, 2007.

7. Amy Brayfield, "Why I Left My Beta Husband," MarieClaire.com, www.marieclaire.com/life/sex/advice/beta-husband (accessed September 23, 2007).

8. Elizabeth Lower-Basch, "Parenting and Mothering," Half-Changed World, April 6, 2006, www.halfchangedworld.com/2006/04/parenting_and_m.html. Lower-Basch is responding to one of my own blog entries at Daddy Dialectic.

9. Natasha J. Cabrera et al., "Fatherhood in the Twenty-First Century," *Child Development* 71, no. 1 (January/February 2000): 131.

10. Kerry Daly, "Reshaping Fatherhood: Finding the Models," *Journal of Family Issues* 14, no. 4 (1993): 517.

11. Elder's conclusions are echoed by a roughly contemporary study: Ruth J. Tasch, "The Role of the Father in the Family," *Journal of Experimental Education* 20 (1952): 319–61.

12. Elder, 106.

13. Daly, 524.

14. Ibid., 525.

15. Trent W. Maurer and Joseph H. Pleck, "Fathers' Caregiving and Breadwinning: A Gender Congruence Analysis," *Psychology of Men and Masculinity* 7, no. 2 (April 2006): 101–12. Also see Trent W. Maurer, "Gender Congruence and Social Mediation as Influences on Fathers' Caregiving," *Fathering* 5, no. 3 (fall 2007): 220–35.

16. Helen Chang, "No-Fault Divorce Laws May Have Increased Women's Physical Well-Being," Stanford Graduate School of Business, January 2004, www.gsb.stanford.edu/news/research/econ_divorce .shtml (accessed July 1, 2007).

17. Laura Dugan, Daniel S. Nagin, and Richard Rosenfeld, "Explaining the Decline in Intimate Partner Homicide," *Homicide Studies* 3, no. 3 (1999): 187–214.

18. Po Bronson, "Do Men Change Diapers?" Social Studies, March 2, 2006, www.pobronson.com/blog/2006/03/do-men-change-diapers-are-new-dads.html (accessed March 5, 2006).

19. Ruth Bettelheim, "Binuclear Man," in *What Makes a Man: 22 Writers Imagine the Future,* ed. Rebecca Walker (New York: Riverhead Books, 2004), 220–31.

20. Constance Ahrons, *We're Still Family: What Grown Children Have to Say About Their Parents' Divorce* (New York: HarperCollins, 2004), passim. For an earlier study of children of divorce, see Frank F. Furstenberg Jr. and Andrew J. Cherlin, *Divided Families: What Happens to Children When Parents Part* (Cambridge, MA: Harvard University Press, 1991), passim.

21. Jason Marsh, "A Better Way: An Interview with *The Good Divorce* Author, Constance Ahrons," *Greater Good,* fall 2007, 20–21.

22. Rhona Mahony, "Divorce, nontraditional families, and its consequences for children," November 20, 1997, www-leland.stanford .edu/~rmahony/Divorce.html (accessed January 5, 2007).

23. Betsy Schiffman, "Women Increasingly Paying Alimony," *Forbes,* March 13, 2007, www.forbes.com/leadership/2007/03/13/women-paying-alimony-lead_cx_pink_0313alimony.html (accessed March 14, 2007).

3. Stay-at-home Economics, or
Five Myths of Caregiving Fatherhood

1. An early reader of this manuscript disputed the idea that reverse-traditional family roles can flip as time goes on: "My sense is that families that go back and forth as to which parent is at home are even more rare than mom-at-work/dad-at-home (MAWDAH) families. I know families that have moved back and forth between MAWDAH and dual-income, but not from MAWDAH to dad-at-work/mom-at-home. Not sure it makes sense to focus so much on that variant." My reader lives in an affluent Virginia suburb of Washington, D. C., where Ivy League degrees are common and so are jobs with the federal government and with assorted partisan think tanks; in contrast, my personal experience in the working-class and bohemian areas of San Francisco has been different. Many couples interviewed for this book—such as Ed and Rachelle in chapter 2, Vince Janowski and his wife in this chapter, and Gopal and Martha in chapter 7—have taken turns making money and caring for babies. This reinforces the idea that reverse-traditional families are diverse. In any event, my point here is *not* that it is normal for families of any type to flip; I have not seen any research that shows it to be normal or abnormal, so at this point, we are guessing and speculating. Instead, my point is that it can and does happen, and when it does, it helps families to survive boom-and-bust cycles. It is better, in my view, for both parents to be capable of work and care.

2. The bias extends to stay-at-home mothers. Researchers and writers such as Pamela Stone and Linda Hirshman have deliberately focused on the choices made by educated and affluent white women. Sue Shellenbarger's otherwise superb coverage of family issues in the *Wall Street Journal* is, not surprisingly, heavily biased toward affluent moms.

3. Heather Boushey, "Are Mothers Really Leaving the Workplace?" Council on Contemporary Families, March 28, 2006, www.contemporaryfamilies.org/subtemplate.php?t=briefingPapers&ext=pr306 (accessed April 1, 2008).

4. Elizabeth Lower-Basch, "Do only rich families have at-home parents?" Half Changed World, October 19, 2005, www.halfchanged

world.com/2005/10/do_only_rich_fa.html (accessed October 19, 2005).

5. In others, such as the countries of the European Union, state subsidies significantly boost the incomes of child-care workers.

6. U.S. Census Bureau, "Who's Minding the Kids? Child Care Arrangements: Spring 2005," www.census.gov/population/www/socdemo/childcare.html (accessed May 30, 2008).

7. Thanks to Elizabeth Lower-Basch for providing updated census data and examples.

8. Sue Shellenbarger, "The Brat Race: In Diapers and on a Day-Care Wait List," *Wall Street Journal,* February 21, 2008, http://s.wsj.net/article/SB120354424298580955.html?mod=todays_us_nonsub_pj (accessed April 25, 2008).

9. Kathryn D. Linnenberg, "Number One Father or Fathering 101?: Couple Relationship Quality and Father Involvement among Fathers Who Live with Their Children," in *Unmarried Couples with Children,* ed. Paula England and Kathryn Edin (New York: Russell Sage Foundation, 2007), 159–82.

10. Jane Waldfogel, *What Children Need* (Cambridge, MA: Harvard University Press, 2006), 61–62.

11. Martin H. Malin et al., *Work/Family Conflict, Union Style: Labor Arbitrations Involving Family Care* (Washington, DC: Program on WorkLife Law, 2004), 6–7.

12. Ross D. Parke, Scott Coltrane, and Thomas Schofield, "New Americans, New Families," *Greater Good,* fall 2007, 22–26.

13. See, for example, John F. Toth and Xiaohe Xu, "Ethnic and Cultural Diversity in Fathers' Involvement: A Racial/Ethnic Comparison of African American, Hispanic, and White Fathers," *Youth and Society* 31, no. 1 (September 1999): 76–99.

14. Quoted in Parke, Coltrane, and Schofield, 24.

15. Linnenberg, 162.

16. Sue Shellenbarger, "More New Mothers Are Staying Home Even When It Causes Financial Pain," *Wall Street Journal,* November 30, 2006, http://online.wsj.com/article/SB116484756909736354.html?mod=Work+%26+Family (accessed April 1, 2008).

17. Leslie Bennetts, "The Feminine Mistake," *The Huffington Post,* March

31, 2007, www.huffingtonpost.com/leslie-bennetts/the-feminine-mistake_b_44690.html (accessed March 1, 2008).

18. Nancy Folbre, *The Invisible Heart: Economics and Family Values* (New York: New Press, 2001), 18.

19. Karen V. Hansen, *Not-So-Nuclear Families: Class, Gender, and Networks of Care* (New Brunswick, NJ: Rutgers University Press, 2005), 182–83.

20. U.S. Census Bureau, "Who's Minding the Kids? Child Care Arrangements: Spring 2005." Tables available at www.census.gov/population/www/socdemo/child/ppl-2005.html (accessed May 27, 2008). For additional background, see Lynne M. Casper, "My Daddy Takes Care of Me! Fathers as Care Providers," Current Population Reports, Census Bureau, September 1997.

21. Hansen, 183.

22. When Scott Coltrane and Oriel Sullivan published a paper summarizing new research into men's changing contributions to housework and child care, Smock responded by denying the importance of progress to date. "Until men begin to take responsibility for invisible household work," she writes, "women will continue to shoulder more family work, and therefore to face more constraints in their freedom to engage in paid work." This is perfectly true but fails to account for the degrees to which society has changed. Men today *are* shouldering household work, and women *are* gaining more options. It's curious to me that people like Smock try to snatch defeat from the jaws of the feminist movement's greatest victories. Coltrane and Sullivan's paper and Smock's response can be read at www.contemporaryfamilies.org/subtemplate.php?t=briefingPapers&ext=menshousework.

23. Anonymous comment on "One Utopia," Daddy Dialectic, January 15, 2008, http://daddy-dialectic.blogspot.com/2008/01/one-utopia.html (accessed January 20, 2008).

24. Society for Human Resource Management, "SHRM 2008 Employee Benefits Report: How Competitive Is Your Organization?" www.shrm.org/hrnews_published/archives/CMS_025886.asp (accessed October 2008; available only to subscribers).

25. Nancy Hatch Woodward, "Make Room for Daddy," *HR Magazine,*

July 2001, http://findarticles.com/p/articles/mi_m3495/is_7_46/ai_
77197989 (accessed May 30, 2008).

26. David Cantor et al., *Balancing the Needs of Families and Employers: Family and Medical Leave Surveys* (Rockville, MD: Westat, 2001), §2.2.4, www.dol.gov/esa/whd/fmla/fmla/toc.pdf (accessed May 30, 2008).

27. Karen Holt, "Good for the Gander," *Working Mother,* October 2008.

28. Reported in Ann Crittenden, *The Price of Motherhood* (New York: Metropolitan Books, 2001), 99.

29. Arlie Russell Hochschild, *The Time Bind: When Work Becomes Home and Home Becomes Work* (New York: Metropolitan Books, 1997), 140–41.

30. Mick Cunningham, "Influences of Women's Employment on the Gendered Division of Household Labor over the Life Course: Evidence from a 31-Year Panel Study," *Journal of Family Issues* 28, no. 3 (March 2007): 422–44.

31. Michael Bittman et al., "When does gender trump money? Bargaining and time in household work," *American Journal of Sociology* 109, no. 1 (July 2003): 186–214; Suzanne M. Bianchi et al., "Is anyone doing the housework? Trends in the gender division of household labor," *Social Forces* 79, no. 1 (September 2000): 191–228; Catherine I. Bolzendahl and Daniel J. Myers, "Feminist attitudes and support for gender equality: Opinion change in women and men, 1974–1998," *Social Forces* 83, no. 2 (December 2004): 759–90. Note that all of these studies still find widespread inequality.

32. Sanjiv Gupta, "Women's Money Matters: Earnings and Housework in Dual-Earner Families," Council on Contemporary Families, September 4, 2007, www.contemporaryfamilies.org/subtemplate.php?t=briefingPapers&ext=womenshousework (accessed October 1, 2007). Gupta found that for every seventy-five hundred dollars a woman earns, the amount of housework she does declines by one hour per week. However, the news in Gupta's study isn't all good: although the number of households where men and women equally share chores has risen dramatically, "old assumptions about women's responsibility for household work remain very widespread." Gupta points out that in most cases, "not only do women spend more time

on everyday housework than do their husbands, they also appear to draw only upon their own earnings to cut down on it, not their husbands."

33. Jennifer L. Hook, "Care in Context: Men's Unpaid Work in 20 Countries, 1965–2003," *American Sociological Review* 71, no. 4 (August 2006): 639–60.

34. Crittenden, 248.

35. Rana Foroohar, "Myth and Reality: Forget all the talk of equal opportunity. European women can have a job—but not a career," *Newsweek,* February 27, 2006.

36. Hugh Heclo and Henrik Madsen, *Policy and Politics in Sweden: Principled Pragmatism* (Philadelphia: Temple University Press, 1987), 176.

37. Crittenden, 247.

38. Karin Alfredsson, "At Home with Dad," Swedish Institute, 2007, www .sweden.se/templates/cs/CommonPage____18298.aspx (accessed May 30, 2008).

39. Anna-Lena Almqvist, "Why Most Swedish Fathers and Few French Fathers Use Paid Parental Leave: An Exploratory Qualitative Study of Parents," *Fathering* 6, no. 2 (Spring 2008): 192–200.

40. Alfredsson.

41. There were 200,000 stay-at-home dads in 2007 in the United Kingdom, which has a population of 61 million. In comparison, the 2007 census officially counts 159,000 stay-at-home dads in the United States, a country with a population of 300 million. In both countries, the numbers have more than doubled since the mid-1990s. It is hard to interpret these numbers, however, because the census count is so flawed; I don't know anything about the quality of the count in the UK or if, for example, the UK's Office of National Statistics counts primary caregivers who work part-time as at-home parents. For a solid overview of stay-at-home dads in the UK, see Blake Morrison, "Family: The Paternal Instinct," *The Guardian,* June 16, 2007.

42. Rob Hincks, "Sweden fosters fatherhood," Swedish Institute, November 25, 2005, www.sweden.se/templates/cs/Article____12972 .aspx (accessed May 30, 2008).

43. Naomi Kresge, "German dads jump at chance to stay home with kids," *Mail & Guardian* Online, December 14, 2007, www.mg.co

.za/articlepage.aspx?area=/breaking_news/breaking_news__inter national_news/&articleid=327812&referrer=RSS (accessed December 15, 2007).

44. Hook, 656.

45. Amy Husser, "Quebecers top the list for stay-at-home dads: StatsCan," *Vancouver Sun,* June 23, 2008.

46. Malin et al., 4.

47. Stephanie Armour, "As dads push for family time, workplace tensions rise," *USA Today,* December 11, 2007. Also see Joan C. Williams and Stephanie Bornstein, "Caregivers in the Courtroom: The Growing Trend of Family Responsibilities Discrimination," *University of San Francisco Law Review* 41, no. 2 (fall 2006): 171–89.

48. Tresa Baldas, "More Men File Work Bias Suits over Family Leave," *Recorder,* July 29, 2008.

49. Woodward.

50. Heller Ehrman LLP, "Work/Life Balance: 'Not Just for Women,'" Roundtable Discussion, Stanford Park Hotel, Menlo Park, CA, January 23, 2007, www.hellerehrman.com/en/optin/work%20life%20 balance%20report.pdf (accessed June 10, 2008).

4. Searching for Community

1. Barry A. Kosmin, Egon Mayer, and Ariela Keysar, *American Religious Identification Survey 2001* (New York: Graduate Center of the City University of New York, 2001), 40. Available online at www.gc.cuny .edu/faculty/research_briefs/aris.pdf (accessed May 20, 2008).

2. Ross D. Parke, Scott Coltrane, and Thomas Schofield, "New Americans, New Families," *Greater Good,* fall 2007, 22–26.

3. Linda George, "The Costs of Loneliness," *Greater Good,* winter 2007–08, 9.

4. For example, see Jacinta Bronte-Tinkew et al., "Symptoms of Major Depression in a Sample of Fathers of Infants," *Journal of Family Issues* 28, no. 1 (January 2007): 61–69. Unsurprisingly, the study finds that unemployment contributes significantly to paternal depression and that this depression can harm relationships with children in their care. Another study presented at the May 2008 American Psychiatric Association meeting in Washington, D.C., found that "fathers of

9-month-olds are about twice as likely as other men their age to show symptoms of major depression, which also hurts their children." Marilyn Elias, "New dads twice as likely to become depressed, study finds," *USA Today*, May 7, 2008.

5. A study released at a meeting of the American Heart Association in April 2002 "found that men who decide to become househusbands and take care of children at home may be putting their health and hearts in danger," reports CNN. "In fact, researchers conducting the study in Framingham, Massachusetts, for the National Institutes for Health found men who have been stay-at-home dads most of their adult lives have an 82 percent higher risk of death from heart disease than men who work outside the home." In the article, lead researcher Elaine Eaker blames these risks on the relative social isolation of stay-at-home dads. Rhonda Rowland, "Beyond tantrum control: Stay-at-home dads face health risks," CNN.com, April 25, 2002, http://archives.cnn.com/2002/HEALTH/conditions/04/24/heart .role.reversal/ (accessed May 15, 2008).

6. This quote is from an e-mail sent by Aaron Rochelen to study participants. The letter can be read online at: "Summary of University of Texas Stay-at-Home Dad Research," Rebeldad, April 2, 2007, www .rebeldad.com/UTStudy.html (accessed April 3, 2007).

7. Andrea Doucet, *Do Men Mother?* (Toronto: University of Toronto Press, 2006), 151–69.

5. Interlude

1. ChildStats.gov, "FAM3.B Child Care: Primary Child Care Arrangements for Children Ages 0–4 with Employed Mothers by Selected Characteristics, Selected Years 1985–2005," http://childstats.gov/americaschildren/tables/fam3b.asp (accessed August 2008). Table derived from U.S. Census Bureau, Survey of Income and Program Participation. Also see U.S. Census Bureau, "Who's Minding the Kids? Child Care Arrangements: Spring 2005," www.census.gov/population/www/socdemo/childcare.html; and Lynne M. Casper, "My Daddy Takes Care of Me! Fathers as Care Providers," Current Population Reports, Census Bureau, September 1997.

6. Returning to Glory

1. Robert L. Griswold, *Fatherhood in America: A History* (New York: BasicBooks, 1993), 231.

2. Paula Giddings, *When and Where I Enter: The Impact of Black Women on Race and Sex in America* (New York: William Morrow, 1984), 63.

3. Scott Derks, *Working Americans, 1880–1999,* vol. 1, *The Working Class* (Lakeville, CT: Grey House, 2000), 39–53.

4. Griswold, 53.

5. Giddings, 246; Paula England, Carmen Garcia, and Mary Richardson, "Women's Employment Among Blacks, Whites, and Three Groups of Latinas," Institute for Policy Research Working Paper, September 11, 2003, www.northwestern.edu/ipr/publications/papers/2003/WP-03-06.pdf (accessed August 21, 2008).

6. U.S. Bureau of Labor Statistics, "Women in the Labor Force: A Databook" (Washington, DC: U.S. Department of Labor, 2007), www.stats.bls.gov/cps/wlf-databook-2007.htm (accessed June 27, 2008). See table 5, "Employment status by sex, presence and age of children, race, and Hispanic or Latino ethnicity, March 2006." For more background, see Lynette Clemetson, "Work vs. Family, Complicated by Race," *New York Times,* February 9, 2006.

7. Pew Research Center, "Fewer Mothers Prefer Full-time Work from 1997 to 2007," July 12, 2007, http://pewresearch.org/pubs/536/working-women.

8. Quoted in Lonnae O'Neal Parker, *I'm Every Woman: Remixed Stories of Marriage, Motherhood, and Work* (New York: Amistad, 2005), 128.

9. For a solid overview of the politics of black mothers and social welfare, see Annelise Orleck, *Storming Caesars Palace: How Black Mothers Fought Their Own War on Poverty* (Boston: Beacon Press, 2005), passim, but especially pages 82–87.

10. U.S. Bureau of Labor Statistics, 3.

11. Giddings, 64.

12. Quoted in Deborah Gray White, *Too Heavy a Load: Black Women in Defense of Themselves, 1894–1994* (New York: W. W. Norton, 1999), 64.

13. Mark Anthony Neal, *New Black Man* (New York: Routledge, 2005), 157.

14. Matthew DeBell, "Children Living without Their Fathers: Population Estimates and Indicators of Educational Well-being," *Social Indicators Research* 87, no. 3 (July 2008): 427–41. Using data from the 2003 Parent and Family Involvement in Education Survey, DeBell finds, "In bivariate comparisons, absent-father status is associated with reduced well-being: worse health, lower academic achievement, worse educational experiences, and less parental involvement in school activities. When socio-economic factors are controlled, father-absence is associated with small deficits in well-being. The findings suggest that the conventional wisdom may exaggerate the detrimental effects of father absence."

15. For an amusing and ferocious overview of the demonization of black men, see Earl Ofari Hutchinson, *The Assassination of the Black Male Image* (New York: Simon & Schuster, 1996). I should note, however, that Hutchinson is strongly antifeminist; long stretches of his book defend black men against black feminist charges of sexism.

16. Daniel Patrick Moynihan, "The Negro Family: The Case for National Action," in *The Moynihan Report and the Politics of Controversy,* ed. Lee Rainwater and William L. Yancey (Cambridge, MA: MIT Press, 1967), 43.

17. Ibid., 75.

18. John J. Dilulio, quoted in William J. Bennett, "What to do about the children," *Commentary,* March 1995, 23–29.

19. Louis Farrakhan, "A Holy Day of Atonement and Reconciliation: October 16, 1995," *The Final Call,* September 1995.

20. Sidney W. Mintz and Richard Price, *The Birth of African-American Culture* (Boston: Beacon Press, 1976), 2.

21. Ta-Nehisi Coates, "Confessions of a Black Mr. Mom," *Washington Monthly* 34, no. 3 (March 2002): 20–24.

22. See, for example, Jennifer Hamer, *What It Means to Be Daddy: Fatherhood for Black Men Living Away from Their Children* (New York: Columbia University Press, 2001), passim; Earl Ofari Hutchinson, *Black Fatherhood: The Guide to Male Parenting* (Los Angeles: Middle Passage Press, 1995), passim; Gloria Wade-Gayles, ed., *Father Songs: Testimonies by African-American Sons and Daughters* (Boston: Beacon Press, 1997), passim; and Marelene Perchinske, ed., *Commitment: Father-*

hood in Black America (Columbia: University of Missouri Press, 1998), passim.

23. Bart Landry, *Black Working Wives: Pioneers of the American Family Revolution* (Berkeley: University of California Press, 2000), 161–62.

24. See, for example, Lillian Rubin, *Families on the Fault Line: America's Working Class Speaks about the Family, the Economy, Race, and Ethnicity* (New York: HarperCollins, 1994), 92; Mohammad Ahmeduzzaman and Jaipaul Roopnarine, "Sociodemographic factors, functioning style, social support, and fathers' involvement with preschoolers in African-American families," *Journal of Marriage and the Family* 54, no. 3 (August 1992): 699–707; and William Marsiglio, "Paternal engagement activities with minor children," *Journal of Marriage and the Family* 53, no. 4 (November 1991): 973–86. For an overview, see National Center on Fathers and Families, "Brief: Fathers Care: A Review of the Literature," www.ncoff.gse.upenn.edu/litrev/fcbrief.htm (accessed June 25, 2008).

25. Mintz, 65.

26. Quoted in Bob Herbert, "A Dubious Milestone," *New York Times,* June 21, 2008.

27. Neal, 156.

28. Coates, "Confessions of a Black Mr. Mom." For an astonishingly vivid first-person account of Ta-Nehisi's upbringing, see Ta-Nehisi Coates, *The Beautiful Struggle* (New York: Spiegel & Grau, 2008). I interviewed Ta-Nehisi and wrote this chapter six months before *The Beautiful Struggle* was published.

29. Meredith F. Small, *Our Babies, Ourselves: How Biology and Culture Shape the Way We Parent* (New York: Anchor Books, 1998), 228.

30. Ibid., 228.

31. Landry, 6.

7. The Astonishing Science of Fatherhood, or Three More Myths about Male Caregiving

1. "In our family, on Father's Day, we celebrate me," writes blogger and self-described lesbian dad Polly Pagenhart. She continues: "My 'fatherhood' of our child is strictly social, invisible to the state until petitioned for as a would-be 'second parent,' and marginally visible

to many even afterwards. But it is the result of an accretion of daily work on my part, ever-changing and, I pray, lasting my entire life. The older our daughter gets, the more I'll learn about what my sort of lesbian fatherhood means, to me and to her. Right now, it's not so complicated." See http://lesbiandad.net/about/ (accessed September 2007).

2. For example, a pamphlet published by the right-wing advocacy group the Family Research Council explicitly compares gay marriage to one Missouri man's demand that he be able to marry his horse. "Homosexual marriage is an empty pretense that lacks the fundamental sexual complementariness of male and female," it says. "Homosexuality is rightly viewed as unnatural." Timothy J. Dailey, "The Slippery Slope of Same-Sex 'Marriage,'" Family Research Council, www.frc.org/get.cfm?i=bc04c02 (accessed April 2007). Another example: "The union of a man and woman is the most enduring human institution," said President George W. Bush in 2004, "encouraged in all cultures and by every religious faith. Ages of experience have taught humanity that the commitment of a husband and wife to love and to serve one another promotes the welfare of children and the stability of society." But gay and lesbian marriage, he said, threatens "the most fundamental institution of civilization." Office of the White House Press Secretary, "President Calls for Constitutional Amendment Protecting Marriage," February 24, 2004.

3. Frans B.M. de Waal, "The Evolution of Empathy," *Greater Good,* fall/winter 2005–06.

4. Louann Brizendine, *The Female Brain* (New York: Broadway Books, 2006), 161.

5. Ibid., 159.

6. Ibid., back cover.

7. The Family Research Council (one of the largest and most ferocious opponents of same-sex marriage) "also believes that the two-worker parent family should not be favored (as it presently is) over the family with one parent at home raising the children, nor that the public school parent should be fiscally favored over the private school parent or the home school parent, especially as these two deliver superior outcomes." Marriage and Family, www.frc.org/marriage-

family#structure (accessed June 2, 2008). Elsewhere on its Web site, the FRC makes it clear that the traditional family ideally consists of a breadwinning father and homemaking mother. "What caused this return with a vengeance to the family disorders of the early decades of the 20th Century?" asks one Christian Right leader. "Part of the answer lies in the continued desire by the industrial sector for women's work, as a way to expand the labor pool and hold wages down. . . . As women moved into the paid labor force on terms equal to those of men, they became more like men in function. In consequence, the economic logic of marriage blurred. . . . A falling marriage rate, rising divorce, tumbling marital fertility, and widespread cohabitation were the predictable results." Witherspoon Lecture, www.frc.org/get.cfm?i=WT02J1 (accessed June 2, 2008).

8. Robert M. Sapolsky, *The Trouble with Testosterone* (New York: Scribner, 1997), 12.

9. Ibid., 156.

10. I am indebted to Ross Parke, a psychologist at the University of California at Riverside, for inspiring the framework that shapes this chapter. His April 2008 presentation at the UC-Berkeley Child Development Center, "Fatherhood: Remembering the Past and Imagining the Future," identified many of the myths and facts to which I refer.

11. Christiana M. Leonard et al., "Size Matters: Cerebral Volume Influences Sex Differences in Neuroanatomy," Cerebral Cortex Advance Access, April 24, 2008, http://cercor.oxfordjournals.org/cgi/content/abstract/bhn052.

12. Ian Deary et al., "Population Sex Differences in IQ at Age 11: The Scottish Mental Survey 1932," *Intelligence* 31, no. 6 (November/December 2003): 533–42.

13. U.S. Department of Justice, Bureau of Justice Statistics, "Prison Statistics: Summary Findings on June 30, 2007," http://usgovinfo.about .com/gi/dynamic/offsite.htm?zi=1/XJ&sdn=usgovinfo&cdn=news issues&tm=118&f=10&tt=2&bt=1&bts=1&zu=http%3A//www .ojp.usdoj.gov/bjs/ (accessed August 21, 2008).

14. Roy F. Baumeister, "Is There Anything Good About Men?" Invited Address, American Psychological Association, 2007. Transcript

available online at www.psy.fsu.edu/~baumeistertice/goodaboutmen .htm.

15. Emiliana R. Simon-Thomas, "Brain Teaser: Are women more empathic than men?" *Greater Good,* summer 2007, 7. Note that mirror neurons are newly discovered; their nature and functions are not completely understood. At this writing some scientists seem to claim that mirror neurons are responsible for tying us all together, while others think that groups of neurons work together to do the job. I think the lay reader just needs to understand that both men and women have little machines in our brains that help us connect to other people.

16. Erno Jan Hermans, Peter Putman, Jack van Honk, "Testosterone administration reduces empathetic behavior: A facial mimicry study," *Psychoneuroendocrinology* 31, no. 7 (2006): 859–66.

17. Jack van Honk and Dennis J. L. G. Schutter, "Testosterone Reduces Conscious Detection of Signals Serving Social Correction," *Psychological Science* 18, no. 8 (August 2007): 663–667.

18. David Leonhardt, "A Diploma's Worth? Ask Her." *New York Times,* May 21, 2008. Also see Christianne Corbett, Catherine Hill, and Andresse St. Rose, "Where the Girls Are: The Facts about Gender Equity in Education," American Association of University Women Educational Foundation, 2008.

19. Alex Williams, "Putting Money on the Table," *New York Times,* September 23, 2007.

20. This chapter contains an underlying assumption that is not at all a safe one: namely, that testosterone and aggression are inherently incompatible with parenting. This might not be the case. Of course, no one should behave aggressively toward children, but it might not be a bad thing for kids to witness a parent playing hard on the basketball court. Aggression exists in the world and inside us; it could be the case that kids need to see parents channeling and controlling aggression in prosocial ways. Kids definitely need the physical play associated with higher testosterone levels. That said, a study by Anne E. Storey et al. ("Hormonal correlates of paternal responsiveness in new and expectant fathers," *Evolution and Human Behavior* 21,

no. 2 [March 2000]: 79–95) found that men with lower testosterone levels spent more time holding baby dolls in a lab and were more responsive to cues like infant crying. Similar results have been obtained in subsequent studies.

21. Sapolsky, 151–52.

22. Katherine E. Wynne-Edwards, "Hormonal Changes in Mammalian Fathers," *Hormones and Behavior* 40, no. 2 (September 2001): 139–45.

23. Carl M. Corter and Alison S. Fleming, "Psychobiology of Maternal Behavior in Human Beings," in *Handbook of Parenting*, vol. 2, *Biology and Ecology of Parenting*, 2nd ed., ed. Marc H. Bornstein (Mahwah, NJ: Lawrence Erlbaum, 2002), 141–82.

24. Yevgenia Kozorovitskiy et al., "Fatherhood affects dendritic spines and vasopressin V1a receptors in the primate prefrontal cortex," *Nature Neuroscience* 9 (2006): 1094–95.

25. Yevgenia Kozorovitskiy, A. Pavlic, and E. Gould, "Fatherhood influences neurogenesis in the hippocampus of California mice." Poster presented at the annual meeting of the Society for Neuroscience, San Diego, November 6, 2007. Available online from Society for Neuroscience Abstracts at www.abstractsonline.com/viewer/viewAbstract .asp?CKey={8E23CD46-2AC3-47B6-BAA9-DF6F8CAB736E}& MKey={FF8B70E5-B7F9-4D07-A58A-C1068FDE9D25}&AKey= {3A7DC0B9-D787-44AA-BD08-FA7BB2FE9004}&SKey={B242A 65E-EB31-4BB9-B985-A5F874B1877A} (accessed May 29, 2008).

26. Summarized in an interview of Richard J. Davidson by Daniel Goleman, available online from More than Sound Productions at www .morethansound.net. For an example of one of the original studies, see Heleen A. Slagter et al., "Mental Training Affects Distribution of Limited Brain Resources," *PloS Biology* 5, no. 6 (June 2007): 1228–35. Also see Richard J. Davidson, "Emotion Regulation, Happiness, and the Neuroplasticity of the Brain," *Advances in Mind-Body Medicine* 21, no. 3/4 (fall/winter 2005): 25–28.

27. Daniel Goleman, "The Power of Mindsight," *Greater Good*, winter 2007–08, 11.

28. Dacher Keltner, "The Compassionate Instinct," *Greater Good*, spring 2004, 6–9. A great deal of neuroscience is, at the time of this writing,

speculative. Researchers see parts of the brain light up when certain emotions are felt or behaviors exhibited, but issues like cause and effect remain unresolved.

29. Leonard et al.

30. Joshua Coleman and Stephanie Coontz, eds., "Unconventional Wisdom: A Survey of Research and Clinical Findings." Prepared for the Council on Contemporary Families tenth anniversary conference, University of Chicago, May 2007. Available online at www .contemporaryfamilies.org/subtemplate.php?ext=unconventional wisdom&t=briefingPapers (accessed January 1, 2008).

31. Simon-Thomas, 7.

32. Robert M. Sapolsky, "Peace Among Primates," *Greater Good,* fall 2007, 34–37.

33. Sapolsky's findings are reported in Eve Ekman, "Power Sickness," *Greater Good,* winter 2007–08, 28–30. Also see Sarina M. Rodrigues, "Burdens of Power," *Greater Good,* winter 2007–08, 29.

34. Douglas P. Fry, *Beyond War: The Human Potential for Peace* (New York: Oxford University Press, 2007), passim.

35. Sarah Blaffer Hrdy and Mary Batten, "The Psychology of Fatherhood," *Time,* June 7, 2007. Available online at www.time.com/time/ printout/0,8816,1630551,00.html.

36. Cai Hua, *A Society without Fathers or Husbands: The Na of China,* trans. Asti Hustvedt (New York: Zone Books, 2001), passim.

37. Mueggler is an expert on southwestern China. In conversation he told me that while the Na arrangement is unique, the influence is felt throughout the region. Mueggler makes clear, however, that southwestern China is not a matriarchal utopia. Child rearing is considered easier than trading or working in fields, and men take care of children in part because it is their privilege to do so. In the cultures of the region, Mueggler implied, women do a disproportionate share of all labor. One can imagine, however, that a feminist-like movement in the region would start from a higher level of power and assume a very different shape than it has taken in the Western world. In citing the Na, I wish only to show an example of men caring for children, nothing more.

38. For an examination of one such family, see my extended May 15,

2007, profile of Jessica Mass and Jackie Adams, the couple mentioned at the beginning of this chapter, on Daddy Dialectic at http://daddy-dialectic.blogspot.com/2007/05/jackie-and-jessicas-story-missing-piece.html: "Though he now lives in Hawaii, the donor, Dave, is close to the family. 'We had a hard time with that in the beginning,' reports Jackie. 'I was very, very possessive, and I didn't want Jessica to lose that feeling of being a parent, because people are so focused on that question of who's the father. But Dave is just such a love, there's such an honesty to him, that it makes me want to open up more and allow this extended family to work out. Today, he's more than an uncle, he's closer than that.'"

39. Ross D. Parke, *Fatherhood* (Cambridge: Harvard University Press, 1996), 73–118. Parke also identifies the gender of the child as influencing father involvement, for the average dad is likely to give more attention to boys. To the best of my knowledge, no one has tested how much attention stay-at-home dads give to sons and daughters.

40. See the following studies for examples: Sarah M. Allen and Alan J. Hawkins, "Maternal Gatekeeping: Mothers' Beliefs and Behaviors That Inhibit Greater Father Involvement in Family Work," *Journal of Marriage and the Family* 61, no. 1 (February 1999): 199–212; Naomi Gerstel and Sally K. Gallagher, "Men's Caregiving: Gender and the Contingent Character of Care," *Gender and Society* 15, no. 2 (April 2001): 197–217; and Sarah J. Schoppe-Sullivan et al., "Maternal gatekeeping, coparenting quality, and fathering behavior in families with infants," *Journal of Family Psychology* 22, no. 3 (June 2008): 389–98. For observations and insights into the relationship between stay-at-home fatherhood and maternal gatekeeping, see Andrea Doucet, *Do Men Mother?* (Toronto: University of Toronto Press, 2006), 229–32. As I have, Doucet found that mothers in reverse-traditional families did not appear to exhibit gatekeeping behaviors, although she found that quality of housework remains "a sensitive issue." This provides additional evidence for the idea that the degree of maternal gatekeeping behavior shapes father involvement: it makes sense that the families with the least amount of gatekeeping would have the most involved fathers.

41. "Doing family work is a way to validate a mothering identity ex-

ternally as it is the primary source of self-esteem and satisfaction for many women," but that "does not automatically mean that they are inhibiting more collaborative arrangements of family work." Allen and Hawkins, 204. For many insightful personal observations about mothering as a source of identity and self-worth, see Daphne de Marneffe, *Maternal Desire: On Children, Love, and the Inner Life* (New York: Little, Brown, 2004), passim. For many women, it seems, motherhood is a source of personal as well as social power. And why shouldn't it be?

42. For an overview of this research, see Scott Coltrane, "What About Fathers?" *American Prospect* 18, no. 3 (March 2007): 20–22.

43. Quote and study information taken from a University of British Columbia press release, "Women's Math Performance Affected by Theories on Sex Differences," October 19, 2006, www.publicaffairs .ubc.ca/media/releases/2006/mr-06-108.html. For another example of recent research into this phenomenon, see Jennifer R. Steele and Nalini Ambady, "'Math is hard!' The effect of gender priming on women's attitudes," *Journal of Experimental Social Psychology* 42, no. 4 (July 2006): 428–36.

44. This line of research is summarized in Rodolfo Mendoza-Denton, "Framed!" *Greater Good,* summer 2008, 22–24. Also see R. Mendoza-Denton, K. Kahn, and W. Y. Chan, "Can fixed views of ability boost performance in the context of favorable stereotypes?" *Journal of Experimental Social Psychology* 44 (2008): 1187–1193; Rodolfo Mendoza-Denton, Sang Hee Park, and Alexander O'Connor, "Gender stereotypes as situation-behavior profiles," *Journal of Experimental Social Psychology* 44, no. 4 (July 2008): 971–82.

45. Simon Baron-Cohen, *The Essential Difference: The Truth about the Male and Female Brain* (New York: Basic Books, 2003), 2.

46. Elizabeth Washbrook, "What Happens When Dad Looks after the Kids?" *Research in Public Policy* 5 (autumn 2007): 6–8. Incidentally, the same issue of the journal contains a study that purports to show a link between working mothers and obesity in their children, which adds up to a kind of one-two punch on behalf of the so-called traditional family, albeit a feeble one.

47. For an easily digested summary of this well-known research, see

Ross D. Parke and Armin A. Brott, *Throwaway Dads* (Boston: Houghton Mifflin, 1999), 17–29. Also see Parke, *Fatherhood,* 44–72 and passim.

48. Ibid.

49. Barbara J. Risman, *Gender Vertigo: American Families in Transition* (New Haven, CT: Yale University Press, 1998), 51.

50. Oriel Sullivan and Scott Coltrane, "Men's Changing Contribution to Housework and Child Care: A Discussion Paper on Changing Family Roles." Paper prepared for the 11th annual conference of the Council on Contemporary Families, University of Illinois, Chicago, April 25–26, 2008. Available online with responses at www.contemporaryfamilies.org/subtemplate.php?t=briefingPapers&ext=menshousework.

51. Ross Parke, M. A. Miller, Melinda S. Leidy, Scott Coltrane, Sanford Braver, Jeff Cookston, and W. Fabricius, "Father involvement and adolescent adaptation in Mexican American and European American step and intact families." Manuscript in preparation at the time of this book's publication. Results of this study were reported to me by Ross Parke and Jeff Cookston; results were also presented on a poster, "Dyadic processes and child outcomes: An analysis of first generation Mexican American fathers and their adolescents." Society for Research on Adolescence, San Francisco, March 2006.

52. NICHD Early Child Care Research Network, *Child Care and Child Development: Results from the NICHD Study of Early Child Care and Youth Development* (New York: Guilford Press, 2005), passim.

53. "The State of the Modern Family," Equality and Human Rights Commission, 2. Available online at www.equalityhumanrights.com/Documents/Gender/Research/State%20of%20the%20modern%20family%20EOC%20research.pdf. Data available from S. Dex and K. Ward, "Parental Care and Employment in Early Childhood: Analysis of the Millennium Cohort Study Sweeps 1 and 2," Manchester: Equal Opportunities Commission.

54. For a summary of research into gay and lesbian families, see the American Psychological Association Policy Statement, "Sexual Orientation, Parents, and Children." Adopted by the APA Council of Representatives July 28–30, 2004. Available online at www.apa.org/

pi/lgbc/policy/parents.html. For a summary of the implications of research into lesbian-headed families and fatherhood, see Ross D. Parke, "Fathers, Families, and the Future: A Plethora of Plausible Predictions," *Merrill-Palmer Quarterly* 50, no. 4 (October 2004): 456–70.

55. Kyle D. Pruett, *Fatherneed: Why Father Care Is as Essential as Mother Care for Your Child* (New York: Free Press, 2000), 58–75.

56. Robert A. Frank, Susan Kromelow, and Michael C. Helford, "Primary Caregiving Father Families: Do They Differ in Parental Activities?" Presentation at the annual meeting of the American Psychological Association, August 18, 2005. Full text available from the American Psychological Association Public Affairs Office.

57. Summarized and quoted in Patrick Tucker, "Stay-at-home Dads," *The Futurist* 39, no. 5 (September/October 2005): 12–13.

58. Sarah Blaffer Hrdy, *Mother Nature: A History of Mothers, Infants, and Natural Selection* (New York: Pantheon, 1999), 226. For a wonderful anthropological overview of research into parenting styles around the contemporary world, see Meredith F. Small, *Our Babies, Ourselves: How Biology and Culture Shape the Way We Parent* (New York: Anchor Books, 1998), 71–108.

59. For a comparison of how public policy has affected father involvement in different countries, see Barbara Hobson, ed., *Making Men into Fathers: Men, Masculinities, and the Social Politics of Fatherhood* (Cambridge, UK: Cambridge University Press, 2002), passim. Also see Ariane Hegewisch and Janet C. Gornick, *Statutory Routes to Workplace Flexibility in Cross-National Perspective* (Washington, DC: Institute for Women's Policy Research, 2008), passim.

60. Hrdy, *Mother Nature*, 211–12.

8. Searching for Heroism

1. Zeno Franco and Philip Zimbardo, "The Banality of Heroism," *Greater Good*, fall/winter 2006–07, 30–35.

2. According to the Department of Labor, married, nonemployed mothers spend three hours a day on housework, food prep, and cleanup, while married nonemployed dads spend just two hours a day

on housework and food chores. Reports *USA Today:* "'When you think about it, the task of caring for kids is logically different from doing the housework,' says Joan C. Williams, director of the Center for WorkLife Law at Hastings College of the Law in California. 'There's no reason that the person who rocks the cradle also needs to pick up the dry cleaning.' This can frustrate breadwinning moms who assume they're getting a package deal. But 'guys have it right here,' says Williams, who has studied the caregiving arrangements of hundreds of families. If all couples negotiated housework and child care separately, 'that would ultimately help a lot of women.'" Laura Vanderkam, "What Moms Can Learn From Dads," *USA Today,* June 24, 2008.

3. This early research is summarized in Michael E. Lamb et al., "Paternal Behavior in Humans," *American Zoologist* 25, no. 3 (1985): 883–94.

4. Judith Stadtman Tucker, "Men and Mothering: An Interview with Sociologist Andrea Doucet, Author of *Do Men Mother?*" Mothers Movement Online, June 2007. www.mothersmovement.org/features/07/06/doucet_1.html (accessed June 29, 2007).

5. This is true in my experience, but I recognize that the only evidence I can offer is anecdotal. We should recognize the degree of flux that exists in definitions of the good mother: many mothers today feel free to assert their autonomy and personal interests, while others are plagued by feelings of guilt that they are never doing enough.

6. Daphne de Marneffe, *Maternal Desire: On Children, Love, and the Inner Life* (Boston: Little, Brown, 2004), xii–xiii.

7. Anne Marie Owens, "Fathers as mothers—there's a difference," *Ottawa Citizen,* November 10, 2006.

8. Misun also shared this story with me: "The other day Clinton, Louise, and I were playing lion. I was the mommy lion, Clinton was the daddy lion, and Louise was the baby lion. And I turned to Clinton and said, 'OK, daddy lion, maybe you should go out and get us some food and bring it back and I'll cook it.' He looked at me completely confused, like, 'What?' So I said, 'OK, here's what we'll do: I'll go get the food, I'll bring it back, and you'll cook it.' And he said, 'OK, no problem, that's what daddy lions do.'"

9. Conclusion

1. Joel Schatz and Diane Schatz, *Peace Trek: Family Coloring Book* (Twin Lakes, WI: Lotus Press, 1986), passim.

2. Avi Sadeh, *Sleeping Like a Baby: A Sensitive and Sensible Approach to Solving Your Child's Sleep Problems* (New Haven, CT: Yale University Press, 2001), 79.

3. Annalee Newitz, "Big Love on Staten Island," *New York,* April 24, 2006.

4. Allan C. Carlson and Paul T. Mero, *The Natural Family: A Manifesto* (Dallas, TX: Spence Publishing Company, 2007), 6.

5. Ibid., 20. I also quoted this passage in the introduction.

6. W. Bradford Wilcox, "Religion and the Domestication of Men." *Contexts: Understanding People in Their Social Worlds* 5 (fall 2006): 42–46.

7. From "Evangelicals and the Public Square," a panel discussion hosted by the Pew Forum on Religion and Public Life, October 11, 2007, Washington, DC. For a transcript, see http://pewforum.org/events/?EventID=156.

8. Associated Press, "Baptist Seminary Launching Homemaking Program," *Dallas Morning News,* August 10, 2007.

9. W. Bradford Wilcox, "Preaching to the Choir," *Wall Street Journal,* August 10, 2007.

10. Carlson and Mero, 11.

11. Quoted in Brian Mann, *Welcome to the Homeland: A Journey to the Rural Heart of America's Conservative Revolution* (Hanover, NH: Steerforth Press, 2006), 226.

12. Michael Gartner, "Live and Let Live," *USA Today,* September 13, 2007.

13. Robert P. Jones and Dan Cox, "American Values Survey." The Center for American Values in Public Life, People for the American Way Foundation, September 2006, http://media.pfaw.org/pdf/cav/AVSReport.pdf (accessed May 14, 2008).

14. For an empirical overview of these trends, see Paul R. Amato et al., *Alone Together: How Marriage in America Is Changing* (Cambridge, MA: Harvard University Press, 2007), passim.

15. Betsey Stevenson and Justin Wolfers, "Marriage and the Market," *Cato Unbound,* January 18, 2008, www.cato-unbound.org/2008/01/18/ betsey-stevenson-and-justin-wolfers/marriage-and-the-market/ (accessed January 29, 2008).

16. *The Rush Limbaugh Show,* "Liberals Reshape Male Role Models," November 8, 2007. Audio and transcript available at www.rushlim baugh.com/home/daily/site_110807/content/01125110.guest.html.

17. For the traditional homemaker side, I submit Caitlin Flanagan, *To Hell with All That: Loving and Loathing Our Inner Housewife* (New York: Little, Brown, 2006). And for the working mother side, I submit Linda Hirshman, *Get to Work: A Manifesto for Women of the World* (New York: Viking, 2006). For the record, I think both of these writers are insane.

18. There are many books on this topic. For an example, see Judith Warner, *Perfect Madness: Motherhood in the Age of Anxiety* (New York: Riverhead Books, 2005).

19. Amie K. Miller, "Does Barbie Need a Man?" *Greater Good,* fall 2007, 27–29.

20. Tara Parker-Pope, "Gay Unions Shed Light on Gender in Marriage," *New York Times,* June 10, 2008.

21. Rhona Mahony, *Kidding Ourselves: Breadwinning, Babies, and Bargaining Power* (New York: Basic Books, 1995), 41–43.

22. Ibid., 216.

23. For a summary of this research, see Barbara J. Risman, *Gender Vertigo: American Families in Transition* (New Haven, CT: Yale University Press, 1998), 93–98.

24. Molly Monahan Lang and Barbara J. Risman, "A 'Stalled' Revolution or a Still-Unfolding One? The Continuing Convergence of Men's and Women's Roles." A discussion paper prepared for the 10th anniversary conference of the Council on Contemporary Families, May 4–5, 2007, University of Chicago. www.contemporaryfamilies .org/subtemplate.php?t=briefingPapers&ext=stalledrevolution (accessed January 20, 2008).

25. Daphne de Marneffe, *Maternal Desire: On Children, Love, and the Inner Life* (Boston: Little, Brown, 2004), 295–303.

26. Jody Heymann, *Forgotten Families: Ending the Growing Crisis Confronting Children and Working Parents in the Global Economy* (New York: Oxford University Press, 2006), 195.

27. Adrian White, "A Global Projection of Subjective Well-Being: A Challenge to Positive Psychology?" *Psychtalk* 56 (2007): 17–20. The map that comes with this study clearly shows that countries with social democratic family policies are significantly happier than others, despite the fact that their weather is often terrible! Swedish, Norwegian, and Canadian winters are far too cold; instead of going to those places, we need to bring their social policies to the United States.

28. For a detailed list of family-friendly policy recommendations, see Moms-Rising and the Progressive States Network, "State Legislative Models," www.progressivestates.org/content/388/state-legislative-models-w-momsrising (accessed June 27, 2008).

29. Quoted in Jeremy Smith, "The Ambiguous Utopian: Kim Stanley Robinson," *January Magazine*, July 2002, http://januarymagazine.com/profiles/ksrobinson.html.

Index

Index